PLAYS THREE

Bernard Kops

PLAYS THREE

THE DREAM OF PETER MANN
ENTER SOLLY GOLD
WHO SHALL I BE TOMORROW?

OBERON BOOKS
LONDON

The Dream of Peter Mann first published
by Penguin Books Ltd in 1960

First published in this collection in 2002 by Oberon Books Ltd.
521 Caledonian Road, London N7 9RH
Tel: +44 (0) 20 7607 3637 / Fax: +44 (0) 20 7607 3629
e-mail: info@oberonbooks.com
www.oberonbooks.com

A catalogue record for this book is available from the British
Library.

ISBN: 978-1-84002-177-6

Cover illustration: Andrzej Klimowski

Typography: Jeff Willis

Visit www.oberonbooks.com to read more about all our books
and to buy them. You will also find features, author inter-
views and news of any author events, and you can sign up for
e-newsletters so that you're always first to hear about our new
releases.

for Erica

Contents

THE DREAM OF PETER MANN

Characters

ALEX
a tramp

MR GREEN
a greengrocer

MRS GREEN
the wife of the greengrocer

PETER MANN
a dreamer

MAN (MR SMALL)
a worker

MR BUTCHER
a butcher

MR FISH
a fishmonger

MRS BUTCHER
the wife of the butcher

MRS FISH
the wife of the fishmonger

SYLVIA
daughter of Mr and Mrs Green

JASON
an undertaker

SONIA MANN
proprietress of the gown shop

PENNY
daughter of Mr and Mrs Butcher

TOM GROOM
a prospective bridegroom of Penny

JOHN

JACK

The Dream Of Peter Mann was first perfomed by Lynoq Productions on 5 September 1960 at the Lyceum Theatre, Edinburgh, with the following cast:

ALEX, Michael Warre

MR GREEN, Will Stampe

MRS GREEN, Peggy Rowan

PETER, Robert Hardy

MR FISH, William Elmhurst

MRS BUTCHER, Eileen Way

MRS FISH, Doria Noar

JASON, Martin Miller

SONIA, Hermione Baddeley

PENNY, Valerie Gearon

TOM GROOM, Oscar Quitak

Director, Frank Dunlop

Set design, Richard Negri

Music, Ricet-Barrier

Lighting, Richard Pilbrow

ACT ONE

The scene is a market-place in London.

Several market stalls are standing empty outside several closed shops. These are: a Butcher's shop, a Greengrocer's, a Fishmonger's, a Gown shop, and an Undertaker's.

The stalls are used as accessory to the shops, and it is from these that most of the goods are sold.

Each shop has an appropriate sign painted above it. The undertaker's sign simply says 'Twenty-Four-Hour Service'.

The gown shop is the largest and has a large shutter with a door in it. Gowns and rolls of material are all around the shop.

Time is the present. It is a beautiful mid-summer morning, and the stage is deserted.

Some CHILDREN are heard singing, then activity begins. One by one the shops are opened; goods are brought out and displayed on the stalls. The gown shop remains closed.

CHILDREN: (*Voices off. Singing.*)
    Peach, Plum, or Apricot!
    How much money have you got?
    If you've got a bob or two.
    I will bring some home for you.
    (*SYLVIA enters from the shop of MR and MRS GREEN. Her arms are full of flowers. She arranges them on her stall which stands outside the undertaker's shop.*
    Voices off. Singing.)
    Apricot, Peach, or Plum!
    We may get blown to kingdom come.
    Let us eat our fruit before
    Our parents go again to war.
    (*ALEX enters, a ragged tramp, with a swagger of dignity.*
    He goes to the fruit stall.)
ALEX: I would like a pound of plums.

MR GREEN: Certainly, sir. (*Weighs them.*)

ALEX: I only wish I had the money to pay for them.

MR GREEN: Clever bloke – aren't you – get away from my stall.

MRS GREEN: What's the World coming to – it's full of lousy good-for-nothings.

(*ALEX bows; as he walks away from the stall he relishes a peach that he has stolen. As the CHILDREN sing he takes a great bite.*)

CHILDREN: (*Voices off. Singing.*)

Plum, Apricot, or Peach,

Hide the stone from out their reach,

So that it falls into the earth.

And brings another world to birth.

(*ALEX wanders around, smells the flowers, and is amused by what he sees. All the traders rush around. The BUTCHER is dressed in evening dress and his wife in a long evening gown. He plucks a chicken and smokes a cigar. ALEX sits down on the pavement outside the gown shop, takes out a pocket chess set, and plays a game of chess with himself. The shutter of the gown shop is thrown open and PETER emerges, yawning.*)

PETER: Good morning morning! Another blinking day.

(*PETER starts to bring out rolls of cloth but in the middle of this he sees ALEX.*)

Playing chess? I'll give you a game.

ALEX: Not on your Nelly – I only play against myself. This way I can cheat to my heart's content and I never lose.

PETER: They say there's more out than in.

(*He returns to his stall. A MAN enters carrying an umbrella and wearing glasses.*)

MAN: (*To MR BUTCHER who is pulling a chicken.*) Please can I have a tasty, ready for the plate, oven fresh, delicious chicken pie?

MR BUTCHER: What did you say?

MAN: Can I have an oven fresh, chilled, ready cooked chicken pie?

MR BUTCHER: (*Brandishing knife.*) Get out of my shop before I mince you.

MAN: (*Going to MR FISH.*) Don't they want customers?

MR FISH: Can I help you? Lovely haddock? Beautiful flaky cod? Whiting? Fresh water trout? Beautiful Scotch salmon? Just been landed out of the sea.

MAN: Fish? Yes! I would like, let me see – (*Consults note.*) Ah yes, a packet of frozen, ready prepared, and absolutely succulent, hygienically-sealed fish fingers, please.

MR FISH: Did I hear you right?

MAN: You should move with the times.

MR FISH: I'll move you, you little eel.

MAN: (*Rushing to MR GREEN.*) What's the matter with everyone here? They are all mad.

MR GREEN: Lettuces are crisp today and radishes are juicy. Aubergines are lovely, mauve and sweet. Green peppers are hot and artichokes are cheap and fresh. What do you want? Some bananas? Oranges? Apples? Lemons? Nuts? Cabbages? Sprouts? Lovely fresh peas?

MAN: Peas? Yes please. A packet of frozen peas, please.

MR GREEN: Would you mind repeating that?

MAN: Packed foods save time.

MR GREEN: Time for what?

MAN: Why, time for – time for – what? Time for time of course. Now you're driving me as mad as yourself. Don't you see we haven't got time, that's why we live out of tins. You're all living in the past, everyone buys at the Superstores, that's why this market's dead.

PETER: That's what I told them. Join together, make more money.

MR GREEN: (*Simultaneously with MRS BUTCHER and MRS FISH.*) All you make is trouble.

MRS BUTCHER: You're a snotty-nosed big mouth.

MRS FISH: Too big for your boots, that's your trouble.

MRS BUTCHER: (*Simultaneously with MRS GREEN and MRS FISH.*) If I was your Mum I'd smack your bum and send you packing. (*To husband.*) It's time you stood up to him, he insults me and you do nothing.

MRS GREEN: (*To husband.*) We ought to get up a petition. He ought to be abolished. Can't you do something about it?

MRS FISH: (*To husband.*) He's a mischief-maker. Please, move yourself, get rid of him.

MR BUTCHER: Well, I may be a weak-kneed, pigeon-livered, hen-pecked has been –

MR FISH/MR GREEN: Ditto.

MR BUTCHER: But now I've made up my mind and I'm determined to do something.

MR GREEN/MR FISH: So am I.

MRS BUTCHER: About time, too. What are you going to do?

MR BUTCHER: I'm going to put my foot down and tell you to go to hell.

MR FISH: (*Together.*) Same here.

MR GREEN: (*Together.*) Me too.

MR BUTCHER: Apart from that, I'm going to do nothing; so leave me alone and give me a bit of peace.

MR GREEN: (*Together.*) You said it. That's telling them.

MR FISH: (*Together.*) That's certainly telling them.

(*They continue working slowly.*)

MAN: I know just how you feel. I get up in the morning, wife's asleep. From a tin of milk and a tin of coffee I make myself a tin mug of tea – Well, it tastes the same – From the refined wheat-free waxed wrapped loaf I make some sandwiches using tinned corned beef. I rush to work in a tin train, packed like sardines, and in the tin factory I make tin cans all day. When I come home, my wife opens a tin of baked beans and stewed steak. I follow her to bed. She lies beside me like a cold chicken pie ready for the oven but I am too exhausted and fall asleep. I dream of tins and tins and tins and tens of thousands of tins and nightmares of tin horses and I wake up screaming, 'Help, help, I've lost the opener'.

MR GREEN: Why don't you make a stand?

MAN: You trying to make me discontented? I shall never come to this market again. (*He is about to stomp off when he sees the flower stall.*) A carnation, please.

SYLVIA: Certainly, sir. (*She fixes one in his buttonhole.*)

MAN: Wish it was a reincarnation.

SYLVIA: Sorry, sir, we don't stock those.

JASON: I have a nice line in tin coffins that would suit you down to the ground.

(*Everyone laughs except the MAN, who stomps off.*)

ALEX: Checkmate! (*He stops playing and goes to PETER.*) *Could you* spare me a fag?

(*PETER gives him one.*)

Got a light?

(*PETER lights it.*)

Could you spare me a couple of bob? I'm down on my luck this week.

PETER: (*Giving him money.*) Now get out of my life, I've got enough worries.

ALEX: Perhaps I can help you, sonny?

(*PETER pushes him to one side and sadly goes to SYLVIA who pretends to ignore him. ALEX follows PETER.*)

PETER: Forgive me for last night. I got carried away.

SYLVIA: Go away.

ALEX: Ah, forgive him, he really is sorry.

MR GREEN: He's talking to Sylvia again. How many times must I tell her the facts of life? He's no good. (*He rushes over to PETER.*) Now you stay away from my girl.

PETER: Pipe down.

(*MR GREEN is afraid and rushes back to his wife.*)

MRS GREEN: Well, his mother's got pots of money, our daughter could do a lot worse.

MR GREEN: Before he was no good, but now you remember the money he's got and he's all right again.

MRS GREEN: Shut up and get on with your work.

ALEX: Leave this to me, son, I'll handle it.

PETER: I'll settle my own affairs.

MR GREEN: Did you hear that? They're having an affair.

MRS GREEN: Shut up.

PETER: (*To ALEX.*) Now out of my way.

ALEX: (*Leans against the flower stall, between them, and takes a large flower, chrysanthemum, and starts plucking the petals, one by one.*) She loves him not, she loves him, she loves him not – (*Soon he is just mouthing the words.*)

SYLVIA: This a friend of yours?

PETER: Never seen him before in my life.

SYLVIA: Birds of a feather.

PETER: Sylvia, listen to me. I dreamed of you last night and the night before. I dream of you all the time. I love you.

ALEX: She loves him?

SYLVIA: (*To PETER.*) Go away.

ALEX: Not!

PETER: Give me a chance.

SYLVIA: I gave you one once.

PETER: Give me another chance. I want to kiss you. You know you love me.

(*He tries to grab her; she pushes him off.*)

SYLVIA: I know nothing of the kind.

PETER: Let's fly away together.

SYLVIA: I want a home.

PETER: I'll build one for you.

SYLVIA: What, with dreams? I want a boy with his feet on the ground.

PETER: Mine are! Mine are!

SYLVIA: My man must have his head screwed on.

PETER: (*Shaking his head madly.*) Mine isn't exactly failing off.

SYLVIA: I want to understand you but it's no use. If you give up your crazy ideas I'll be pleased to reconsider you. I'm a respectable girl and I need to settle down.

PETER: You once said you loved me. Down by the river, remember? And in the roundabout at Hampstead Heath and in the tube near Oxford Circus.

SYLVIA: You've changed. You were always so quiet; you were such a steady boy with your nose to the grindstone. When you swung the hammer the bell always rang.

PETER: How beautiful you are, lovelier than any flower. Throw away your flowers and come with me. Vision of purity, bloom of innocence.

SYLVIA: You're blooming daft.

PETER: Daft with love. Isn't that strange, we've lived here all our lives together and now we're strangers.

SYLVIA: You're beyond me.

PETER: (*Tries cuddling her again.*) I'll make you a queen. What do you want? Tell me.

SYLVIA: I want what every girl wants. To be courted slowly with chocolates. I want a lovely engagement ring, big and sparkling. I want everything planned. To be married in

white and with flowers and bridesmaids. A choral wedding
with everyone crying. I want to be pure on my wedding
night. You're too impatient.

PETER: I'm normal.

(*She fusses with flowers.*)

ALEX: (*With the last handful of petals, throwing them away.*) She
loves him not.

PETER: Women! They make me sick.

ALEX: I was married once; you can't tell me anything about
women.

PETER: I'll show her. She'll change her mind one day and
then she'll beg me to marry her. Guess what I'll do?

ALEX: What?

PETER: Marry her, of course. Oh, I wish I could leave.

ALEX: Wish I could settle down.

PETER: I'm shut in here.

ALEX: (*Lost in his own dream.*) 'Cos I'm not getting any
younger.

PETER: I want money, sure, like the others, but I want
something more.

ALEX: The nights get colder.

PETER: I don't get on with the yobs round here. I think of the
future.

ALEX: I'm lonely.

PETER: I want to be stinking rich, open the most super-
colossal Superstore you ever saw. If only I had the courage
to just go.

ALEX: Come with me.

PETER: That's not a bad idea. Do you mean it?

ALEX: Sure, I'll show you the ropes.

(*They laugh and shake hands heartily.*)

PETER: I'll have my fling with every so and so and reap my
wild sluts. (*He jumps on to the stall.*) Girls of the world. Hear
me. Dolls, damsels, virgins, skirts, floozies, listen to me!
I'm coming your way, don't be impatient! I've got time
for all of you. Casanova, Don Juan, Yul Brynner, stand to
one side: Mann is coming to show you how to make love.
Girls! Stop crying for me, stop chewing your pillow cases,

take down those photos. I'm coming in the flesh to make *your* flesh tingle. It'll be the thrill of a lifetime.

ALEX: Hip! Hip! Hoor...

(*ALEX applauds but it falls on silence and all in the market shake their heads.*)

Come on, let's go.

PETER: (*Jumping down.*) Sorry, I'd like to but I can't.

ALEX: Why not?

PETER: All the mountains have been climbed, all the deserts have been crossed and all the records smashed.

ALEX: Got a fag?

(*PETER gives him one. ALEX pockets it.*)

PETER: There's nothing for me to do but get old and fat and pass on the business to my horrible kids. There's nothing worth living for and nothing worth dying for. I'm fed up. Why did you have to come and make me unhappy?

ALEX: What, me?

(*PETER brings out rolls of material from the shop and displays them. JASON notices ALEX and stands close, considering him for something. Meanwhile –*)

MR BUTCHER: (*To wife.*) When will they come home?

MRS BUTCHER: Stop worrying and clean those chickens.

MR BUTCHER: My own daughter gets married and you won't even let us take the day off.

MRS BUTCHER: We are essential workers. If we closed they'd all become anaemic or vegetarian or worse.

MR BUTCHER: What could be worse? Are we inviting them all to have a drink? (*He indicates the market people.*)

MRS BUTCHER: That means more expense. Oh, well.

MR BUTCHER: We must have some celebration, now we're dressed up like this.

MRS BUTCHER: Maybe, we'll see. Just get on with your work.

MR BUTCHER: (*Reading from a newspaper.*) It says that the fallout from one hydrogen bomb will kill ten million people. Some fallout.

MRS BUTCHER: Listen, when you get to our age, the only fallout that should worry you should be your teeth and your hair. Don't yap so much, we have a very busy day.

JASON: (*To ALEX.*) Excuse me, I couldn't help overhearing your conversation. How would you like to earn a fiver?

ALEX: Whose throat do I have to cut?

JASON: Just get rid of that young man.

ALEX: How?

JASON: Spin him a yarn, a tall story. Get him away from here. As far as possible.

ALEX: Why?

JASON: He's driving us all dotty.

ALEX: (*Taking money.*) All right, you talked me into it.

JASON: Incidentally, can I interest you in a life insurance policy? Down payment, one fiver?

ALEX: Who'd collect?

JASON: I am also local agent for the never-never furniture company, a qualified midwife, a marriage broker, and an undertaker. Jason is at your service from the cradle to the grave. And between you and me, as soon as Peter's out of the way I'm going into the gown industry by marrying his mother. Thank you, good day.

ALEX: (*Happily wanders to PETER's stall.*) Haven't had a pair of new socks since the Coronation. I'll treat myself. (*To PETER.*) A pair of socks.

PETER: Show us the colour of your money. Good. Let's see what I can do you for. Now, these socks were made for the King of Egypt but because you're a punter they're going to you.
(*ALEX takes his old socks off and puts the new pair on.*)
Now I've only got fifty pairs left – step right up – Phew – (*He holds his nose.*)

ALEX: What about a shirt?
(*PETER gets a shirt and holds it like a bullfighter would his cloak. He fans the air with it, then he tries it on ALEX.*)

PETER: We've got the best shirts in the world. Shirts from the finest silk hot from first-grade cockney silkworms. Shirts for mere cash from Kashmir. (*Sings.*) Pale hands
I love beside the Gaswork wall – Flannel from the Channel, Cretonne for Cretins! Come on, step right up you

silly sods, get your crappy crêpes here.

(*The new shirt is much too big for ALEX, but PETER, by pinching it in, makes it appear a perfect fit.*)

There you are, a perfect fit!

ALEX: You're a very good salesman.

PETER: I would be if there were some customers. When a market goes down there's nothing you can do about it. Once upon a time my spiel left them spellbound but where are they? Look at it, Nylon Négligées, Lingering Lingerie, Beautiful Brassières, Combinations, Pants, and Petticoats and yards and yards of cloth all waiting for the moth. I feel useless.

ALEX: Nonsense. You've got imagination, you can go a long way. Especially North and South. That's where you'll find it.

PETER: What?

ALEX: Gold. In the Yukon.

PETER: Don't be crazy – you're fifty years late.

ALEX: Well, not exactly gold. Something better. Uranium!

PETER: Uranium? Where?

ALEX: Tons of it, mountains of it, handfuls of it. I'll take you to it.

PETER: They've got Geiger counters at the surplus store.

ALEX: We'll go North and stake a claim. The great uranium fever is sweeping the world. We can't wait to blow ourselves to smithereens.

PETER: Sounds terrific. (*He dances around the stage and then shouts at ALEX.*) U – R –

ALEX: I am?

PETER: U – R – A – N – I – U – M – URANIUM!

(*He claps his hands and dances around from one stall to another.*)

Uranium, uranium, boom, boom, boom!

(*They shake their heads and now PETER dashes to the flower stall where he sings to the indifferent SYLVIA.*)

Big bang bong bang – boom – womb – ZOOM!

Get this in your cranium,

Stuff your old geranium,

I'm off to find uranium – boom – boom – boom!

ALEX: (*Patting PETER on the back.*) That's my boy. We'll go just as we are. All we need is that Geiger counter and a little cash and we're in business.

PETER: How much money?

ALEX: How much you got?
(*PETER doesn't reply.*)
That's enough. Almost.

PETER: We'll make a fortune and I'll come back and buy up everything. I'll open the biggest, most fabulous Superstore and everyone will work for me. Great conditions! Five months' paid holiday a year, three-day week, sun lounge, hospitals, clocking-in machines ringing a hymn, like church bells. URANIUM! My friend, we're in business. (*He sees SONIA coming out of the shop singing 'Ochi chornya, Ochi krasnya'.*) Almost.

ALEX: Who's she?

PETER: My mother.

ALEX: Isn't she fat!

PETER: You said it. I'm sure one day she'll just float away. (*ALEX buys some fruit and eats it. JASON goes to SONIA and puts his arm round her waist. She throws it off with virginal indignation.*)

SONIA: (*To JASON, as he walks away.*) You're soon put off.

PETER: Listen folks, I'm about to leave you.

SONIA: Come here.

PETER: I've got the urge to go.

ALL: Hurray!

PETER: But I'll be back.

ALL: Ohhhhhhhh!

PETER: And I'll break your chains and set you free.

JASON: Sonia, what's he talking about?

SONIA: Mind your own business, Peter! What are you talking about.

PETER: U.R. – U.R.A – U.R.A.N.I.U.M.

SONIA: I've got news for you. You're going mad, you madman. Now come down, do you hear?

PETER: This is Peter Mann the Uranium King – I'm on my way.

SONIA: Ooh! If you don't come here I shall die, I shall faint, I shall scream.

(*He dances in and out of shops embracing fruit and vegetables and chickens; he finally ends up kissing a cod.*)

PETER: (*Sings to tune of 'Serenade in the Night'.*) Farewell, little fish, my most passionate lover. Though I love you so – Now I really must go – in search of another – I've made up my mind, I'm going.

SONIA: You're out of your mind. You're not. Where?

PETER: Away.

SONIA: Why? Haven't you got everything you want?

PETER: Yes, but I want something more.

SONIA: Don't you love me?

PETER: Yes.

SONIA: Well, then, if you need a few extra pounds, just ask me. Shall we go away to Brighton for a few days?

PETER: No. Look, Mum, I want to go alone and come back rich.

SONIA: But you're rich now.

PETER: I never see money.

SONIA: I'm keeping it for a rainy day. It's in the safe, safe and sound.

PETER: You are an old miser.

SONIA: Don't I feed you? Don't I give you everything you want? Pineapple and cream and chicken and cheesecake – everything he wants.

PETER: Sorry, Mum, but I've got to go.

SONIA: It's in the blood. I knew it. Shall I remind you how I slaved for you, how I brought you up?

PETER: You've told me a thousand times.

SONIA: Oh, Peter –

PETER: Here we go again.

SONIA: What a beautiful child you were.

(*PETER now mouths her words and apes her expressions.*) The things I did for you. Everything I sacrificed to make you happy and safe. I won't talk about your father, but you, you were the apple of my eye, so I left the old country on my own; that takes some doing, eh? A woman starting life again all on her own, and I was pregnant, seven months gone. I remember the journey on that boat.

PETER: I've heard this so many times before.

SONIA: Don't interrupt. You were just a bump inside me, hanging over the rail of that ship – did you kick! So I landed seven months pregnant; know what I did?

PETER: Yes.

SONIA: No, you don't. I hadn't a bean so I scrubbed floors and didn't understand a word of the language, and then you were born – with all that carbolic and brooms and mops, your big black eyes and soft curly hair.

PETER: Please pipe down.

SONIA: You were so beautiful. Any customers yet this morning?

PETER: Just one. This market's dead.

SONIA: How much have you taken.

PETER: A pound.

SONIA: Is that all? How dare you tell me such bad news? I think I'm going to have a stroke.

PETER: At the third stroke the time will be time I left. She's been on the verge of this stroke for fifteen years. Mum, thanks for everything but I'm really going. Just give me your blessing and a few quid.

SONIA: What do you want for lunch, Peter darling? A bit of roast chicken? Some boiled salmon?

PETER: It's no good, Mum. I want to find myself, I want to find love. (*Points to SYLVIA.*) And she won't have me.

SONIA: Only a mother could love you. No one else would have the patience or the insanity; anyway, darling, you're too good for her. That's the trouble – you're too good for anyone and I'm too good for you. (*She prepares to pretend to weep.*) Stop making me cry – my eyeblack will run. (*She sobs a bit, then when that doesn't work speaks again.*) Look, Peter darling, what are these fires raging in your head? Have a nice, cool lemonade and put them out. No more talking. Now run along, there's a good boy; take these pieces of cloth to Miller's warehouse, and yesterday's money to the bank.

(*PETER takes the money from her and takes several lengths of cloth. JASON goes to SONIA.*)

ALEX: We all set now? You ready?

PETER: First I've got to go on an errand. Carry these. (*He gives ALEX the cloth.*) This is the most beautiful blue, it's going-away blue.

ALEX: Blue is blue.

PETER: No, blue is for the seas and for the sky, for steel and smoke. And yellow, just look at this yellow.

ALEX: Yellow is for jaundice.

PETER: No, yellow is for deserts and for the cornfields, for spring flowers and lemons and sunshine. Yellow is for life. Don't you see? Every colour leads you somewhere, every colour is a country, every shade is a place, every piece of fruit, every flower, every fish, everything in this market tells me to go and find something, to find myself.

ALEX: You're right, blue is more than blue, yellow is more than yellow.

PETER: And I'm more than I am. Let's go – by the way, what's your name?

ALEX: Alex.

(*They shake hands.*)

What have you got in your hand?

PETER: Money.

ALEX: Let me carry it.

PETER: No.

ALEX: Don't you trust your best friend?

PETER: Sure, but not as far as money's concerned.

ALEX: Look, you've got everything because you've got imagination. You're the richest person I know – it would be a pity to get all clogged up with money. I'm down to earth, let me arrange the sordid details.

(*He dances around PETER and covers the boy with the cloth which PETER unwinds and rewinds as they dance together.*)

(*Sings.*) Hi! Hi! Dance and sing, money doesn't mean a thing. You must give it all to me if you want the golden key. Hi! Hi! Sing and shout, it's time to throw your money out, if you throw it in my purse – I'll give you the Universe.

(*PETER gives ALEX the money.*)

Hi! Hi! Dance for joy, the spinning world is now your toy – and you'll become the greatest King for money doesn't mean a thing.

(*They laugh.*)

SONIA: Who is that man dancing with Peter?

JASON: Just a tramp.

SONIA: I thought so; he has a shifty face.

JASON: Peter will be safe with him, I'm sure.

SONIA: I hope so. He's such a good boy.

JASON: I wonder, though, if he'll be safe with Peter?

SONIA: What did you say?

JASON: I said I have business to discuss with you later.

SONIA: As long as it's not monkey business.

(*PETER and ALEX dance off together, singing.*)

PETER/ALEX: Hi! Hi! Dance and sing, money doesn't mean a thing – not much!

(*They exit.*)

MRS BUTCHER: (*To MR BUTCHER.*) All right, if you must you can tell them now.

MR BUTCHER: Friends! As you know, my daughter, Penny, is being married. They'll be back from the church shortly and we want you all to have a drink with us.

MRS BUTCHER: More expense. I don't know – oh well, it might have been worse. What a lucky escape I've had. That madman Peter Mann could have been my son-in-law.

MRS FISH: That was a lucky escape.

MR BUTCHER: So we'll all forget work for a few hours and enjoy ourselves. What about it?

(*Silence as people carry on working.*)

A change is – as good – as a rest – ? A few drinks? – you're only – young once? What's the world coming to?

SYLVIA: (*Goes to them.*) Would you like to buy some flowers?

MR BUTCHER: Certainly dear. Some lilies for purity.

SYLVIA: That's a laugh.

MRS BUTCHER: Well, Sylvia dear, you'd better hurry up. My Penny's beaten you to the bedpost.

SYLVIA: When I marry it won't be on the rebound. I could get married whenever I wanted but I'm going to make sure it's the right one.

(*They choose the flowers. The market people drift back to their respective stalls. SYLVIA still talks with MR BUTCHER.*)

When Mr Right comes along, I'll know all right. We'll have the same opinions about everything. My man will be a man; he'll have to be. I'll have four bridesmaids, and two matrons of honour. The organ will play and it will be a spring day – before the sixth of April. We'll have a nice semi-detached house and two children.

MR BUTCHER: Hope you'll be as happy as I hope Penny will be.

(*He returns to his work and she to her stall.*)

JASON: There's a wonderful feeling in the air today. BIRTHS – MARRIAGES – DEATHS – The only things worth living for. Sonia we must marry at once.

SONIA: Go away, you smell like a church.

JASON: I'll get you in the end.

SONIA: I don't doubt that. Only trouble, mister, is that I shall be in a box and no good to anyone six feet under.

(*MR BUTCHER whispers into JASON's ear.*)

SONIA: Ladies and gentlemen, may I act as master of ceremonies? Our dear friend's daughter has been married. Let's put all the stalls together and make a good spread. Come on, rouse yourselves.

MR BUTCHER: Let's get together, folks, let's have a party.

MRS FISH: Oh – all right.

MRS GREEN: (*Agreeing but grudgingly.*) Silly waste of time.

JASON: Come on you miserable, greedy, money grabbers.

SONIA: He's talking to himself again.

JASON: Wake up, make it lively. This is a wedding. Bring out the bunting, make merry, look alive, if you can.

SONIA: I'll lend some white cloth to cover the stalls. White for purity, wasted on the younger generation. When I was a girl everyone was pure, today virgins are as rare as unicorns – still, I'll give white cloths to keep up appearances.

SYLVIA: And I'll lend flowers to decorate.

JASON: Come on, ladies, look alive, you're not dead yet – worse luck.

(*The men think this an ideal opportunity to play cards.*)

MRS GREEN: Look at them, we slave away and they play rummy. (*To husband.*) Haven't you got anything better to do?

MRS FISH: (*To MR FISH.*) Please have some consideration
    for me, for a change.
MRS BUTCHER: (*To MR BUTCHER.*) Just you wait till
    I get you inside.
MR GREEN: The broken record's on again.
MR FISH: For Pete's sake, leave me in peace.
MR GREEN: It's a celebration, a day of joy.
MRS GREEN: Should be a day of mourning.
MRS FISH: The day I got married was the worst day of my
    life.
MRS GREEN: The day I got married all the flags flew at half
    mast.
SONIA: All the days that I got married all the whistles blew.
JASON: Come on, ladies, let's get cracking, as the woodworm
    said in the mahogany coffin.
    (*JASON and SONIA organize the women. The stalls are
    covered with white cloths, then fruit and drink.*)
MR BUTCHER: That's me down the drain. It ain't my lucky
    day.
MR GREEN: Unlucky in cards, lucky in love.
MR BUTCHER: Do you know, I like women.
MR GREEN/MR FISH: What?
MR BUTCHER: I certainly do – but not my wife.
    (*The men continue playing. SONIA and JASON stand to
    one side as the women get the tables ready.*)
WOMEN: (*Singing as they work.*)
    Money is time and time is money.
    Might as well die if you haven't any.
    Money makes the world go round.
    Oh praise thee, sweet almighty pound.
    Money is time and time is money.
    If you are broke it isn't funny,
    And our love will not grow old,
    Provided it is set in gold.
    Money is time and time is money.
    If you're rich the world is sunny,
    For money opens every door.
    Give us more and more and more and more and more –

(*Their voices trail off.*)

JASON: (*Pulling SONIA close.*) Now we are alone at last.

SONIA: Please, I'm not in the mood to be made love to. Besides, I'm a sick woman, I've got kidney trouble and neuralgia, lumbago and backache, sciatica, chilblains, a carbuncle, and a boil; plus a slight attack of mice in the attic, a plague of pigeons on the roof, and guitars in the ears. Apart from that I'm all right. Who wants you when you're old? Who cares?

JASON: I want you, and Sonia, I have a confession to make – you love me.

SONIA: You should live so long.

JASON: Darling, for days I've been in a daze. Marry me and we'll combine our businesses and play monopoly all day and night. I love you.

SONIA: You liar, you're after the money I might have saved.

JASON: I wasn't even thinking of your lousy five thousand three hundred and fifty-eight pounds. Oh, Sonia, be a sport and marry me. I love you so much I could murder you.

SONIA: If you do I won't talk to you no more. No, my heart is with my money.

JASON: Where?

SONIA: In the safe and the safe is in a safe place.

JASON: You see, Sonia, we should amalgamate. The more businesses I own the better. One helps the other out.

SONIA: (*Fluttering her eyelashes.*) What do you mean, Jason? I'm only an ignorant girl.

JASON: Please don't come too close. You take my breath away and you know how much I love talking. I will explain. All my trades are interrelated. As an undertaker I make room in the world for more children – more children means more marriages – more marriages means more children – more children means more insurance policies, more furniture on the never-never, more people dying of worry.

SONIA: Oh Jason, what a clever man you are.

JASON: (*Pinching her.*) Lend me a broom and I'll sweep you off your feet. (*Sings.*)

Let Jason help you getting wed.
He sell you a double bed,
The pills to make your mattress sing,
A hears, a horse, anything.
Sonia, you must marry me.

SONIA: I don't believe in marriage; not even for mothers and fathers. I have always wanted to be the other woman.

JASON: When they die I pass the dresses to you – when they buy dresses, you sell them thick clothes in summer and thin clothes in winter – everyone will be dead in no time. We'll make a fortune. Excuse me, my love, but I forgot to put out my special sign.
(*He goes into the shop and comes back with long canvas sign which he fixes to the front of the shop.*)
It cost me a fortune – (*Reads sign.*) Jason's contemporary parlour of rest. Sleep in well-designed peace. Visit your loved ones at cut rate. Excursion coaches leave here for Highgate Cemetery every Sunday. (P.S. Watches and old gold bought.)

SONIA: You'd sell your own mother.

JASON: I'm just a poor orphan. My mother was too stingy to have me. Sonia, I'm all yours.

SONIA: You bore me, darling.

JASON: (*He tries to embrace her.*) Sonia! You're driving me mad.

SONIA: There ain't no such thing as a happy marriage. Sure, lots that pretend to be happy – impressing others as unhappy themselves.

JASON: Sonia, you're melting my bones. (*He tries to squeeze her.*)

SONIA: (*Shakes him off and wags a finger at him.*) Now don't get fresh.

JASON: How should I know what I'm doing. Marry me and I'll even find you a wife for Peter.

SONIA: You'd really do that for me? You must really be infatuous with me. I don't believe you. You'd never find a girl for my boy.

JASON: Of course I would. I swear upon my trade union card. (*Takes several papers out of pocket.*)

SONIA: No one is good enough for my sonny boy.

JASON: (*Ardently.*) Sonia, my darling, on my knees I beg. Marry me.

(*Gets on his knees after he has brushed the dust away.*)

SONIA: (*Ignoring him.*) Guess how many times I've been married?

(*He shrugs and gets up.*)

JASON: Twice?

(*She shakes her head and he holds three fingers up; she shakes her head and he gulps and holds four fingers up.*)

Not – four – times????

SONIA: (*Nodding dreamily.*) How clever of you to guess right.

JASON: It makes no difference – I still want you.

SONIA: (*Dreams away.*) Most of my husbands came and went in the Russian Revolution. Some great friends of mine take the salute in Red Square these days. I won't mention any names. But when they smile and wave they are really saying 'Where are you Sonia? Remember the fun we had together? Come back to Russia?'

JASON: Now I know where her son gets it all from.

SONIA: All my men were gay, handsome, and dashing, and all died young – all except Peter's father who was miserable – tired and ugly. Beautiful Dmitri was my first, he had sexy green eyes and died in Leningrad in the summer palace in the middle of winter – died of chess.

JASON: Asthma?

SONIA: No, in the middle of a game that lasted five days. The winner was my second husband – Boris – the black-hearted scoundrel of the back streets of Moscow – that's where he died of German measles in the French hospital. I found out later he was having an affair with a Lithuanian nun. I gave her nun. His funeral was smashing…

JASON: Yes? Who did it?

SONIA: You wouldn't know him.

JASON: I might.

SONIA: Max my third – died beside me in bed – we were eating marshmallow and listening to Irving Berlin – he knew how to make love. Beautiful Max with the sad black eyes. Peter's father was my fourth and here I am – never saw Russia from that day to this.

JASON: Marry me and I'll take you back.

SONIA: They don't like undertakers in Russia. Come to think of it they don't like them anywhere. I love Russia.

JASON: Why did you leave?

SONIA: To get away from my memories.

JASON: Did you?

SONIA: No. (*Sings, to Stephen Foster's 'Beautiful Dreamer'.*)

    Beautiful Russia, Queen of the earth,

    Land of my memories and place of my birth,

    Beautiful Russia, Queen of the sea,

    At night I hear you calling for me.

    Ain't it funny – people are the same all over the world – except from Warsaw – never trust anyone who comes from Warsaw.

JASON: (*Indignant.*) Why not?

SONIA: I have a feeling about it, that's all.

JASON: But I come from Warsaw – !

SONIA: Never trust yourself then.

    (*During the last scene it has been getting slowly darker and now everyone in the market looks up at the sky.*)

JASON: Even the days are too stingy to last long, these days.

    (*A flash of lightning followed by a crash of thunder.*)

MR BUTCHER: It's going to pour. Listen everyone, come and shelter in my shop and we'll all have a nice drink till my daughter gets here with her new husband. They're all welcome, aren't they, dear?

MRS BUTCHER: Well, we may as well kill two birds with one stone, seeing there's no customers about.

    (*Some more lightning and thunder make them all react nervously and they quickly go into the Butcher's. There the men play cards and the women natter. JASON keeps on following SONIA around, in and out of the crowd. There is subdued merriment inside the shop but the storm continues.*)

MRS FISH: Come on, Mrs B., show us their bedroom – I bet it's pretty.

MR FISH: That's an idea – show us the bed – I bet it's springy.

MR GREEN: Make them an apple-pie bed. Let's sew up his
pyjamas.

MRS GREEN: Don't be dirty.

MR BUTCHER: Why not? You're only young once – let's all
have a giggle.

MRS BUTCHER: Follow me – It's all pink and beautiful –
and an interior sprung blissful mattress.

(*Dirty laughter from the men as they follow MR and
MRS BUTCHER upstairs. When they are no longer seen,
PETER and ALEX enter.*)

ALEX: But don't you see, if she's only saving the money for
you, why not take it now? We could do with that extra
capital.

PETER: But that would be stealing, wouldn't it?

ALEX: Not at all, the money's yours, besides you're taking it
for a good cause, aren't you? With that behind you you'll
make a million.

PETER: Yep, you're right.

ALEX: What good is money in a safe? It's got to be circulating
to do some good. Let's get it, then.

PETER: I'm ready.

ALEX: Just one little word of advice, because I want my
conscience to be clear.

PETER: What is it?

ALEX: No matter how high you jump you always return to
earth. Never lose sight of it, or you might come down with
a bump. Is that quite clear?

PETER: Clear as mud. Come on, look! The safe's up there, on
that ledge.

(*PETER and ALEX stand by SONIA's shop and PETER
points to the safe.*)

ALEX: Grab it quickly and let's get away from here.

PETER: Inside that safe, packets and packets of lovely, filthy
lucre. (*He climbs onto a chair and fiddles with the safe.*) Two –
to – the left – ah – one to the right – four to the – left and
it's – OPEN! (*He pulls hard at the safe door.*)

ALEX: No time for dreaming. Quick.

(*PETER pulls harder and the safe falls on his head. He*

tries to retain his balance but cannot and falls backward off the chair and onto the floor. Spectacular sparks and stars seem to ignite around him and in the sky. ALEX slaps PETER's face.)

ALEX: Wake up, wake up. You all right?

(PETER stands up slowly. In a daze he opens the safe and takes the money, and, as he does so, the light returns; but although full on it is different from before. The shadows cast seem more unreal, the sky behind looks more intense and vivid.)

PETER: I've got what I want. My dream's come true.

ALEX: Dreams or no dreams, let's get going.

PETER: Nothing can stop me now.

(He turns and shakes his head and activity begins once again inside the Butcher's shop; the people come down and are dressed differently; their clothes and characteristics are slightly more stylized and emphasized. The women look like busy owls shaking their heads, disapproving of their husbands who are all lounging about smoking and drinking and playing cards. SONIA is fussing around and giving everyone a word, like a queen at a garden party, and JASON is trying to keep up with her, visually proclaiming love at every opportunity. He is dressed more sinisterly. SYLVIA is looking at her flowers.

PETER and ALEX are about to exit.)

JASON: *(Coming out of shop.)* Ladies and gentlemen – here they come –

SONIA: *(Rushes out.)* Here comes the bride – dadadedum – dadadedum –

(PENNY and TOM enter, she in bridal gown and he in dress suit. She is sad and he is happy. The people come out and dance around them and throw confetti – they seem gay but don't make much noise.)

MR FISH: Isn't she pretty? Isn't she nice?

MR GREEN: Pelt them with confetti, rose petals, and rice.

MR BUTCHER: Penny darling, my joy's complete.

MRS FISH/MRS GREEN: She'll learn soon enough that life's not so sweet.

MRS BUTCHER: Well, come on, everyone, let's go back inside.

ALL: Isn't it lovely to see a bride?

MRS BUTCHER: Penny, you look beautiful. Thank God it's Tom and not Peter. I'm so happy for you I could cry.

PENNY: And I'm so unhappy for myself I could scream – throw confetti over me, I don't want to see him.
(*They pelt the couple with confetti and dance around the stage in single file and go back into the shop; PENNY sadly tags on at the end of the line.*)
(*At the door.*) You coming, Peter?

PETER: No, I'm going. (*She sadly follows the others into the shop.*)

PENNY: (*To TOM.*) Would you mind if I go upstairs? I've got a terrible headache.

TOM: Not at all, darling – you stay up there, that's a good place to be. I'll come up presently.

PENNY: Thank you, Tom, you're so sweet. I don't want to see him. (*She goes upstairs.*)
(*SONIA comes to the door and SYLVIA looks out of the window.*)

SONIA: Peter, Peter, come inside; it's getting windy and you'll get a cold.

PENNY: (*Upstairs on the fire-escape or leaning out of window.*) Peter, Peter, I love you still and I always will.

SYLVIA: Peter! Pull yourself together and I'll give you another chance. Maybe.

PENNY: I love you; take me away with you.

SYLVIA: If you loved me, you'd settle down.

SONIA: If you love me there's chicken for supper.

PETER: Three women in my life but the one I want doesn't want me. Who cares? That's the way it goes. I'm off. I'm going up in the world before the world goes up before me.

SONIA: And tomorrow, Peter, if you're a good boy, I'll boil you some salmon and garnish it with cucumber.

PETER: Girls! Supergirls! Peter supermann is coming your way –

SONIA: Or maybe some halibut and white lemon sauce followed by peaches and cream.

PETER: Your dream's coming true – and I don't care what
colour you are, red – yellow – white – blue or green –
my Superstore is open for you – whether you are father
inferior or mother superior Peter's Superstore stocks
everything for everyone. I don't care what you wear and
where you wear it – I don't care what you do and where
you do it. Boom. Boom. I'm coming your way – watch
out for me in the sky. Zoom – zoom – Peter supermann
– supermanic – supersonic – boom – boom – superboom
– super – super –

SONIA: Come home and have a nice plate of soup.

PENNY: Peter, I'll wait for you anytime, anywhere.

SONIA: Perhaps turkey and tongue and mushroom sauce and
lobster on Wednesday –

ALEX: You've got the money, you've had your say, now let's
get going.

SONIA: (*Comes out.*) Peter, come in, there's a good boy.

PETER: I'm finished listening to you. I'm leaving for the good
of myself and for the good of you and I'll return rich –
You'll see.

SONIA: Peter, what have you got in your hand?

PETER: This is it, I've taken the money – good-bye Mum. A
loan – you – understand – ?

SONIA: Money? Peter, don't joke about money –
(*All the people come out of the Butcher's shop, stand around,
and shake their heads.*)
Peter, what have you done? (*She rushes into shop.*)
(*PENNY comes down to door.*)

ALEX: Peter, let's get gone.

SONIA: Darling, the safe's open – tell me you're only joking.

PETER: (*His arm around her.*) I've taken it for the best – you'll
see – I'm doing this for you – for all of us.

SONIA: I think I'm going to die. Put it back, sonny boy.

PETER: You'll see, I'll make you proud of me. Good-bye.

SONIA: Go away. No, come here – How could you do this to
me?

PETER: Don't cry.

SONIA: All my life I slaved and what have I got? Look! See?
He's going – walking out on me. Now I've got nothing

except memories, but what use are they in your old age? Who wants a destitute widow with four photos on the mantelpiece? Who'll miss me? Does he care? Go on – Go! Go! Think I care? Everything is gone – Hope you enjoy yourself – I don't think – you've stolen everything – all the money I was saving for a rainy day.

PETER: (*Sings.*) There's a woman down the road, thought she'd

last forever,
So she saved ten thousand pounds for the rainy weather.
But now she's dead, yes, now she's dead,
The worms are chewing through her head,
In the rainy – wea-ther.
(*SONIA weeps.*)
Good-bye, Mother. Thanks. I'll be seeing you.

SONIA: (*She suddenly stops crying as PETER moves to one side with ALEX.*) Good riddance. Ain't it strange how troubles come these days, piling up on each other, more and more. Everything comes these days and nothing goes – 'cept him – Go – Go – It makes my eyes sore to look at you.

PETER: Come on, Alex, I'm ready now.

ALEX: Don't be upset – women are emotional things – she'll get over it. We all do.

SONIA: It'll do him no good. He started off on the wrong foot.
May he lose more blood than sea in the ocean –
May he get run over and smashed –
May the ground open up and swallow him –
May the sky fall on him –
(*After her outburst, pathetically and quietly.*)
Peter, please take care of yourself, don't catch cold.
(*SONIA, weeping, runs into the shop. The people go back into the Butcher's.*
PETER sadly plucks a flower from the flower stall and he and ALEX move and pass the Butcher's; PENNY still stands by the door.)

PENNY: Take me with you, please take me with you. I can't face it here without you.

PETER: All right, come along. You asked for it.
(*He pulls her out of the window and carries her off across his shoulder. ALEX follows him off quickly. The stage*

darkens and in the Butcher's shop we see them dancing.)

SONIA: (*Comes out of the shop.*) He was only kidding; he won't go far. (*She calls him.*) Peeet-ter – Peeeter – Where are you, darling? Supper's ready. It got dark suddenly. As you get older days don't last so long. Tuesdays and Thursdays become one and soon they all roll in together. Then just dark and light, dark and light, until – only dark, I suppose. Still, I mustn't grumble, I must count my blessings.

(*TOM, who has been upstairs, comes out of the shop and looks around.*)

He won't go far, will he?

TOM: No, have you seen my bride?

SONIA: (*Shaking her head slowly as if she realizes something.*) Come here, sonny boy, I want to tell you a few things about life.

(*He approaches and sits down beside her. He leans against her and she strokes his hair. The fading light goes out.*)

End of Act One.

ACT TWO

The dream continues but it appears that twelve years have passed. The stalls are empty and look menacing, and grotesque shadows are thrown. The shops are no longer used for selling and are all boarded up except the gown shop and JASON's funeral parlour. Before each shop is a separate little trench and before the trench a mound of earth – each mound has a crude wooden board stuck in it – reading 'FISH', 'BUTCHER', and 'GREEN'. Hooters are heard and dogs are howling. Moonlight, and in JASON's shop three figures are seen. They are indistinct and are gazing through the window. One of the figures is very small and has a tall man on each side. Their cigarettes glow in the dark.

PETER enters, followed by PENNY and ALEX. He is now thirty and has an untidy beard. He wears the clothes of a weary traveller, clothes that are utilitarian but worn out. ALEX looks more like a tramp than ever, and PENNY looks seductive in a crude way. They are all weary but furtive, looking over their shoulders as they enter. ALEX carries the few bundles. They are all obviously feeling cold.

PETER: This is it. This is where we stay tonight.

ALEX: Don't like the look of it.

PETER: I'm not asking you. (*He points to his old stall.*) We'll make ourselves comfortable here. Seems safe enough.
    (*ALEX shrugs and puts the things down. PENNY starts preparing some food for them while ALEX unpacks. PETER sits down and smokes. The two tall men come out of the shop, but are not seen by the trio. They are about to pounce on them, but the little man pulls them back. We briefly see that the little man is JASON.*)

PENNY: Doesn't he know where we are?

ALEX: Doesn't seem to. It's changed so much it had me fooled.

PENNY: Shall I tell him?

ALEX: Not yet. Can't stand another blow up. Peace at any price, that's my motto from now on.

PENNY: So that's my home then – my old safe womb – (*She shrugs and carries on with the food.*)

(*We now hear a high shrill sound, far away and dreamlike. We don't at first realize that it is JASON in the shop calling PETER's name.*)

JASON: PEEEET – TERR – PEEET – TERR – PEET – TERR –

(*He carries on like this. PETER suddenly jumps up.*)

PETER: Who's that? Did you hear that?

ALEX: It was just a dog howling.

PETER: No. Someone's calling me.

PENNY: There are plenty of mad dogs about.

JASON: PEET – TERR.

PETER: I told you. Now will you believe me?

PENNY: It's your imagination; it's just kids playing.

(*PETER walks around hut but does not see his mother's shop. He sits down for a moment and wipes his hands over his eyes like a confused man.*)

ALEX: (*Sitting down.*) Oh my poor plates of meat! Got a corn plaster, darling?

(*PENNY searches in her bag and gives him one.*)

(*Takes off shoes and socks and puts plaster on.*) What a relief! I've got one foot in the grave, and the other's got ingrowing toenails.

(*They both laugh.*)

PETER: (*Rushes over.*) What's going on here? What have you got to laugh at?

ALEX: Nothing and everything.

PETER: Well, stop it then. I don't feel like laughing. You got me into this bloody mess and now you expect me to get us out of it. (*To ALEX.*) A fine bloody guide you turned out to be. Uranium! You lousy liar – it was always the next country where we would strike it rich – the next field was greener – Well, I was the green one all right – Stole all my mother's money and it all led nowhere. And now I'm a no one with nothing. This is where we break up. This is the end of the road.

ALEX: You said it, this *is* the end of the road. This is where I came in.

PETER: What do you mean?

ALEX: This is your home?

PETER: *Home.*

ALEX: Sweet Home.

(*PETER sweeps all the things off his old stall and then rushes to his mother's door.*)

PETER: Mother! Open up! Let me in, I'm home. (*He bangs on the door.*)

(*When he realizes that there is no response he bangs on all the doors but avoids JASON's where the men duck out of sight.*)

Hey there! Where's everyone? Listen everybody – I'm home!

(*He bangs and rattles on all the doors again until he is back at his mother's door. ALEX looks on, but PENNY stretches herself along the stall and lies down.*)

Mum! Where are you? This is me! Wake up! Peter Mann's come home.

ALEX: (*To PENNY.*) No wonder everyone's run away.

PETER: (*Returning to ALEX.*) Don't understand it and I don't like it. (*To PENNY.*) What are you doing lying down?

PENNY: This is the position you got me used to.

PETER: The position you begged for. (*Once more he returns to his mother's shop.*) Open up! Let me in! (*When he sees it is quite hopeless he quietly sits down outside.*) A house to let, no rent to pay, knock on the door and run away. I used to play that. But where are the kids now? They've all gone. I'm all alone. (*He closes his eyes.*)

PENNY: (*Gets up and goes to him.*) Please, Peter, pull yourself together.

PETER: Leave me alone.

ALEX: Pull up your socks, son.

PETER: I might if I had some.

(*He reveals the fact that he has no socks; they both laugh.*)

What have I got to laugh at? I'm fed up with supporting you.

ALEX: That's rich – I did all the supporting, I did all the odd jobs.

PETER: Liar.

PENNY: Shut up the pair of you. Lying on my back I supported the both of you.

PETER: Get out of my sight – Get lost.

ALEX: (*Starts to walk away.*) All right, if that's the way you want it –

PETER: Hey. Come back – where are you going?

ALEX: You just told me to –

PETER: Trust you to walk out on me when the going gets a bit tough.

ALEX: Oh – I wish you'd make up your mind. (*He wanders near JASON's shop, tests the walls, and sings.*) Oh, the walls are thin in London town – they wouldn't need much blowing down, so workers of the world unite, before we vanish in the night – my dreams are thin and wearing thinner, no one expects me home for dinner, oh, comrades of the universe, there's nothing better but plenty worse. (*He sits down.*) Think I'll have a game of chess. (*Takes pocket chess out and starts playing.*) Oh dear, what a life – now let's see, my right hand won last time – stop talking to yourself, Alex, stop talking, you'll spoil the game – I must have silence when I play – Oh all right – shut up – Thank you.

PETER: (*Sitting outside mother's shop and PENNY lying on the stall for a moment are composed in their separate worlds.*) No one! Can't trust anyone – look at him – look at her – What can you do? What can you do with them?

(*JASON creeps out behind ALEX. Quietly he beckons JOHN and JACK who grab ALEX quickly and quietly; they carry him struggling into the shop.*)

(*Looking up just after they have all gone into shop.*) What did I tell you? Run out an me – you'll be the next –

PENNY: Never. I'll never leave you.

PETER: Go, who cares? (*Gets up.*) Alex? Where are you? Come back – I didn't mean it –

(*PENNY gets up and goes to him.*)

PENNY: Don't be afraid, I'm with you.

PETER: Afraid? I'm afraid of no one – go on – get cracking, you whore – there's your own street door – (*He knocks on MRS GREEN's door.*) Sylvia, where are you? I'm home.

PENNY: Grow up – For years I've been hearing about stinking Sylvia – why didn't you carry her off?

PETER: Sylvia! Let me in!

PENNY: Listen, Peter, I love you for what you are – I'm real – I'm not a vision –

PETER: You said it – You're a tart, a trollop, you make me sick.

PENNY: I'm what you made me, but I don't hold that against you. Don't you see, you're all washed up, but I don't care because I am also –

PETER: What can I do? Penny, where can I go?

PENNY: We'll start again here – Business as usual.

PETER: Not here. Never crap on your own doorstep.

(*He turns away from her and goes back to his mother's shop. PENNY sadly returns to her mother's door.*)

We haven't been gone long – go home – they'll forgive you.

PENNY: Maybe, but I'll never forgive myself.

(*JASON's men grab her and take her inside.*)

PETER: Penny, come here – where are you? Mum, let me in – Sylvia! Alex, where are you? Penny, don't leave me!

(*JASON comes out. PETER sees him across the stage but does not recognize him at first. They stealthily creep towards each other. JASON is dressed in frock coat and top hat and carries a baton under his arm.*)

Stop! Don't come closer.

JASON: (*Taking out a cosh, holds it in striking position, then offers it to the young man.*) It's dangerous to be out alone these days – can I interest you in a cosh, or a knuckle-duster? Haven't I seen you before some where? On Tele maybe or in the rogues' gallery.

PETER: Jason, it's me.

JASON: (*Shines a torch in his face.*) Strike a light, look who it ain't. So the salmon has come back to be tinned, definitely grade three.

PETER: I've been through a hard time.

JASON: Can I interest you in some life insurance or a ticket to the policeman's ball?

PETER: Stop joking – Where's everyone?

JASON: Indoors, afraid and shivering under bedclothes.

PETER: Why? Afraid of whom?

JASON: Of strangers – like you.

PETER: *Me?* I'm not a stranger.

JASON: (*Takes out a mirror.*) Take a look at yourself – Would you trust that man? Never! Can I sell you a razor?

PETER: But it's me, Peter Mann –

JASON: Try and tell them that. Now look, I like you and want to help, but I know you won't be welcome here.

PETER: But this is my home!

JASON: It was, but *twelve years* is a long time.

PETER: Twelve years? But I only left – a few months ago.

JASON: That's the way time flies.

PETER: But it seems like yesterday. What can I do?

JASON: Sorry, if your face don't fit you're out in the cold. Good-bye.

PETER: I want my mother. She'll vouch for me. (*Bangs on door.*) Mum! Where are you? (*To JASON.*) Where can I go?

JASON: That's your headache. Now – be a good boy and go. The people won't come out until you've gone. And they've got to work in order to get the food to make them work. Ta ta.

PETER: I won't go. You can't scare me. I know my rights. I'll call the police.

JASON: At your service – I am the police – why do you think I wear this hat? Here's my badge. Now do I have to blow my whistle for my two legged bow-wows?

PETER: But what happened? What are these holes for? Everything's changed. Why?

JASON: Twelve years ago you had an idea and went to look for it – URANIUM! The fever spread here and everywhere. They stopped making love, stopped buying and selling, neglected the business, and everything went to rack and ruin. To cut a long story sideways, everybody started digging, each his own little pitch. People were like animals, and the governments ran away – everywhere the same story. Westminster barricaded itself from Marylebone, streets cut themselves off from each other – everyone cringing in his little corner. Nobody wanders out and nobody wanders in – or (*Makes a throat-cutting sign with his hand across his throat.*) Twelve years, and we're still digging, and found nothing but worms, bones, and nails, and we're tired but who knows? Something may turn up. The most intelligent person in each district usually takes charge of things – that's me –

(*He blows his whistle and the men come on.*)

– who usually hires tough guys, that's them –

(*Indicates the two men who by now are close to PETER.*)

– to get rid of scroungers and strangers – that's you. Good day.

(*PETER makes one last desperate attempt to break into his mother's shop and get away from the men – he is about to throw his weight against it when she opens the door and he falls inside.*)

SONIA: They fall at my feet these days.

(*JASON waves his men away.*)

What can I do for you, sonny boy?

PETER: (*Picking himself up.*) Mother! I'm home. (*He tries to kiss her.*)

SONIA: I may be an attractive woman, but I draw the line at cradle snatching.

PETER: Mother – I'm home – it's me – Peter. Please forgive me.

SONIA: I forgive you, but who are you? Peter? Peter? Let me see?

PETER: Mother – they're after me – don't let them get me.

SONIA: Who?

(*She looks around and JASON puts his finger to his temple denoting PETER's madness; SONIA nods.*)

PETER: Help me, please; I'm hungry, cold, and tired.

SONIA: You're a nice-looking kid but I can't help you.

PETER: But I'm Peter – your son.

SONIA: I have no son.

PETER: It must be my beard – you don't know me because of this.

SONIA: If I had a son do you think I would let him grow a beard – sorry, son.

PETER: (*With horror walks away.*) Penny, where are you? Alex – let's get away from here. (*He searches for them.*)

JASON: So you don't know him?

SONIA: (*To JASON.*) When you've got money everybody's related to you. When you've got nothing you've got no one.

JASON: We'll have to make an example of him – he's an impostor.

SONIA: Pity – such a nice kid, too – still, we can't take any chances these days, besides look at his face – it's all jaw and no forehead.

(*All the people come out and start digging in the trenches. They look tired and take no notice of each other or of PETER. They are furtive and wear rags.*)

PETER: Alex! Quick! Come back – let's get away from here!

(*JASON blows a whistle; JOHN and JACK appear, and all the people stop working. PETER backs away from them and falls in a trench. They grab him and pinion him, and the market people applaud.*)

Let me go – let me go.

(*They tie PETER to a stall.*)

JASON: Bring the others!

(*JOHN and JACK go off and bring back ALEX and PENNY who are tied up – one on each side of PETER.*)

PETER: Oh, there you are – at last. If it hadn't been for you I wouldn't be here.

ALEX: Who led us here in the first place?

PENNY: Stop arguing, you two – we're all in the same boat.

(*The market people gather around and now seem quite happy with the proceedings.*)

JASON: Well, friends – let's have some hush please. As you can see we have strangers. What shall we do with them?

MR BUTCHER: Maybe they know some new card games.

MRS BUTCHER: Don't trust them.

MRS FISH: They might steal from us.

MR FISH: They'd find it hard.

MRS GREEN: What do they want?

MR GREEN: (*To PETER.*) If you want my old woman – it's a deal.

MRS FISH: They might be spies from Bow, or murderers from Soho.

MRS BUTCHER: Or thieves from Shepherd's Bush after the gold fillings in my teeth.

MRS GREEN: Or white slavers after virgins.

MR GREEN: They'd go bankrupt round here.

JASON: Silence! I don't care who they are or why they've
come – All I know is they are up to no good –

SONIA: Oh, smack their bums and send them packing.

JASON: No! I am the law here! And I don't know about you
but I'm tired of spies and foreigners – we must show the
world who we are.

JOHN: Hear –

JACK: Hear!

PETER: I've been too stunned to speak, lost for words to see
how my old friends have changed, but now I'm appealing
to you – Please – look – look at my face – I'm Peter Mann
– shave off my beard, honestly – I swear
I am – on the Bible!

JASON: Bible? (*He shrugs.*) Don't use that dirty word – you
make the ladies blush. *We* don't have books any more.
Haven't you heard?

PETER: Look, you know who I am.

PENNY: It's no good, Peter; they don't want to recognize us.

PETER: Sylvia! She's the one. Yes. Sylvia! Sylvia! Where are
you?

JASON: Bung up his gullet, boys, he's splitting my ear drum.

PETER: I promise not to scream.

(*JASON waves his men away. SYLVIA comes out of
Green's house. She looks much fatter now and is getting
grotesque to look at.*)

SYLVIA: Did someone call me? (*She goes up to PETER.*) What
is this? (*She sniffs and shudders.*) They pong.

PETER: Oh go away. Sylvia – where are you?

SYLVIA: I'm Sylvia – who are you?

PETER: Peter. But you're not Sylvia. SYLVIA! SYLVIA!

JASON: I warned you.

SYLVIA: Peter? I don't know you.

PETER: If you are Sylvia, tell them to let me go, for old time's
sake. Remember the times we had together – I was the first
to touch you – you said so.

SYLVIA: The bloody nerve – how dare you. I'm a respectable
girl – I'd never mix with the likes of you.

PETER: Oh go away – go away – I can't bear to look at you.
Gag me, blindfold me, I don't care any more.

ALEX: (*Calls JASON over.*) Get it over quickly, he's a sensitive
lad.

(*JASON nods.*)

And please untie me, I won't run away. Anything will seem
like a picnic after travelling around with him.

JASON: You have my sympathies. (*He unties ALEX who starts
to play chess again.*) Dear friends – quiet please.
I demand that we set an example with this liar.

JOHN: You said it.

JACK: You certainly did.

JASON: For your good. For the good of the community
I demand the full works.

JOHN: Hear –

JACK: Hear!

JOHN: He must die –

PETER: Hey – a joke's a joke –

(*JOHN puts his hand over PETER's mouth.*)

JASON: Then the outside world will know that we don't like
strangers in the market-place.

MRS BUTCHER: Quite right!

MRS FISH: Serves him right.

MRS GREEN: We've got to be careful.

SONIA: Count me out – you're all doing your nut.

JASON: We'll let the others go – both of them – (*Indicating
ALEX and PENNY.*) After they've seen what we've done to
him they will tell the world.

ALEX: King out of danger.

PENNY: I won't go without him – if you kill him you can kill
me too.

JASON: Silly girl. Why are you dying to die? You'll do as
you're told.

(*JACK releases PENNY and she goes to ALEX who
continues to play chess.*)

PENNY: How can you play at a time like this?

ALEX: He's got out of worse scrapes.

PENNY: No, this time it's serious.

ALEX: He'd talk his way out of hell.

PENNY: They'll kill him. Alex, we must do something.

ALEX: Don't worry. Call me when he goes green around the
gills – I'll believe it then.

(*PENNY rushes to PETER.*)

JOHN: Three cheers –

JACK: For Jason – Hip – Hip – Hip –

SONIA: *Horrors!* You give me the horrors.

JOHN/JACK: For he's a jolly good fellow – for he's a jolly
good fellow –

JASON: For I'm a jolly good fellow –

SONIA: That's something I can deny.

JASON: *Sonia!* Aren't you proud of me? Everyone is safe
again, thanks to me. Marry me tomorrow and we will
merge in every way.

SONIA: Not on your life – business and pleasure don't mix.

JASON: (*To PETER.*) Well, how do you want to go out? (*To
JOHN.*) Take the gag off and let him have a few last words.

PETER: Mum, save me. Penny, help me.

PENNY: If only I could.

JASON: Have you a last wish?

PETER: Yes. I don't want to die.

(*The gag is replaced.*)

JASON: You're mad, death is very fashionable these days –
the very best people are dying like flies.

ALEX: Please be quieter. My knight is in a sticky position.

MRS BUTCHER: Come on, Jason, let's get cracking.

MR BUTCHER: If you must do it – quick and clean –
through the forehead with a bullet.

MRS FISH: Put a sock in it. We haven't seen a good show for
years.

MR FISH: Bash him on the head, then – that's the best way –
and slit his gullet.

MR GREEN: Chop him up, peel him, boil him, bake him,
mash him – do what you like but get it over with – the
poor boy's had enough.

MRS GREEN: Trust you. You want everything quick – have it
and turn to the wall – well, women are different.

MRS BUTCHER I love a bit of ceremony.

MRS FISH: It's not often we can let off steam.

JASON: (*To PETER.*) If you know any prayers, say them now.

SONIA: Let the poor boy speak.

(*The men are playing cards, and altogether there is a festive air around. SYLVIA and JACK bring on drinks from JASON's shop while JOHN guards PENNY and ALEX.*)

(*SONIA is offered a drink by SYLVIA.*) No thanks.

SYLVIA: It's very nice – it's a Bloody Mary – Tomato juice and vodka.

(*She hands the drinks around.*)

SONIA: Take off his gag.

(*JASON does so.*)

PETER: HELLLLLLLLLP.

JASON: Save your breath, you ain't got much coming.

PETER: This is my home – where I worked – you must know me. That was my stall. Step right up, you know me – I'm the one – everyone knows me – I'm the man – Peter Mann.

JASON: Poor boy's demented.

PETER: I sold cloth here – I know all the patter. Give me a chance. Alex – tell them you found me here.

ALEX: I found him here. (*Continues with chess.*) Sssh – this is crucial.

PETER: Penny darling – tell them.

PENNY: Please believe him, this was my home, too. What's the matter with all of you? *Stop it!* Oh, Peter, what can I do? Let him go! Use me as an example. Kill me. I haven't got much to lose – only the things I don't even have. Peter, I'm staying with you.

PETER: My stall – (*He breaks away and jumps on stall.*) My stall – (*He stands before it between the two men.*) Step right up – Ladies and gentlemen – I've got a little line today – the finest, toughest, purest, softest, guaranteed drip-dry, heat resistant, mothproof cloth this side of the Table Mountain – you there – feel it – smell it – see that mark? Made by Mann for Man – I'm knocking them out – not fifty shillings – not forty, not thirty-five, not thirty but going to the first

ten lucky punters for a measly nicker – Show us the colour
of your money – That's the best colour in the world – I'm
mad – I'm crazy, I'm stone bonks – I should be locked
away giving such bargains. Look at these shirts – Come on,
buy, you silly sods – Nylon négligées, lingering lingerie,
and beautiful bras for bonny bits of –

(*The men get hold of PETER.*)

JASON: Don't worry, son, I've got a padded coffin just your
size, and it's almost closing time.

PENNY: (*Rushes to him.*) Peter –

(*The men try to drag her away.*)

No, let me hold on to him –

JASON: All right, let her stay – I was in love once. I was
young once.

SONIA: Don't kid me – you were born just as you are.

PETER: Penny – now I know – if I had another chance
I swear I'd be different – it's you I really want.

PENNY: I know, darling. Hold on – I'm holding on to you.
You're not alone.

PETER: We're all alone in the end. Penny, forgive me.

MR BUTCHER: Get a move on.

MR FISH: Look at them, love's young dream.

MR GREEN: If had a fiddle I'd play 'Hearts and Flowers'.

MRS GREEN: Shut up – these men – lovely show, ain't it?

MRS BUTCHER: Proper smashing.

MRS FISH: Real romantic.

SYLVIA: Popcorns! Chocolate! Cigarettes! (*She wanders
around.*)

ALEX: Checkmate!

JASON: All right, boys, this is it.

(*JOHN and JACK stand PETER on the stall and tie his
outstretched hands with white ribbons which they tie to
either end of the stall. PENNY clutches his feet and buries
her face into his flesh.*)

Now, something spectacular like stabbing.

(*JOHN and JACK take out knives and are about to fall
on him.*)

PETER: I want say a few last words.

JOHN You've said enough.

JACK: You said it.

JASON: All right boys – I know how you must be feeling – like turkey to roast and no shillings for the slot. A few last words and be quick about it –

PETER: God guide me –

JASON: No prayers, no philosophy – hurry up, my boys are already on time and a half.

PETER: Where was I? Oh yes – listen God – I didn't mean to steal – Seriously – look here – What? I can't hear you – come closer – I'm so lonely – everyone's gone – even you –

JASON: No filibustering.

SONIA: Leave the poor devil alone – he's talking to God.

JASON: He's a liar.

SONIA: Would God talk to a liar?

PETER: Oh guide me – I'm afraid – I've got land sickness, sea sickness, and sky sickness – get me out of this and I'll make it worth your while – oh – Dad! Dad! Come home – where are you? Stop wandering – Oh God come home – the days play fast and loose with me and the noose of night strangles my prayers – please understand even if you're not there – just in case – come downstairs and pull your pyjamas up – take the cotton wool out of your ears – stop tripping over your beard – lead me out of this – lift me up – hold me – lift me up – not too far from earth – put me down not too far from the stars – Dad – come home – Oh God – Where am I? Where are you? Who am I? Who are you? What am I? Why am I? When am I?

JASON: Enough – that should put you in his good books. Carry on, boys.

SONIA: (*Rushes to them just as the men are about to lunge their daggers in.*) WAIT!

JASON: What now?

SONIA: You cannot kill him – he's my – son – that's who you are.

PETER: Mother – thank God! The nightmare's over.

SONIA: You area silly boy – why didn't you tell me? (*She climbs up beside him.*)

JOHN: What now, boss?

JACK: Yes, what next?

JASON: Be patient, boys – we'll iron the whole thing out – have a fag.

(*They do.*)

Sonia – are you sure he's your boy? Why didn't you recognize him before?

SONIA: I wasn't too proud of him – wanted to forget him – but blood is thicker than water. Why didn't you tell me?

JASON: If you didn't recognise him why should I?

SONIA: You know everything. After my money still – you naughty, nasty old man. I'm surprised with you.

JASON: Are you sure you're sure?

SONIA: I heard him cry for help – a mother knows – yes under all that bum fluff he's all mine. Untie him.

JASON: I'll think it over. We won't be hasty. (*He goes and speaks softly to his two men.*)

SONIA: Please hurry up, I've got a chicken in the oven.

(*PENNY embraces PETER and to avoid her parents she goes to talk to ALEX.*)

MRS GREEN: What a bloody shame – looks like the show's over.

MRS BUTCHER: It's always the same. Nothing ever happens round here.

MR BUTCHER: Good luck, son – but go while the going's good.

MR FISH: Back to work, then – come on –

(*All the wives drag all their husbands back to their respective trenches.*)

PETER: Thank you – how can you forgive me? How can I repay you? I'm free! Free again – free – I'm flying – nothing can stop me – I'm alive – (*He flaps his arms and though he is still tied with ribbons he resembles a bird.*) I'm saved – cockledoodledo. Mother – I want to kiss you.

SONIA: Mother? Look, when they untie you, you hoppit – I've got enough worries. I'm not your mother – and if I was I wouldn't want to be.

PETER: But you are. You said you were.

SONIA: I couldn't bear to see you suffer – not even you – so I took pity. I've got a heart, ain't I? But I'm a hard woman, so don't take advantage.

PETER: But you *are* my mother – you really are. I'm Peter.

SONIA: I have no son – apart from being a low life he's also touched – poor boy – Listen, I took pity on you but when they untie you – you fly. Only I could have done it, only I can influence that body snatcher, so take my advice and toodle loo.

PETER: But – I am – you are –

JASON: (*As his men untie PETER.*) Welcome home, Peter – I'm so pleased I bumped into you before you leave.

PETER: Leave? What do you mean?

JASON: You can't stay here – it's too small for the both of us.

PETER: I won't go – you need me here.

JASON: Sonia – either he goes or I stay.

SONIA: Sort it out between you – my chicken's nearly done.

PETER: Chicken? Oh, Mum, I'm starved.

JASON: We've got enough mouths to feed without you.

SONIA: (*To PETER.*) You heard what he said – Tata, sonny boy –

PETER: But –

SONIA: Look, son, I saved your life – what more do you expect? Chicken as well? In these times – ?

JASON: You heard what she said. Even your mother's had enough – Good-bye. (*He turns to SONIA.*) Sonia, at last – now I know you're free. No longer holding on to pipe dreams in the sky – and now you've got rid of your son – maybe you'll listen to reason. Marry me.

SONIA: But what's your real reason? Because I can cook? *No!* Because I'm beautiful? *No!* Because I might have a few bob saved? *Yes!*

JASON: Marry me now – I'll marry us – I'll sell myself a ring – buy some furniture and insurance from myself – and we'll keep it in the family. I love you – you're so lovely – so gay – so tender and understanding – so – my shape – I dream about you.

SONIA: You dirty old man – you make me shiver, besides you don't wash behind your ears –

JASON: You do things to me – I'm your slave. I can't live without you. Oh, Sonia, how like a woman you are –

SONIA: That's only a coincidence. Let's talk about you for a change. What do you think of me? Good-bye.

(*SONIA goes into her shop.*)

JASON: I think you're a horrible, terrible, ugly old woman – a heartless monster, with no fine feeling. (*He turns to PETER.*) Now you go quick before we string you up a gain. We don't want you round here.

(*The two men close on him.*)

PENNY: Come on, Peter, let's get going.

(*One man gives ALEX a prod.*)

ALEX: The people in the next field may be greener. Oh my poor legs – will I ever rest?

PETER: (*To the people in the separate trenches.*) Listen everyone – listen to me – dreamers, schemers, slaves, slobs – Down your tools and listen –

JASON: Don't listen to him if you know what's good for you. Jack – John! Frogmarch him away.

PETER: I've got something to tell you. Something to sell you.

(*JOHN and JACK have grabbed him, but the people come out of their trenches.*)

MR GREEN: Leave him alone – listen to what he's got to say.

MR BUTCHER: He can't make things worse.

PETER: There needs to be a new spirit – a new feeling – a revival of hope.

MRS BUTCHER: Hope? What's that?

ALEX: Hold on to your safety belts, here we go again.

MR BUTCHER: (*To JOHN and JACK.*) Let him go – speak up, son.

MR FISH: Where there's life there's hope.

PETER: I can give you hope.

MRS FISH: Will hope light the gas? Will it fill the belly?

MR BUTCHER: Let him go or we'll brain ya –

(*The three men stand ready to hit JOHN and JACK.*)

JASON: All right, let him go.

PETER: (*Stands on a soapbox.*) Thank you one and all – Now, what are you digging for?

MR BUTCHER: Uranium!

PETER: Exactly! Then I'm the boy for you. We must organize, co-operate, work together.

MRS BUTCHER: Work together? You mad?

PETER: Why are you digging your own grave – erm – trench – ? You there? What have you found? Nothing! Many hands make light – how does it go?

ALEX: Too many cooks spoil the broth?

PETER: Oh shut up, Judas. You must pool resources – pull together – work in harmony – share the labour, share the treasure. You must dig a supertrench – and you need me as supervisor.

ALEX: Yeah, the supermanic depressive visionary.

PENNY: Leave him alone. He's trying. You've been needling him for days.

ALEX: (*To PENNY.*) Let's go.

PETER: There's nothing you don't know about uranium – ask my friends here – is that right?

ALEX: Absolutely – he doesn't know – a thing.

PETER: You want me – and I want you to want me – I promise you the earth –

ALEX: They'll get it all right.

PETER: What have you got to lose?

MRS BUTCHER: Nothing!

JOHN: Shall we do him, boss?

JACK: Give the word.

JASON: Not yet.

PETER: We'll become strong again – this place will be the centre of the world – we'll set an example to all the streets in the country – what do you say?

MR FISH: Sounds like hard work.

PETER: Sure – but who's afraid of hard work?

MEN: We are.

PETER: Nonsense – you've had no incentive – nothing to work for – but now we must dig, dig, dig – off with your coats and on with the job. Up with your hearts and down with your shovels.

(*This is met with silence.*)

What's the matter with you all?

MR BUTCHER: We're afraid.

PETER: What of?

MR FISH: This, that, and the other.

MR GREEN: Especially the other.

MRS GREEN: I'm afraid of myself.

MR BUTCHER: I'm afraid of my wife.

MRS BUTCHER: I'm afraid of my brother.

MR FISH: We're afraid of each other.

MR GREEN: I'm afraid of my mother – and she's scared to
death of me.

MRS GREEN: Who could blame her? I'm afraid of my
shadow.

WOMEN: We're afraid of having kids.

MEN: We're afraid of sterility –

MRS FISH: Afraid of virility.

MR BUTCHER: Afraid of frigidity.

MRS GREEN: Rigidity.

MRS FISH: Potency.

MR FISH: Impotency. Oh, we're so afraid.

PETER: I'm afraid you all worry too much.

MR BUTCHER: What's the answer?

PETER: I am. Peter Mann.

MRS GREEN: If only we could believe that.

WOMEN: We need someone to lead us.

MEN: We need someone to need us…

PETER: Your worries are over, because – I'm taking over.

ALL: Hurrah – hurrah –

> (*They lift him up and carry him around the stage. SONIA
> comes rushing out and so does TOM-GROOM looking just
> like in Act One, only much older – his wedding clothes still
> on but looking rather dilapidated. JASON retires to the back
> of the stage with his men, and ALEX sits down and plays
> chess: PENNY tries to keep close to PETER, but SYLVIA
> keeps on coming in between her and the happy group.*)

PETER: Listen, everyone – and when we find uranium – we'll
open the greatest – longest – highest – grandest Superstore
– you ever saw – selling the most wonderful superfood
in the world – lovely fresh salmon – peaches and cream

– fat turkeys – hams and tongues – lobster and barons of
beef – legs of pork – shoulders of veal – lettuces the size of
currant bushes – cucumbers – tomatoes – dates – melons
– olives – kippers – marmalade –

SONIA: Peter! You are my Peter – my son – you're back – at
last you're back.

PETER: (*The people put him down.*) At last you know me – Oh,
Mum, I'm starving.

SONIA: Where have you been? I've looked all over for you!
You bad boy – you're so pale and thin – your eyes are
bloodshot – too many late nights, eh?

PETER: Days and nights have been the same. Let's go inside.

SYLVIA: Oh, Peter – darling Peter – I love you – I've been
waiting for you – please don't leave me again.

PETER: Sylvia – I dreamed of this moment.

SONIA: Jason, I want you.

JASON: Sonia darling.

(*He embraces her; she pushes him off.*)

SONIA: (*Takes off JASON's hat and puts it on PETER.*) Here is
my son and he's taking over.

JASON: I'll be happy to place myself and my boys at his
disposal – at a slight cost, of course. Oh, Sonia, Sonia, it
seems like I've lost you again. Never mind – I'll get you in
the end.

SONIA: Don't be dirty. Come, Peter, I've got a bone to pick
with you – a nice roast chicken – and some lovely soup to
start with – oh what can I do with you? Do me a favour,
shave that beard off. Oh you drive me mad – you'll be
the death of me – what a son I've got! Did you miss me,
darling? What did you do with that money? Where have
you been? Thief! Liar! Worm – darling – am I happy to see
you!

SYLVIA: Peter, we'll get married as soon as possible.

MRS GREEN: Let's all have a party.

MRS FISH: That's a marvellous idea.

(*They all become merry.*)

PETER: (*About to enter house.*) No! This is the time to work –
we must dig – break down barriers – dig together – fast

and deep – Now is the time – I'll see you all later.

(*PETER, SONIA, and SYLVIA go inside where they drink.*)

ALEX: What did I tell you? He's out of trouble and we're out in the cold. Typical! Look at him! We worry ourselves sick, and greedy-guts in there guzzles himself sick. I'm a bloody mug and you're a bloody fool.

PENNY: You're right, Alex. Lets get away from here –

(*The people start digging again – this time more feverishly – watched by JOHN and JACK. PENNY goes close to TOM-GROOM, watching him.*)

JASON: (*To ALEX.*) Excuse me, how would you like to earn a fiver?

ALEX. How many people must I kill?

JASON: Just get rid of Peter Mann. Spin him a yarn – get him away from here – as far as possible.

ALEX: Nothing doing, I'm in the middle of my game.

JASON: Twenty pounds?

(*ALEX shakes head.*)

Forty? Forty-one? Fifty? Seventy-five? All right – I'll have to do it. One hundred pounds?

ALEX: Not interested. Sssh – my left hand is sensitive. (*Playing chess.*)

JASON: You must take him away.

ALEX: And stop shouting. My right hand suffers from ear trouble. Good night.

JASON: In that case I shall go inside and enjoy the party. I'm a realist – what else could any honest undertaker afford to be?

(*He knocks on the door and PETER opens it and inside they all dance; ALEX plays quietly, and PENNY talks to TOM.*)

TOM: Are you lost, Miss?

PENNY: Yes, I have been but I've come home. Tom!

TOM: How do you do? You know my name? Of course. I'm the fellow who's pointed at and jeered after. I have a room here. (*Points at MR and MRS BUTCHER.*) You've got a nice face.

PENNY: Are you still waiting?

TOM: What else is there to do?

PENNY: You must love her a lot.

TOM: I'm not sure anymore – I've just got into the habit.
I like you.

PENNY: You poor boy. You're so different from the others; I
wish I had someone like you.

TOM: I know what you are, but I don't care. I need something
so bad. Please come with me inside.

PENNY: How long will you wait for her?

TOM: For ever, I think.

PENNY: Then there's no chance for me.

TOM: Sure there is. Come and pass the time with me. I'll look
after you. (*He grabs her.*) Let me kiss you.

PENNY: Leave me alone. She'll never come now. Men! For
someone like me, for a slut, you'd dirty your dream.

TOM: I've waited so long. She'll understand. Believe me,
you're the first I've noticed.

PENNY: Bitched by myself. That's something to tell the
looking-glass. She'll never come now.

TOM: Please let me help you. Let me love you. Help me.

PENNY: Come on – I'll kill two birds with one stone –
besides I don't want to see him again.

TOM: (*To MRS BUTCHER.*) Can she stay with me?

MRS BUTCHER: What you do in your room is your own
affair. As long as you pay for it.
(*PENNY sadly follows TOM into the house.*)

MR BUTCHER: I've seen that girl before, somewhere.

MRS BUTCHER: You have, have you? Get on with your
work.
(*Everyone is digging when PETER and SYLVIA, JASON
and SONIA come dancing out of the house.*)

SYLVIA: Mr Jason get for me – a long white gown – a double
bed –

PETER: With a springy spring –

SYLVIA: A wedding ring, a motor car – a frigidaire –

PETER: Not so frigid –

SYLVIA: A three-piece suite –

SONIA: And lots to eat.

SYLVIA: Jason get me everything.

PETER: Put up the banns, pull down the blinds – For my
    darling you are mine – We'll be rich and great – the very
    greatest – every gadget we get will be the latest –

ALL: All jump into bed – good-bye maidenhead –

PETER: Oh tonight you will be mine –

ALL: Up with the lights – let's all get stinking tight – we're
    gonna have a smashing time.
    (*Everyone dances around and the four dance back into the
    house. The people in the trench work furiously but now are
    all happy. Drink has appeared and they are all swigging it.*)

ALEX: (*Finishing the game.*) Checkmate. (*He sits down on a stall
    and covers himself over as the Act ends.*)

End of Act Two.

ACT THREE

Five more years have passed. It is summer. At the back of the stage, where the shops stood, there is now a modern-looking building. This is the shroud factory. The trenches are now gone, but downstage there is a concrete slab that covers a passageway down into the earth; this has a very heavy door with the word 'SHELTER' in red lettering.

The undertaker's and the gown shop still there, but look very prosperous. The shutters of SONIA's shop are up but there are no more gay-looking dresses and no more materials.

Flowers surround the door and windows and inside there is great luxury, though the furniture is a terrible mixture of contemporary and nouveau riche.

Inside SONIA lies on a divan, asleep. SYLVIA is with her, looking very fat, in fact very much the way SONIA did in Act One.

SYLVIA looks obscene with gaudy clothes and a great deal of chunky jewellery. Her hair is dyed platinum blonde and she is heavily made up. PETER is with them, but is looking outside, where all the stalls have been pushed away from the centre of the stage.

On one stall languish PENNY and ALEX; he is playing chess.

The market people have lost the hunted, haunted look of the previous Act: now they are vacant and robot-like. They are all dressed in dull uniform dungarees and are seated centre-stage in a circle. TOM-GROOM addresses them. In the factory JASON stands between his two men.

TOM: Come on, once again –
MEN: We're tired.
TOM: Come on, on your feet – all together – One, two – One, two, three – We don't want a shroud factory. One, two, three, four – Where is our Superstore? Oh, what's the use? What are we on strike for if you're goona sit down?

WOMEN: This is a sit-down strike.

TOM: That's what you think. Up you lazy bastards –
(*They all groan as they slowly get up.*)
One, two – three, four – We don't want war – One, two,
three, four, five –

ALL: We want to stay alive. (*They all carry little posters as they
walk around and around – reading.*) – We demand more
money – we want peace. No Union – No Work.
(*JASON suddenly rushes out followed by JOHN and
JACK.*)

JASON: Now come on, back to work, and then we can start
negotiations.

TOM: We stay on strike till we get our rights.

JASON: Everything will get better, we are thinking of you all
the time. And if you want a union – well, certainly,
I will organize it and run it for you.

MR BUTCHER: We want a Superstore, not a superwar.

JOHN: You'll get what you're given.

JACK: Shall we do them, boss?

JASON: No – we are all sensible people and we can talk it
over. Please, my children, what do you want?

TOM: We all dug together, didn't we? And we found it but
what happened? Peter Mann told us that so much uranium
made the world a dangerous place to be so we couldn't
have our Superstore just yet and we were palmed off with
promises.

MR GREEN: We haven't even got a decent place to live.

TOM: So he gave us full employment and now we work the
clock round in this shroud factory and he's the richest man
in the world – and we haven't got a Superstore.

JASON: But these are old arguments – And when we have
enough shrouds and everyone in the world is protected
I personally promise you will get your Superstore. Now
back to work for everything will turn out all right. Besides,
what use is food if you're dead?

MRS GREEN: It's always been promises, promises, promises.

MRS FISH: Things don't get better, they get worse.

MRS BUTCHER: Everything is dearer. And look at the state
of the world.

TOM: Yes, we want protection like him. We want shelter. The world is on the brink but he'll be safe. Down there in his deep shelter. Because he's the richest he's got the deepest place to hide. We want protection.

JASON: There will not be a war, take that from me – it's only rumours you hear. Maybe a little limited war but the shrouds will protect you. Now, please for his sake – you know how he worries about you; besides poor Sonia is dying.

TOM: So are we dying. We're being wasted. We work all the time, we're going to get blown up any minute – come on everyone –

(*JASON retires to talk to his men as they march round again.*)

MEN: We found a fortune in the ground and scooped it out.

WOMEN: And in its place we set a concrete mound –

MEN: But now it isn't safe above the ground –

WOMEN: We truly have inherited the earth.

MEN: We stay on strike – we're sick of senseless work.

ALL: No peace on earth until we rest in earth.

(*The men sit down and play cards. The women stand and gossip. JOHN and JACK watch them as JASON rushes into SONIA's house.*)

JASON: Peter, you must do something – get them back to work. Only you can do it.

PETER: We're all going to die.

JASON: Thank God, otherwise where would I be? Peter, do something.

PETER: I brought it to this and there's no escape.

JASON: We need more shrouds. You must stop dreaming – after all the world isn't coming to an end even if we do all get blown up. I'm an optimist.

PETER: I must take my mother down.

JASON: Do what you like, but first get them back to the bench. And don't worry. Whatever you do, I'll look after the business.

PETER: *That's* my main worry. (*He goes outside.*) Listen everyone – (*He walks into the centre of the people.*) I'm one of you. We did this together. This factory – look at it – once again we can hold up our heads with pride – we led the world and we set the example – we built this Empire – all eyes are on us – and as you know we pulled the world together, it is our shrouds that cover the world – every Peter Mann shroud factory in the world got the prototype and the hope and incentive from us – I was the Mann. I had the idea. I created this new industry for you – Only by working hard can we be saved; we can be saved and we must be saved. We can negotiate but it must be by strength – the enemy must know that our goods are Empire and second to none – there will be no war, I promise – cross my heart – but only, I repeat, only if each member of the community plays his part – shrouds are essential – they are for the defence of freedom and liberty – when this crisis is over I promise you – remuneration, superannuation – abolition of taxes, free television sets, and the greatest Superstore full of food – remember what it was like? Real food – three-hour day – four-day week and beautiful homes for your happy children – this is my solemn promise – now let me see you all – all of you – go back to work and everything will be forgotten.

TOM: Three cheers for dear mister Mann. Hip, hip, hip. –

ALL: Hooray – hooray –

(*They line up and troop back into the factory, followed by JOHN and JACK who watch them. There they work like automatons, fast and silent.*

PETER goes back inside, to his mother.)

PETER: Mother, wake up, there's not much time.

SONIA: Oh, I was dreaming so beautifully.

PETER: Come on down, war will break out any moment.

SONIA: I'll be dead anyway in a couple of hours. What the eye doesn't see the heart cannot grieve. Now, wheel me outside, it's nice out there – the birds don't notice the crisis.

SYLVIA: (*Rushing to PETER as he prepares to take his mother from settee to a very grand-looking invalid chair.*) Take me down with you. Peter, I believe you.

SONIA: Peter, who's she? Huh! Your wife!

SYLVIA: Shut up, you interfering old bitch.

SONIA: Who's old? Come, Peter, I've only got a short time
left – You owe me at least that much.

(*SYLVIA confers with JASON as PETER pushes his
mother outside. JASON follows them, and SYLVIA follows
on.*)

PETER: Now you must rest and take it easy.

SONIA: Now he worries about me – now, when it's too late.
All my life he drives me to this point and now he wants to
prolong my agony.

PETER: In a minute we'll be down in the shelter and safe.

SONIA: I'm not going anywhere, except you know where and
I don't mean that place, either.

PETER: You're perfectly well.

SONIA: Well? How dare you say I'm well. I won't last the
night – still, it'll make a change.

JASON: Sonia, marry me while there's still time.

SONIA: I would if I could but I can't, because you'll be
burying me tomorrow. Being married and being buried is
almost the same thing for a woman. I'm going to be a man
next time.

JASON: Marry me now.

SONIA: Sorry, darling, I want to go unattached. I'm not
taking any chances. Maybe the devil's got designs on me.
I'm feeling wonderful; all the pains are gone. If this is
death why didn't I have more of it? Jason, no funny stuff,
bury me near the gasworks – no, no – cremate me and turn
me into an egg-timer – your boiled eggs should only have
three minutes, Peter.

JASON: You worked hard enough, Sonia.

PETER: Mother, you won't die. You're not the dying sort. You
can't, I won't let you. Who'll cook and take care of me?

SYLVIA: Don't waste your time with her; can't you see she's
out of her mind?

SONIA: If you're sensible, thank God, I'm mad.

JASON: Sonia, we have witnesses – we could become one
here and now.

SONIA: Don't be a dirty old man, you dirty old man.

JASON: Huh, the pot calls the kettle black.

PETER: Shut up.

SONIA: Peter darling, if you are that scared you'd better shelter – and if you're frightened of being alone – take her. (*Points to SYLVIA.*) Even she's better than nothing.

PETER: I want to go but I don't want to go without you. I'm torn two ways.

SYLVIA: You heard what she said, take me. I'm your wife, I demand to go.

PETER: Shut up – can't you see my mother's dying? (*To JASON.*) And you shut up – you've been robbing me for years. You're not getting your hands on her money also.

JASON: What money?

PETER: The money she's leaving me.

SONIA: Don't be too sure.

JASON: You are a mad crank who's gone balmy, and on top of that you're out of your mind.

SONIA: If they do this today what will they be like tomorrow? Time, gentlemen, please. I'm dying to get some peace.

JASON: I loved her; you ruined everything.

PETER: I love her and from now on I'm finished with you.

SONIA: Have you no respect for the dying?

JASON: When she's dead you can take care of yourself – if you can.

PETER: When she's dead I'm taking over everything. Completely.

SONIA: Listen, I'm not dead yet and what's more – if you go on like this I won't die.

PETER: Don't threaten me.

SONIA: Listen, Peter, you'll have to fend for yourself – a few cooking hints. To make an omelette crack the eggs first, throw them in the pan, and light the gas.

PETER: The bloody world is gonna burst before our very eyes.

JASON: You're mad.

SONIA: When you come to think about it – everyone who made a terrible fortune has been out of their mind – There was the man with motor cars in America and that man who struck it rich with frying oil and my Uncle Sydney.

JASON: Be serious, Sonia.

SONIA: To make a soufflé separate the white from the yellow
– whisk the white, fold in the yellow, and in seventeen
minutes it's nice and brown and golden.

SYLVIA: Peter, please, we can start all over again – we've got
everything down there –

SONIA: Even a swimming pool and a picture palace. (*To
'Beautiful Dreamer'.*) Beautiful cheesecake, creamy and rich,
tender roast chicken and smoked salmon sandwich. By the
way, son, drink a lot of milk.

SYLVIA: What's all her money worth now? You can't buy a
visa into heaven.

SONIA: That's what you think. I've just been having a chat
with their immigration officers. Nice boys. Peter, do
yourself a favour. Buy a yacht – drift over the south seas
and buy a few islands – use one island for a living room
and another for a bedroom – leave your terrible wife, take
Penny with you. I have something to confess, Peter – I
loved your father the most.

PETER: Why drag him up? Go to sleep, Mum, you must be
tired.

SONIA: No, you go to sleep. I'll sing you a song.

PETER: You'll make me cry. (*Sits by her.*)

SONIA: Why? It's me who's dying. Hush. I'll sing you a going
to sleep song. (*She strokes his hair as she sings.*)
When Peter was a little boy, he heard the angels sing;
They flew into the living-room and said, 'You will be king.'
'Of what will I be king?' Peter did reply.
'You'll be king of your domain, underneath the sky.'
'Where, oh where, is my domain? Who and where am I?'
'In your heart and in your brain – now go to sleep my boy.'
When Peter was a little boy, he heard the angels sing;
They flew far from the living-room when they proclaimed

him king.
(*PETER is almost asleep, but SONIA slumps forward
over him.*)

PETER: Help me, oh, she's gone.

SYLVIA: She's at rest now.

JASON: Well, how do you want her buried?

SONIA: You soon got over loving me.

JASON: But I thought – oh –

SONIA: I've changed my mind. I don't want to die in the afternoon. Besides I'm thirsty.

JASON: I'll get you some water.

SONIA: Don't be bloody daft, I want wine. I want to be drunk when I go out – drunk and dancing, dancing and singing. I'll show 'em.

PETER: *Who?*

SONIA: (*Pointing at the sky.*) Those who come and go.

PETER: Listen, everyone, isn't that beautiful? My mother's talking to the angels.

SONIA: They're just like people. Already they've been on the tap talking about partnerships and singing 'Buddy can you spare a diamond'. Where's the wine? (*She stands.*)

PETER: Mother, please don't exert yourself.

JASON: But, Sonia, you're dying – this isn't decent.

SYLVIA: Let her finish it off quick.

SONIA: I'll dance into death – poke out your tongue at the dark and say here's mud in your eye and fluff in your keyhole. (*She dances a few steps, singing.*) Dancing in the dark – Jason, may I have this waltz with you?

JASON: What waltz?

(*She now dances to PETER when JASON moves away with horror. PETER moves backward, also afraid.*)

SONIA: Peter, dance with your mummy.

PETER: (*Trying to draw her towards the shelter door.*) I'll dance with you downstairs.

SONIA: Who will dance with me? Who? Who? Who?

ALEX: (*Who has moved forward with PENNY to watch the proceedings.*) I will.

SONIA: Who are you?

ALEX: A friend of the family.

SONIA: Do you come here often?

ALEX: I live here, over there. Don't you know me?
(*He takes her in his arms and they dance.*)

SONIA: Why didn't you come sooner? Have you got some wine?

ALEX: Something better. I've been saving this for a special occasion – champaigne. (*He pretends to pop a bottle and they both dring straight from it.*)

SONIA: I name this battle ship *Potemkin* – may God forgive me and all who sail in me.

(*Music is heard and they dance round faster and faster.*)

Faster, faster, hold me tight.

PETER: (*Tries to intervene.*) Stop it. Leave her alone.

SONIA: Faster. Another swig, my lovely man. They're all gone. Just you and me – why did we miss each other? Why did you come too late?

(*ALEX cannot keep up with her and soon she breaks away from him and dances by herself watched by the others who stand around her. She moves tragically and almost drops several times but ALEX stands forward and seems to encourage her to move. She smiles and carries on but gradually during the course of this next song she slows right down and stops.*)

Dance before you die, dance into the sky – dance into the dark – do not ask me why – while your legs can move – make the most of them – while your arms can wave – oh wave me away – dance while you still live – live while you're alive – every moment snatch yourself a chance and dance – before you dance into the dance into the – d-a-rk.

(*She stumbles, looks around at PETER, and falls dead. Everyone rushes forward and stands round her except PETER who moves back; PENNY goes to him.*

JASON blows a whistle. JOHN and JACK come out and are ready to move her.)

PETER: Leave her alone.

JASON: I'll handle this. Stand back everyone.

ALEX: So long, old girl, I'll be seeing you.

(*JASON directs the men who bring a little market barrow and wheel her off into his shop.*)

SYLVIA: You're free now – now we can go down.

JASON: I'll handle everything.

SYLVIA: Good – I won't be long – I'll get the valuables. (*She rushes into the shop and frantically sorts out things.*)

PETER: There's no time to lose.

(*He sees PENNY who is about to push off with ALEX.*)

Penny, please, don't go without me.

PENNY: So you're coming then? Good.

PETER: No, you must come with me, I want you. Come, let's go down.

PENNY: No.

PETER: But you love me. You said you did.

PENNY: I do, but I will not come with you. If you give up everything now and come with me we might be happy – but we must leave right now.

PETER: Wait. I can't leave – my mother died here –

ALEX: Come on, Penny – I smell rain – I smell thunder and it looks like a big storm. So long, son, take care of yourself.

PETER: Penny, come back – I love you – Alex, don't leave me.

ALEX: You got what you wanted. Was it worth the price?

PENNY: I loved him – but I waited too long – you understand, don't you?

ALEX: Of course I do – Come on, no more words.

(*They go off.*

As ALEX and PENNY leave, the people in the factory stop and come outside – the whistle has sounded a tea-break and they smoke and sit quietly staring ahead.)

TOM: Here, where are you going?

(*PETER has just decided to go down the shelter and his hand is on the door. SYLVIA still frantically tries to pack things. PETER pulls back.*)

PETER: Oh bless you – Bless you all – As you know, my dear mother has died and I am going on a little holiday. I'm off to visit our dear dark cousins in the commonwealth of Lambeth and Camden Town – our illustrious history is bound together in a sacred bond – in one broad Superstore of – of prosperity and knowledge – I cherish memories of progress and – er um – that kind of thing – etcetera – etcetera – Work hard and good-bye –

(*He waves his hand grandly as the whistle blows. They all still stare at him as he enters the shelter.*)

JASON: Get them back to work. We're wasting time

JACK: (*Rushing there.*) Didn't you hear the whistle?

JOHN: Tea-break's over – back to work.

MR BUTCHER: We were watching Mr Mann saying good-bye.

MR FISH: He's going on holiday.

MR GREEN: He's not going, he's gone.

JOHN: Yes, yes, come on then – good-bye, Mr Mann.

JACK: Wrap up warm. For he's a jolly good fellow –

JOHN: For the sake of Auld Lang Syne. There'll always be an England –

JACK: As long as you are mine.

> (*JASON sounds the work whistle again and they all stream back. JOHN carries three boxes to JASON and JACK some ledgers.*)

JASON: Well, he's out of the way. What have you got there?

JOHN: Latest samples. Want to see them?

JASON: In a moment. What's the latest figures?

JACK: (*Consults book.*) Skegness and Shoreditch working to capacity – fifty thousand produced last week. Glasgow, Helsinki, and Camberwell are working day and night on the special Empire Shroud – Whitechapel and Tel Aviv are concentrating on the Kosher for Passover brand –

JASON: Goody, goody!

JACK: Bristol, Birmingham, Bangalore, and Manchester are taking on extra staff, Marseille, Welwyn Garden City, Munich, Amsterdam, Chicago, Lima, and Samarkand cannot cope with the orders pouring in.

JASON: In fact, everything in the garden is lovely – roll on Shroud Tuesday we'll all have some pancakes. Peter Mann may be the richest man in the world, but I'm the richest man on the world. What are we working on here?

JOHN: (*Undoes the boxes and takes out three shrouds.*) The very latest shroud –

JASON: Of course, designed specially for the Cobalt war – one for Russia, one for America, and one for England.

JOHN: Isn't the world saturated with improved designs?

JACK: Won't they explode the bomb to see if the shrouds work?

JOHN: Isn't the whole economy geared to shrouds?

JASON: You ask too many questions.

(*SYLVIA comes rushing out of the shop, her arms laden with heavy furs and several cases – she is almost bent double with the weight of things hanging from her shoulders. She is dressed in several coats and is over-laden with jewellery. As she rushes she drops many things; each time she tries to pick them up she drops other things – eventually she reaches JASON, near the door of the shelter.*)

SYLVIA: Peter! I'm ready, Peter! Where are you? Yoohoo! I've got everything worth while.

JASON: I'm afraid you left it a bit late.

SYLVIA: What do you mean? Where is he? Peter? The door's – shut?

JASON: Yes, and it cannot be opened from the outside and your dear husband is downstairs.

JACK: Singing to spiders –

JOHN: Chattering to rats.

SYLVIA: But I'm his wife – open the door, I've got to join him. What can I do?

JASON: That's your problem, we've got work to do.

SYLVIA: Help me! Help me – I'll be killed. (*She rushes around with panic, trying to hold onto her things.*) Mum, Dad where can I go – help me –

(*The people troop out of the factory.*)

MRS GREEN: What's the matter?

SYLVIA: Mum, help me. Peter's gone.

MR GREEN: Oh yes, Miss Toffeenose, now your old man's run off without you, you come crying back. I told you so.

MRS GREEN: Why didn't he take you on holiday with him?

SYLVIA: He's not on holiday, he's –

JASON: Back to work everyone.

JOHN: Come on, break it up.

JACK: Look lively, get cracking.

TOM: Hold your horses. Where is he?

SYLVIA: He's down below, where I should be – where we should all be – Don't you know – Don't any of you realize – The Bomb's gonna explode now. Now! Get that into your thick heads.

MR BUTCHER: The Bomb?

MR FISH: You sure?

(*They start rushing around and trying the door with much fury.*)

MR GREEN: Oh, God!

MRS GREEN: What's he got to do with it?

MRS BUTCHER: What can we do?

MRS FISH: Where can we go?

MR BUTCHER: Where can we hide?

TOM: There's nowhere to hide. We must stick together. Now quiet. Don't let's panic.

JASON: He's right. I assure you nothing will happen and if it does you'll all be protected, adequately.

SYLVIA: Open the door.

ALL: Yes, open the door – let us down – we don't want to die.

TOM: We demand protection, we demand shelter – come on all together – One, two, three, four – who are we dying for? One, two, three, four, five – we want to stay alive.

(*They march round and round, this time joined by SYLVIA.*)

SYLVIA: There isn't time – we've had it.

TOM: We're not dead yet.

JOHN: (*Taking out revolver.*) They soon will be.

JACK: Shall we show them, boss?

JASON: Not that way – Slogans. (*He walks to the marching circle of people.*) Friends, I want someone to make the gesture now – go back to work – I promise you all the best shroud the world has seen –

TOM: Open the door.

JASON: I can't.

(*The people continue marching round, and JASON and his men stand near shouting slogans.*)

Leak-proof shrouds will keep the worm out, keep the body in – they're guaranteed moth-proof!

JOHN/JASON/JACK: (*To Jingle Bells.*) Peter Mann Shrouds, Peter Mann Shrouds, are just the job for you. Buy one for your wife and kids, and your pussy too.

JASON: Recommended by the Houseproud Magazine, the Birth Control Centre, and the Death Watch Committee.

Ladies and gentlemen – I beg you for your own sakes –
you must be protected – We must fight them in the shrouds
and on the shrouds; we must never surrender.

TOM: Thought you said there'd be no war.

JASON: I promise you – you can take my word for it and
I double-cross my heart – You'll all get a rise – wages
are going up on Friday – you have my promise as an
undertaker and a gentleman. War? Nobody ordered war –
shrouds are to prevent war – I predict peace for a million
years.

(*At this moment the sirens start blowing. Everyone freezes.*)
Don't panic! It's a false alarm! (*He takes a transistor radio
from his pocket and twiddles with it.*) The radio will confirm it.
(*Atmospherics are first heard, then a calm voice.*)

VOICE: Ladies and gentlemen, the four-minute warning went
three minutes ago. Broadcasting will now cease. Good
evening!

(*Everyone panics. MR and MRS BUTCHER grab the
Red shrouds, MR and MRS FISH grab the Star-Spangled
shrouds, and MR and MRS GREEN grab the Union Jack
shrouds.*)

MR BUTCHER/MRS BUTCHER: (*Sing.*)
The people's shroud is deepest red,
You'll get a shroud when you are dead,
And you, my friend, may kiss my arse,
I have the foreman's job at last.

MR FISH/MRS FISH: (*Sing.*)
Oh, say, can you see,
My Star-Spangled shroud?
Keep up with the Jones's
And die with the crowd.

MR GREEN/MRS GREEN: (*Sing.*)
Rule, Britannia,
Britannia rules the shrouds…
(*There is a great searing flash, a rumble, then complete
silence. No one is left. A huge enveloping shroud comes
down, like a curtain, and covers almost the whole stage.
Only the shelter door stands in front of it.*)

PETER: (*Opens the door, cheerfully peers out.*) Good! It's all over!
Where's everyone? Jason! You can all come out – It's all
blown over. That's funny, I wonder how long
I was down there? (*He sees the shroud.*) What's this? Let me
out –
(*A voice like PETER's speaks to him.*)

PETER: Peeeeet-ter – Peeeet-ter!

PETER: Who's that? Where is everyone?

VOICE: Dead.

PETER: Dead? What do you mean? (*Getting impatient.*)
Where's everyone?

VOICE: There's not a person left in the world, just shrouds –
shrouds covering the dead world. Want to buy some?

PETER: Then where are their bodies? You're joking.

VOICE: All vaporized – Phufft, nice and hygienic. Well, that's
that – that was life.

PETER: What about me?

VOICE: A shadow on a bit of charred earth. Good-bye.

PETER: But there must be people – how can they work if
they're not alive? How can we make money and be free
and rich?

VOICE: That's your problem and you haven't much time to
solve it. Bye.

PETER: No! Don't go. We'll split fifty-fifty. I'm afraid.

VOICE: In a few moments you'll die. All sensation will be
gone. You'll be a no one with nothing – just like everyone
else.

PETER: Come out. I'm not afraid of you. I can't die. I'm
starting again. The world's beautiful and it's mine. I can
roam the vast deserts – I can fish in the great seas –
I can fly through the mountains. This is my earth – I am
– invincible – impregnable, invulnerable – I am – feeling
sick. (*Reassures himself.*) I've taken my pills,
I thought of everything, I'll be all right.

VOICE: You're dying – look at you – crawling about
now. You're dying from cancer, from the mushroom of
greed and lust and jealous, apathy, hypocrisy, stupidity,
dishonesty.

PETER: That's the way I was born.

VOICE: That's the way you chose to go.

PETER: Penny! Wait for me – Alex! I'll catch you up – come back for me a little way – I'll change – don't go without me. I'll show you, I'll show you all. This little bargain's not all sold out – don't touch me, death –

I don't want to die – that's the trouble with this place – The law's always after you. Won't let an honest trader spiel in space. (*He staggers and falls down.*) What's the matter with me? I can't stand up – no – no – no. Stay away – my eyes are heavy – my legs are heavy – and

I'm so cold. I'm falling… Falling down…hurtling down, down…crashing endlessly through space… I feel wonderful…free…flowering… Let me die with my eyes full of flowers! In the dark a Daffodil might light my way – O, Lilac, lull me –

I will float like a Lotus on the endless lake –

O, Chrysanthemum – look, I am old – I go to kingdom come – Show me the way. It is night and I grow cold.

I was my enemy – weep for me, Anemone – Mauve, blue and red. Tulips, touch my lips – for I am dead – lost in the black forests of my head.

ENCLOSE ME MIMOSA, WITH YOUR SMELL OF ALMONDS.

O, Rose, what river flows by the Lilies-of-the-valley of death?

(*A shape is seen on the other side of the cloth. It comes close to PETER.*)

Let the scent from all the flowers of the world converge on me – All colours merge and sing to me – YES, THEY SING! YES! YES!

Spring – winter – autumn – summer, dance around me and roll into one blazing light –

I enter the flowers. (*He stands up and is ecstatic.*)

I go into the glow of Crocus – INTO THE ETERNAL SKY OF BLUE-BELL – INTO THE BURSTING SUN OF SUNFLOWER AND POPPY –

My eyes close – so good-bye Violet – I go to God – if he will have me.

(*He is sprawled on the floor and the figure behind the curtain comes right round and approaches. PETER jumps up full of fear.*)
GO AWAY! DON'T TOUCH ME! WHY ME? WHY PICK ON ME? I DON'T WANT TO DIE!

SONIA: (*Taking off hooded cloak.*) Hello, Peter – I've come for you.

PETER: (*Falls against her.*) MOTHER! HOW LOVELY YOU LOOK – I thought you were death – I'm cold.

SONIA: Come, Peter – rest now – I'll sing you a song.

PETER: I'm dying.

SONIA: Hush now!

PETER: (*He yawns as he lies within her arms.*) Oh – I'm so tired. How glad I was to see you.

SONIA: (*Sings.*) When Peter was a little boy – he heard the angels sing –

PETER: Help me – don't let me die –

SONIA: He flew into the living-room and said, 'You will be king –'

PETER: Give me another chance – I'll be good.

SONIA: 'Of what will I be king?' Peter did reply…

PETER: You see I know the difference –

SONIA: 'You'll be king of your domain –' Peter be a good boy –

PETER: Mother, hold me.

SONIA: (*Sings.*) They flew away from his domain when they proclaimed him king.

PETER: Oh, Mother, I'm dead. (*He slumps across her.*)
(*SONIA leans ever PETER and the stage goes completely dark. Sparks and stars seem to strike the sky. When the lights come on again the huge shroud has gone, everything is as it was in Act One. THE DREAM HAS ENDED. SONIA has gone and it is ALEX instead who leans over PETER who is lying on the floor of his mother's shop. SONIA is with JASON celebrating with the others inside the house of MR and MRS BUTCHER. Music is heard from there.*)

ALEX: Wake up! Peter, wake up! (*He slaps PETER's face.*)

(*PETER sits up, holds his head and shakes it, and then stands up and looks dazed.*)

PETER: I'm not dead! Boy, have I been dreaming.

ALEX: Look, let's get the money – let's get going.

(*PETER lifts the safe from the floor and puts it on a chair.*)

Don't you want to go now?

PETER: I'm going –

ALEX: Good. Uranium, Uranium, boom, boom – Get the money, what's the matter with you?

PETER: I'm starting with nothing – that way I've got nothing to lose. It was such a crazy mixed-up dream. You were in it and I destroyed the world.

ALEX: You knocked yourself out.

PETER: Telling me. It all began with me pinching the money. So no money this time. World, here I come! One, two, three, four, five – It's bloody great to be alive. Let's get going before Penny gets back – married. Oh God, she's so beautiful. I was such a stupid fool. I love her, I love her. Why didn't I see it before? Why did I have to wait for a dream to show me?

(*Meanwhile, PENNY has entered the street wearing her wedding gown. She looks very unhappy and is followed by TOM who holds her bouquet very dejectedly. She leaves TOM all alone and leans against the wall of SONIA's shop, where she weeps. ALEX slowly puts the safe back on to the shelf, and PETER wanders outside and sees PENNY who pretends she is not crying.*)

I hope you'll be happy.

PENNY: I hope you'll be happier.

PETER: It's too late now, you're married so that's that.

PENNY: I couldn't go through with it.

PETER: What? Am I awake? (*Pinches himself.*) Pinch me.

(*She does.*)

Ouch! Just say that again!

PENNY: I couldn't marry Tom. If it's not you, it's not anyone.

PETER: PENNY! I love you. I've been such a swine but I love you.

(*They embrace and kiss and just look at each other. Soon they are dancing round and round to the music from the Butcher's shop. They dance into SONIA's shop and ALEX*)

joins the other people who have danced into the street.)
WOMEN: (*Seeing TOM.*) They're here!
MEN: They're here.
WOMEN: Three cheers!
MEN: Three cheers!
> (*They dance around the dejected TOM. SONIA and JASON dance together. ALEX, greatly admiring SONIA, taps JASON on shoulder.*)

ALEX: Excuse me. My God, every acre a woman.
> (*SONIA is flattered as he dances away with her. They dance faster and faster. Then they sway cheek to cheek.*)

You're beautiful!
SONIA: I know.
ALEX: You dance divinely.
SONIA: You don't, but you do have a nice shoulder to lean on.
ALEX: Hundreds of women have said that.
SONIA: Stay to dinner.
ALEX: Not enough have said that. You're ravishing.
SONIA: I agree, but I was even more sensational a few years
ago.
ALEX: You inspire me. (*He seems to be creating a poem on the spur of the moment.*) WHAT MYSTICAL LIGHT SHINES BETWEEN YOUR EYES – ? COME, LET US WRITE OUR LOVE UPON THE SKIES – LET'S DREAM TILL DOOMSDAY – DRUNK WITH LUSTY WINE – OH, FULL-BLOWN BEAUTY – PASSIONATE – DIVINE.
> (*He smiles at her, very pleased with himself, but she suddenly gives him a whack and nearly knocks him off his feet.*)

SONIA: You rat, take that! You wrote that for me, so you said,
twenty years ago.
ALEX: *Sonia!* Sonia, forgive me.
SONIA: *Alex!* Only you could shoot such a line and have me
believing it twice.
ALEX: Only you could have made me say it twice.
SONIA: Only you could wriggle out of everything.
> (*He holds her and tries to move her around to the music. She is stubborn at first, but gradually succumbs.*)

How we danced! Like a dream. All the cups and

competitions we won! We danced like this through the *Palais de Danses* of Moscow, Paris, and Hammersmith.

ALEX: No, not Hammersmith.

SONIA: That's right. Not Hammersmith! How dare you come back. (*She swipes him again.*)

ALEX: Forgive me! I want to settle down, to turn over a new leaf. (*He tries to kiss her.*)

SONIA: My name's not Eve. (*She acts seductively.*)

ALEX: You're my wife, my lovely wife.

SONIA: You're my husband, my lousy husband. (*She gives him another crack.*)

ALEX: We all make mistakes. Forgive? Sonia, how old are you now?

SONIA: How old do you want me to be?

(*They cuddle and kiss, but JASON breaks them up.*)

JASON: Sonia, even though you flirt, I still want to get married to you. The bedspring's been oiled and the bubble's in the wine, so let's get down to business.

SONIA: Sorry. It seems I'm married to this man for better or worse.

JASON: That man? There's no accounting for taste. Well, an undertaker must be practical.

(*JASON goes to SYLVIA and pinches her on the bottom.*)

Come here, my dear. Florists and undertakers have a lot in common, they should get together.

(*The market people are still dancing around TOM, pelting him with confetti and rice.*)

MRS BUTCHER: Where's my daughter then?

MRS FISH: Yes, where's the bride?

TOM: It's no good you dancing. She wouldn't go through with it. She's run off after that Peter Mann again.

ALL: Oh dear!

(*Everyone picks up the confetti and rice and then they quickly return to their stalls and get ready for business. ALEX and SONIA start dancing again, and PETER and PENNY dance out of the house. The two couples collide.*)

SONIA: My no-good son! Come, let me introduce you to your no-good father.

PETER: You? My dad? That settles it, I'm off.

ALEX: My son? My goodness. And you'd pinch your own mother's money?

PETER: Yeah, who tried to talk me into it?

SONIA: What's that?

ALEX: Oh – nothing – Come here, son. Wanderlust, eh? It's in the blood.

SONIA: If he takes after you I feel sorry for him and sorry for you and I feel sorry for myself. So let's all go inside and live happy ever after.

PETER: No! We're off. We've made up our minds.

PENNY: We love each other and that's all that matters.

PETER: And I've learnt a few things. I know what I do want – I want Penny – I know what I don't want – Superstores and Uranium.

MARKET PEOPLE: (*Sing.*)

MONEY IS TIME AND TIME IS MONEY;

IF YOU'RE BROKE IT ISN'T FUNNY – (*Etc.*)

(*They carry on chanting in the background as they work.*)

SONIA: Now he runs away. Trust him – you give them everything and this is how they repay you. Kids of today.

ALEX: It's right they should go. Give us a chance for peace and quiet.

PETER: Dad, that's the first sensible thing you've said.

SONIA: Ah, good riddance! And who'll look after you, sonny boy? Her? She's not good enough for you, darling.

MRS BUTCHER: My Penny's fit for a king.

SONIA: Maybe, but not good enough for my Peter.

MRS BUTCHER: They deserve each other, they're both no good.

SONIA: How dare you talk that way about him? They're both wonderful kids. Go, go – with my blessings – all right – think I care? Go – wrap up warm – they drive you mad. Eat well and don't get run over.

PETER: This is it. Ready?

PENNY: Ready when you are.

(*They are about to go when they see the market people working furiously.*)

MARKET PEOPLE: (*Sing.*)

> MONEY IS TIME AND TIME IS MONEY,
> MIGHT ASWELL DIE IF YOU HAVEN'T ANY –

PETER: (*Breaks in on them.*)

> MONEY IS TIME? AND TIME IS MONEY?
> YOU MISERABLE LOT, YOU'RE NOT EVEN FUNNY.
> THE GRAVE DEMANDS NO ENTRANCE FEE,
> WHY WAIT FOR DEATH TO SET YOU FREE?
> SO PRAISE YOUR SWEET ALMIGHTY POUND,
> BUT SPEND IT WHILE YOU'RE STILL AROUND.

Don't you see – you can always make money, but you can't always make merry. You're saving up for nothing, going nowhere, hoarding nothing, losing – everything – What will YOU bid for LIFE? Here it is. A kiss in the dark. The one and only – all shapes and sizes – lovely, lousy, terrible, terrific. Magnificent! Ridiculous! But it's the only one we've got. A great opportunity never to be repeated – a unique bargain – going – going – so make the most of it before it's gone!

(*He grabs hold of PENNY and the market people seem to be happy – they have stopped work and stand around the couple.*)

> DOCKERS! DOCTORS! SAINTS OR SINNERS!
> TAILORS! SAILORS! LOSERS! WINNERS!
> SHIRKERS! WORKERS! BANKERS! BROKERS!
> MISERS! WHORES! WIDEBOYS OR JOKERS!
> MAKE THE MOST OF LIFE BEFORE
> YOU ARE NO MORE – YOU ARE NO MORE.

MR BUTCHER: The boy's right!

MR FISH: Absolutely right!

MRS GREEN: Let's give them gifts.

MRS BUTCHER: Let's do them proud.

JASON: (*Measures PETER.*) I'll send it on.

(*TOM gives them the bouquet of flowers and the market people load them up with gifts as they sing.*)

MR FISH: (*Sings.*) Don't argue over fish,

> There's plenty in the sea;
> There's cod for you, skate for you
> And Dover Sole for me.

MR GREEN: (*Sings.*) The earth is very fruitful,
So take this fruit I'm giving.
Oh pardon me, that's half a crown,
I've got to make a living.

Who wants to buy a chicken?
The very best I've got.
Here, take my wife as well!
Ten bob for the lot.

JASON: And don't fight over coffins,
There's plenty to go round.
Personally, I'm getting cremated,
But don't spread that around.

PETER: We're all in this together,
A dream of endless space,
The earth is but one country,
The world's a market place.
(*Everyone cheers as PETER and PENNY go off. SONIA and ALEX go into the house. The market people stop cheering and laughing and go back to work as if their lives depended on it – and chant.*)

MARKET PEOPLE: MONEY IS TIME AND TIME IS MONEY –
MONEY IS TIME AND TIME IS MONEY –
MONEY IS TIME AND TIME IS MONEY –

The End.

Appendix

Full versions of songs

(Pages 13 and 14.)

Peach, Plum, or Apricot!
How much money have you got?
If you've got a bob or two,
I will bring some home for you.

Apricot, Peach, or Plum!
We may get blown to kindom come,
Let us eat our fruit before
Our parents go again to war.

Plum, Apricot, or Peach!
Hide the stone from out their reach,
So that it falls into the earth
And brings another world to birth.

Peach, Plum, or Apricot!
The world's gone mad, the whole damn lot.
To hell with them, let's dream and fly,
There's more in life than meets the eye.

(Page 23.)

Uranium, uranium, boom, boom, boom!
Cling clang, zing zang!
Boom, womb, ZOOM!
Get this in your cranium,
Stuff your old geranium,
I'm off to get uranium, boom! boom! boom!

Uranium, uranium, boom, boom, boom!
Bing bang, zing zang!
Boom, womb, ZOOM!
I'm a crazy, hazy, zany un,
A raving stark insanium
But I'm off to get uranium, boom! boom! boom!

Uranium, uranium, boom, boom, boom!

Ring rang, zing zang!
Boom, womb, ZOOM!

I've a super manic panium
Inside my super branium
And I'm off to get uranium.
Boom! Boom! Boom!

(*Page 29 and 30.*)

Money is time and time is money.
Might as well die if you haven't any.
Money makes the world go round.
Oh praise thee, sweet almighty pound.
Money is time and time is money.
If you are broke it isn't funny,
And our love will not grow old,
Provided it is set in gold.
Money is time and time is money.
If you're rich the world is sunny.
For money opens every door.
Give us more and more and more and more.
For money makes the church bells ring –
Oh thank you, God, for everything.

(*Page 31.*)

Let Jason help you getting wed.
He'll sell you a double bed,
The pills to make your mattress sing,
A hearse, a horse, a diamond ring.
I'll buy a husbnad just for you,
Or perhaps you'd like a kangaroo.
Life insurance? A samovar?
A Cadillac or caviar?
A virgin parrot newly caught?
Picture postcards? You know the sort.
What you want I bet I've got –
A 'cello or a chamber – orchestra.
I can suit you for a fee,
In the end you'll come to me.

The name is Jason, don't forget –
What you want I can always get.

(Page 38.)

There's a woman down the road, thought she'd last forever,
So she saved ten thousand pounds, for the rainy weather,
But now she's dead, yes, now she's dead,
The worms are chewing through her head,
In the rainy wea-ther.

There's a geezer down the lane, had fifty thousand nicker,
But he couldn't find a cure for his wonky ticker.
The money's saved but he is dead,
The worms are breeding in his head,
Gobbling up his tic-ker.

There's a broker lived up West, had no time for eating.
Made a fortune out of foam, the kind they use for seating.
He got so rich and got so thin,
The worms will make quick work of him,
Eating up his sea-ting.

(Page 43.)

Oh, the walls are thin in London Town,
They wouldn't need much blowing down.
So workers of the world unite,
Before we vanish in the night.

My dreams are thin and wearing thinner,
No one expects me home for dinner.
Oh, comrades of the universe,
There's nothing better but plenty worse.

The streets are cold in London Town,
No one smiles, all look down.
Where are our dreams of liberty?
Oh, what became of you and me?

The streets are full with empty eyes,
Oh, workers of the world arise.
Can't you hear the sirens call?
Comrade death unites us all.

We're all together on the rocks,
A crawling lot of crooked crocks,
Just one chance in eternity.
Oh, shake your chains and dream you're free.

(*Page 62.*)

Put up the banns, pull down the blinds,
For my darling you are mine.
Don't let's wait, I can't last forever,
Take the plunge, it's either now or never.
Rush up the stairs, better say your prayers,
I've got the twinkle in my eye.
We'll make love, the loveliest, the longest,
And we'll fight to see who is the strongest.
Come over here or I'll come over there
Watch out for my adrenaline.
Jump into bed, good-bye maidenhead.
Tonight you will be really mine.
Put out the light, here goes, so hold me tight,
We're going to have a smashing time.

(*Page 69.*)

When Peter was a little boy, he watched the angels fly,
Around him in the garden, where the clothes hang out to dry.
They sang to him of heaven, a hymn of hope and joy.
'Oh, bring it down to earth,' he said – 'why hide it in the

sky?'

When Peter was little boy, he heard the angels sing;
They flew into the living-room and said, 'You will be king.'
'Of what will I be king?' Peter did reply.
'You'll be king of your domain, underneath the sky.'
'Where, oh where, is my domain? Who and where am I?'
'In your heart and in your brain – now go to sleep, my boy.'

When Peter was a little boy, he heard the angels sing;

They flew far from the living-room when they proclaimed

him king.

ENTER SOLLY GOLD
a comedy

Characters

A PROSTITUTE
35 years old

SOLLY GOLD
35 to 40 years old

A POLICEMAN

RITA
a tailor's wife, 45 years old

JOE
a tailor, 45 years old

AN OLD WOMAN

MORRY SWARTZ
60 to 65 years old

MILLIE SWARTZ
55 to 60 years old

ROMAINE
28 years old

SARAH
23 years old

MELVIN
26 years old

HERBERT FINK
50 to 55 years old

SADIE FINK
50 years old

ALAN FINK
25 years old

Enter Solly Gold was first perfomed at the Mermaid Theatre, London on 22 January 1970, with the following cast:

PROSTITUTE, Jennie Stoller

SOLLY, Joe Melia

POLICEMAN, Jon Rumney

RITA, Judith Harte

JOE, Gabor Vernon

WOMAN, Juliet Duncan

MORRY, David Kossoff

MILLIE, Stella Moray

ROMAINE, Esta Charkham

SARAH, Georgina Simpson

MELVIN, Francis Ghent

HERBERT, David Lander

SADIE, Pamela Manson

ALAN, Michael Lewis

Scene 1: Prologue

Street scene. Dark stage and simple setting. A row of small houses near Aldgate in London's East End. The set is in a stylised manner and the interior can be seen as well as the exterior. When action takes place in a particular house or area that place is simply lit up. It is one o'clock in the morning; late summer. A PROSTITUTE stands outside her street door and SOLLY enters. As she sings, he sizes her up from afar.

PROSTITUTE: (*Sings.*)
> Yours for a short time, how about it honey?
> I'll give you five minutes, if you've got the money.
> You can have me once or have me all night.
> I'm very very versatile if the price is right.
> I can be naughty if you pay me cash,
> Now don't be so bashful, come and have a bash.
> If you want what I've got you can have it honey,
> I'll give you five minutes, if you've got the money.
> (*She beckons SOLLY.*)
> Hello darling, do you want a good time with a bad girl?

SOLLY: Do you mean me?

PROSTITUTE: Why not? I'm not particular. I'll take anyone, as long as they're not jockeys or fishmongers, or Negroes.

SOLLY: What's wrong with jockeys? Some of my best friends.

PROSTITUTE: Whores are not horses, they tend to dig their heels in and treat the bed post like a winning post and fishmongers stink.

SOLLY: What's wrong with Negroes?

PROSTITUTE: You've got to draw the line somewhere. Come on, don't let's waste time.

SOLLY: Changed my mind, I thought you were fatter.

PROSTITUTE: You don't know what you want – eff off, go on.

SOLLY: But maybe I could stretch a point just this once.

PROSTITUTE: Make up your mind or it'll soon be closing time. Now come on, I want cash on delivery.

SOLLY: How much will you charge me to have a chat?

PROSTITUTE: Cut it out. What do you take me for? None of that kinky stuff for me, at least not unless you make it worth my while.

SOLLY: You mean you charge more for talking? Why?

PROSTITUTE: Cos I've heard it all before. How much do you think psychiatrists charge for listening? Five quid for five minutes, that's the fixed rate.

SOLLY: I could become Catholic for less and they'd listen for nothing.

PROSTITUTE: Take it or leave it, that's the standard charge.

SOLLY: How much do you charge ordinary rate for the ordinary thing?

PROSTITUTE: Two quid and no beating about the bush.

SOLLY: Two quid? You're a profiteer! It was only thirty bob before I left.

PROSTITUTE: You're living in the past, grand-dad, prices are rising all the time.

SOLLY: Sorry I wasted your time, fact is I've been daydreaming in the middle of the night. I'm flat broke – stoney – skint – haven't even got a bed for the night – take a look at the soles of my shoes.

PROSTITUTE: You're breaking my heart.

SOLLY: I'm hungry too, haven't eaten for days.

PROSTITUTE: Don't come the old acid with me. You might have heard of sentimental tarts with soppy hearts but yours truly is not like that – times are hard, can't even walk the streets these days. The likes of you should be shot – you've got no morals, no principles, that's your trouble.

SOLLY: Well, this is as far as I can go tonight.

(*He sits on his case.*)

PROSTITUTE: Your mother should see you now.

SOLLY: My mother! Mum! I can just see her now. I was bad to her but she forgave me – she knew in her heart of hearts that I wanted to help her – she was a famous debutante – Martha Goldberg – I dragged her down
and she died in the workhouse – I was just too late –
I arrived in my Rolls to take her to the south of England.

PROSTITUTE: Poor boy – (*She shakes herself.*) What! You've got the spiel all right. You never had a mother. Bet you could melt the heart of a judge. Well, I'm off,
I hear the Swedish Navy are pulling in tonight. I hope you don't catch cold and die of pneumonia. So long.

(*She goes.*)

SOLLY: What time is it?

(*A clock strikes one.*)

Thank you!

(*A POLICEMAN enters and watches SOLLY.*)

My watch is stopped; wonder if I can pawn it for a few bob?

(*He doesn't see the POLICEMAN.*)

What can I do about kip tonight? Coo, I could kip right here and now I'm so tired – so here we are back in the old country – It's so old it's got one foot in the grave and the other foot's got ingrowing toenails.

(*He takes his shoes off, and his socks, and starts cutting his toenails. The POLICEMAN who was just about to pounce has temporarily held off.*)

What am I gonna do for cash? For the old lolly? Must think of something. But there's one thing I'm sure of – I'm not gonna work – never! Never! – never!

(*He stands on the case – mocking the Hyde Park orators.*)

Comrades, if you want work you can have it, as for me, work's too much like an occupation – I've committed no crimes, work is all right for workers, just the job for the working class, but for Solly Gold? There's only one thing he wants, money! And there's only one way he wants to get it – by doing nothing.

POLICEMAN: What do you think you're doing?

SOLLY: (*Jumping off case and quickly putting on his shoes.*)
Hello, Officer – I remember you from way back. I've just returned from a world trip and do you know the world's nothing to write home about. They wouldn't let me stay in the States so I returned here – to little old England, the greatest littlest country this side of the universe.

POLICEMAN: What are you doing?

SOLLY: Isn't it obvious? I'm out here studying the stars – contemplating the infinite.

POLICEMAN: I'll contemplate your what-you-may-call-it if you don't move sharpish. What have you got in that case?

SOLLY: My worldly goods, Officer.

POLICEMAN: You're a saucy bastard, aren't you? Open up.

SOLLY: (*Opens it.*) One toothbrush – you know – for cleaning the teeth. (*Goes through the motions.*) One shoe brush – for brushing the shoes and one clothes brush for –

POLICEMAN: Alright, alright – what else?

SOLLY: That's the lot – I've flogged the rest. Three brushes and a brain, that's all I've got.

POLICEMAN: Where have you come from?

SOLLY: I've just landed – from Australia. Started on the boat as a dishwasher. By the time I got to Gib I was head steward, but by the time we got to Tilbury I'd lost my position, my clothes and my money all in a card game. That's the way it goes – up and down – everything's up and down. Ever been to Australia?

POLICEMAN: No.

SOLLY: Do yourself a favour – never go.

POLICEMAN: You said they threw you out of America, why?

SOLLY: Because I was a member of the blue and white shirts when I was five.

POLICEMAN: What were the blue and white shirts?

SOLLY: How should I know? But I'm going to get into the States, you see. It's my spiritual home. It's dog eat dog there, that's the way I like it.

POLICEMAN: Got any family here?

SOLLY: No – no family – no one. (*Sings.*) My mother got struck by lightning, my father crashed in a plane, my sister drowned in the Serpentine, my brother got shot down in Spain. My cousin died in a madhouse, my aunt from the sting of a bee, my uncle jumped off a skyscraper – Oh, what's gonna happen to me?

POLICEMAN: I don't believe you.

SOLLY: I don't blame you. No, chum, the things I do remember I try to forget and the things I try to forget, I try to forget that I'm forgetting.

POLICEMAN: You'd better hop it out of here or I'll run you in.

SOLLY: A nice feller like you wouldn't do that to me. Where shall I go?

POLICEMAN: Go up to the West End – another crook there, more or less, won't matter – so beat it. I'm on my rounds now and if you're here when I come back I'll lock you up.

SOLLY: You've got me wrong.

(*POLICEMAN starts to go.*)

Oh, what's the use. Thank you! Thank you! You're a very nice man – I think the English police are wonderful –

POLICEMAN: None of that moody. I'll be back in five minutes – so watch it. (*He goes off muttering.*) Spiv! Lazy good-for-nothings –

SOLLY: I resemble that remark, I may be good for nothing but I'm not lazy. He should try living on his wits. Conning people is a full-time job – you've got to use your loaf to get through this bloody world without work and believe me it's a damn sight harder than your union would let you work – and I'm always on duty – twenty-eight hours a day.

(*He shouts after the POLICEMAN, then picks up case and moves, but after a few feet he notices light in a window of a tailor's shop: he knocks on the door and falls on his face – on the doorstep.*)

(*Groans.*) Oh help me – help me-oh God –

(*The tailor's wife comes to the door, opens it.*)

RITA: (*Calls.*) Joe! Joe! Come here, someone's in trouble.

JOE: Who isn't?

(*He is busy sewing in the interior.*)

RITA: But he's on our doorstep.

JOE: So? We won't charge him any rent.

SOLLY: (*Desperate.*) Help me – oh lady – I'm in terrible trouble.

(*He pulls on her skirt and at the same time tries to look up her legs; she doesn't see this.*)

RITA: We've got enough of our own, son.

SOLLY: If you only knew – I can't face it.

JOE: Tell him to go somewhere else – I've got this armhole to finish.

SOLLY: (*Loud.*) I'm so choked – I can't talk – you're a Jewish woman, aren't you? *Sholem Alecheim.*

RITA: I don't care what your name is – what do you want?

SOLLY: I'm gonna die – I'm spitting blood. Oh God, that it should happen to me. I'm gonna die.

JOE: Tell him please not on our doorstep – bring him in.

SOLLY: (*As he is helped inside.*) No tongue can tell the things I've suffered.

RITA: Just take it easy, son – try and relax. Oh the poor boy – he's as white as a sheet.

JOE: What's he doing out this time of night?

SOLLY: Oh I'm all water, my legs are just like water – I can't go on. Take me too – kill me also.

(*He collapses on the floor. JOE won't leave the machine so RITA pulls him into a chair.*)

I'm just like water – water.

JOE: Rita, fetch him some water.

SOLLY: Haven't you got something a bit stronger?

JOE: Rita, bring him some of that Palestinian wine.

SOLLY: I prefer brandy if you've got it.

(*RITA brings him wine.*)

JOE: I'm only a poor tailor.

SOLLY: Alright, I'll settle for this, I'm not so particular – Oh no, I don't believe it – Becky – where have you gone?

RITA: He's delirious.

SOLLY: Nice wine – thank God I found you up.

RITA: You'll always find us up – he says he can't afford to sleep.

JOE: Alright. (*To SOLLY.*) So, what's your story?

SOLLY: I can't talk, not yet. Just let me sit here. I'll be alright in a minute. Could I have another glass of wine?

JOE: Alright. Now listen, you don't feel so well, have a little rest, put your feet up and in two minutes you'll be as right as rain and be able to leave.

RITA: He drives me mad. Joe, can't you see he looks like death, what's the matter, 'fraid you'll lose a few stitches? Work is all he knows. Never marry a tailor. (*She tells SOLLY.*) That's what my Aunt Sophie said. He borrows a few hours from the next day, then a day from the next week and a few weeks from the next year and then he dies owing all that time.

(*She goes to JOE.*)

What's the matter with him, Joe?

JOE: I don't like the look of him.

RITA: He's a Jewish boy, he can't be bad.

JOE: Yeah? What about Schnorrer Morry?

RITA: Can't you stop working? Can't you ever get away from that machine?

JOE: You can grumble; did you ever go without?

RITA: Yes, without you, all my life. I'm married to a sewing machine.

(*Returns to SOLLY.*)

You feeling better, son?

SOLLY: Oh Becky! Becky! What's the matter with you? Why don't you jump – save the children – the children!

JOE: I don't want him having delusions on my sofa.

RITA: Oh shut up!

SOLLY: Becky, my poor wife – all burned. (*Bursts into tears.*)

RITA: What happened to her? It's good to tell someone.

SOLLY: I'm a traveller, I only heard before. I live in Glasgow – and my wife – oh – God rest her soul – died this morning with the children.

RITA: Died? Oh, you poor feller.

JOE: (*Leaves machine.*) How?

SOLLY: Oh, it was such a big fire, there were twenty engines, masks they had on. They all got burned to death, my Becky, my little Renee, the twins, Michael and Angela – they were so beautiful. Becky had long black hair – she was a picture.

RITA: Oh, I'm so sorry.

JOE: I wish we could help you.

SOLLY: I wish I could help myself. I've been wandering in a daze, I haven't eaten.

RITA: The good die young. Don't talk no more, rest.

SOLLY: No, no, it eases me, I've cried enough. Becky tried to save them – she stood on the parapet with all the children in her arms – little Renee, she was such a lovely dancer – tap and ballet. What can I do?

RITA: Let me make you something to eat.

SOLLY: No, I couldn't, I'm all choked. Alright, if you insist, a chicken sandwich with some mustard pickle or some smoked salmon – nothing much – something light.

(RITA goes off to prepare it.)

I must go to Glasgow – now! I must give them a decent burial.

JOE: Stay here tonight, go tomorrow morning.

SOLLY: I must fly tonight – I'll have to charter a plane –

JOE: Of course, I understand.

SOLLY: I wonder if you could help me? God is good, in times of stress. He sends good friends. You know your friends when you're in trouble. Listen – I need a few quid for the plane fare – the banks are closed and I must fly tonight.

JOE: How much?

SOLLY: At least twenty-five – yes, that will cover me. Oh, Becky, Becky, by my mother in the grave I'm sorry – forgive me, I tried to be a good husband.

JOE: I'm afraid I can only afford five.

SOLLY: That's no use, make it twenty then.

JOE: What about ten?

SOLLY: I'll tell you what, I'll settle with fifteen and try and manage with that.

JOE: Alright, fifteen it is!

(He gives SOLLY the money.)

SOLLY: It's a deal.

JOE: Done!

(They shake hands on it.)

SOLLY: It's only a loan, mind. I'll send it back tomorrow morning.

JOE: There's no hurry, wait till the afternoon. I'll get it.

(SOLLY lies back, smokes and pours himself another drink. JOE meets RITA coming in with sandwiches.)

I must be crazy, I'm lending him money.

RITA: It's good to know you've got a heart, we must all help each other. I'm pleased with you; he's the first person you've lent money to in the past twenty years.

JOE: Ah well, he's different – you can see it, it's obvious, he's a decent boy in trouble. I'm a good judge of character.

(JOE goes off and RITA brings the sandwiches to SOLLY.)

SOLLY: You're so kind – how can I repay you?

(Stuffs the sandwich into his mouth.)

You're too good. I bet no one appreciates you.

RITA: You can say that again. My husband takes me for granted.

SOLLY: When you're dead, then he'll appreciate you, just like me and Becky.

RITA: Try and look forward now, we have to get over things, life goes on.

SOLLY: You're very nice, you're an angel. Has anyone ever told you that? You've got a light in your eyes; does he ever say a kind word to you?

RITA: He hasn't got time. He's not a bad boy exactly, just got no time.

SOLLY: I'd have time for someone like you, I would – you're so nice – Oh comfort me – my Becky is dead.
(*She pats him on the shoulder and puts her arms around him.*)
I'm so lonely, let me cuddle you.
(*He pretends to cry and soon he is completely embracing her and touching her hair.*)
Oh, you're lovely, so lovely, just like my Becky.

RITA: No – no – I shouldn't –
(*She tries to break away as she realises he is getting amorous.*)

SOLLY: You're lovely, you're a good woman – so big and kind. I'm in trouble, don't leave me – I need you – you're strong and fat – and oh –

RITA: Please, you'd better stop.

SOLLY: You're just my size – don't go – come closer. Can you blame me – you're so lovely, you're a friend, a real friend. You're just the right size – I'm mad about you.
(*He tries to kiss her but she breaks free and still they speak quietly, urgently.*)

RITA: How could you? With your wife just dead? How could you get fresh with me – no-one's ever done that to me. How could you?

SOLLY: How should I know what I'm doing – I'm so sad and emotional. It was a sudden urge, blood is thicker than water.

RITA: With your wife just dead how could you do it?

SOLLY: Don't tell your husband, he wouldn't understand.
I'll come back some other time – I'm mad for you and so
unhappy.

RITA: Men! Men make me sick.

SOLLY: Me too. I was being affectionate; you're too good
for your husband. I'll make it up to you somehow. Please
forgive me, I'm only human and you're a beautiful woman;
kiss me and tell me you forgive – for poor Becky's sake.

RITA: (*Wanders off and looks in a mirror.*) How could you do
that to me?
(*JOE returns.*)

JOE: Here you are, fifteen quid.

SOLLY: You're a pal, how can I repay you?

JOE: With money.

SOLLY: I'll be on my way now, God bless you all, my Becky
will be so pleased, I mean as she looks down on all this.
Goodbye! May you live long and die happy – may you live
to be a hundred and three.

JOE: Don't do me no favours.

SOLLY: You're one in a million, both of you. I must fly now.
(*He leaves the house and lingers outside, but the light goes
off him for a moment.*)

JOE: Nice feller, ain't it funny how the good always suffer?

RITA: How could he do it to me?
(*She rejoins her husband.*)
I knew there was something fishy all along.

JOE: Well darling, I gave him the money.

RITA: Money? You bloody fool! You stupid silly sod! Didn't
you see how he mauled me – he tried to rape me and you
gave him money? Couldn't you see that he was just a lying
thief? You gave him money? Why didn't you give me away
while you were about it?

JOE: I wish I did.

RITA: Go on, back to your sewing, you silly so and so.

JOE: Why don't you go to bed? I've got a busy night ahead.

RITA: Why don't you drop dead? It's all your fault. Yes,
I'm going to bed and don't wake me up whatever you
do – cos the answer's no. You've had it from now on; you

don't know how to treat a lady – you don't appreciate me. It's alright, I'm not so bad looking; people still think I'm attractive. I'm not finished yet. Good night.

(*She goes to bed, the tailor continues sewing and the light in the room darkens. SOLLY is now seen again, counting the money. The PROSTITUTE comes up to him.*)

SOLLY: What happened to the Swedish Navy?

PROSTITUTE: They've got an attack of German measles on board. Bang goes another night's business. I'll have to sleep.

SOLLY: Don't go, I've changed my mind, I need a room and I fancy something so I may as well kill two birds with one stone.

PROSTITUTE: No one's gonna kill this bird – My my, you've got a wad there. I'm in the wrong racket.

SOLLY: How much you charge for all night?

PROSTITUTE: Special rates for night work – time and a half.

SOLLY: Do me a favour, I want it cut price. How much?

PROSTITUTE: A fiver.

SOLLY: Come off it, I'm only a poor working man.

PROSTITUTE: Oh alright, four.

SOLLY: Make it two.

PROSTITUTE: You out of your mind? Don't you know about the cost of living index? Three pounds ten and that's my final word.

SOLLY: Two pounds fifteen, on the nose.

PROSTITUTE: You'd auction your own mother – alright, three quid and not a penny less.

SOLLY: Right, it's a deal.

(*They shake on it.*)

PROSTITUTE: That's done. Let's go.

SOLLY: You're not as fat as I would like but you can't pick and choose all your life.

(*They exit into her door and the stage darkens completely – now there is a passage of time and the stage lightens again and it is dawn – a cock is heard crowing and SOLLY comes out of the PROSTITUTE's door, yawns and does some exercises.*)

A cock crowing? In Whitechapel? Impossible.

(*It crows again. He looks over a fence beside a third house.*)

Chickens – that's handy. Come on you pretty little darlings – come and get stuffed. Oh boy, that takes me back… chicken soup, stuffed neck, chopped liver, giblet pie. There's one, two, three, five, eight, eleven birds in all, and one lovely rooster – beautiful bird. Looks as if you've had a heavy night like me. Never mind – I'll cut your throat and then you can have a long sleep and then I'll flog you and your girl friends down the lane.

(*He is about to climb over the fence when an old lady comes out of the house with some food for the chickens.*)

WOMAN: What do you want?

(*He jumps back quickly but soon relaxes.*)

SOLLY: I want you. Good morning, my good woman, I'm the bird inspector.

WOMAN: Bird inspector? What do you want? Where are you from?

SOLLY: As a matter of fact I've been inspecting a bird all night. I'm from the Ministry of Agriculture and Poultry; I've been inspecting your birds.

WOMAN: What's wrong with my birds?

SOLLY: What's right with them? They're suffering from foot and mouth disease and they're all having a nervous breakdown. This won't do. This is a serious business.

WOMAN: Please sir, I can't help it; since my husband died I've been struggling to carry on alone.

SOLLY: Your husband dead?

WOMAN: Yes, a week ago, did you know him?

SOLLY: Of course I did, who didn't?

WOMAN: Who didn't know my Hymie? Who didn't know him and love him? He was such a wonder, he knew everyone.

SOLLY: Wonderful Hymie, with the heart of gold. As a matter of fact he owes me some money.

WOMAN: Money? He never owed anyone.

SOLLY: I mean the government. He never paid his last instalment of the Chicken Registration fee – didn't you know he owed us ten pounds?

WOMAN: Chicken Registration? No, I didn't know – he took care of everything, I'm so lost without him. I'll pay you.

SOLLY: Poor Hymie, the world won't be the same without him.

WOMAN: It's good to talk to you – I haven't spoke to a soul since he died.

(*She gives him the money.*)

You make me feel better – I'm glad you liked my husband so much.

SOLLY: (*Looking over the fence.*) The birds will have to go of course.

WOMAN: Why?

SOLLY: Neurotic birds are a menace to society – they're totally maladjusted and what's more I'll have to kill them here and now, I'm afraid. And that will be of course another six pounds disposal fee –

WOMAN: Take them, kill them. Who can be bothered feeding them anyway? Who eats eggs since Hymie died? Here, six pounds.

SOLLY: I'm letting you off light – because I like you and Hymie was a friend of mine. Actually I could report you because you didn't register the disease and then it would mean a heavy fine and even imprisonment, but Hymie was a wonderful guy, and also there will be just one further charge, two pounds ten shillings for the death entry certificate which we will send you in a matter of a few days.

WOMAN: (*Gives him more money.*) Take it, take it, who cares anyway.

SOLLY: I'm letting you off light.

WOMAN: Thank you, thank you – I know, you're very kind. Death is an expensive business – all I've done since my husband died is lay out, lay out.

SOLLY: I hope I'm not leaving you too short.

WOMAN: As my husband always said, you can always find money for bread and coffins.

SOLLY: (*Puts away money.*) Now please, I will need a sharp razor to cut their throats.

(*She goes inside and he jumps over fence and inspects the birds. She returns and hands him a cut-throat razor. He sets to work though we cannot see his hands or the birds but*

*very soon amidst a flurry of sound and feather, he emerges
with a cluster of dead birds.)*

We'll send you receipts.

WOMAN: One minute, do you know anyone who could use
some clothes? I've got some, my husband's things, they're
in marvellous condition. I can't bear to see them anymore.

SOLLY: I might be able to help you out, let's have a look.

WOMAN: Do me a favour, pull out that trunk.

(He puts the chickens down and pulls out a large suitcase.)

Only the best, as you can see – take it all.

SOLLY: A rabbi's clothes?

*(He holds up some jackets and trousers and soon lifts out
some rabbi's clothes.)*

WOMAN: But you knew my husband was a rabbi, didn't you?

SOLLY: Who didn't know? From Tel Aviv to Tell me the Tale
he was famous – the best rabbi in the racket. It's just that I
didn't think you'd part with such personal items.

WOMAN: You're right I wouldn't. Don't touch the Rabbi's
clothes and his Bible. Take everything else – I can't bear
to see them anymore. I must go now and sweep up. Thank
you.

(She goes inside.)

SOLLY: These clothes are not worth a light – she must be
blind, they're all moth eaten; but this Rabbi's gear might
come in handy – and I hear there are some very hot
tales in this black book. Well, Solly boy, you're not doing
too bad – last night you had sweet Fanny Adams and this
morning you're worth twenty odd nicker, a dozen chickens
and this odd clobber. You're in business somehow. The
world owes you a living, my boy, and you've come to
collect.

(He kneels down and prays.)

Oh, Rabbi Hymie – forgive me but I mean well – I'm a bad
boy, but I've got my part to play, and I promise to spread
love and happiness everywhere I go – cos money don't
bring happiness so I'm gonna take it away from them.

(He suddenly gets an idea.)

Solly boy, you're a genius and you're in business.

*(He quickly puts the Rabbi's clothes on and puts the chickens
in his case.)*

First I'll go from door to door, flogging these kosher
chickens for charity, my charity. Thank you, Rabbi Hymie,
you're a pal – I'll walk in your shoes. (*As he changes shoes.*)
And take the word of God – promises of redemption, love,
kisses – anything they want – as long as they're happy.
Watch out, world, I'm coming! Hendon! Golders Green!
Hampstead Garden Suburb! – I'm knocking on your door!
(*He does a little dance and some mock prayers.*)
I'm Rabbi Solomon Goldstone, I'm knocking on your door
With a new kind of religion and a brand new kind of law
If you can't get in heaven, he'll fix it in a flash
I've got the right connections, if you have got the cash.
(*He exits hurriedly.*)

End of Prologue.

Scene 2

*The next day. Interior. Living room of the house of MORRY
SWARTZ. Known as The Castle for obvious reasons. First
because they've named it that and secondly because they've tried
to furnish it and make it appear very grand. The furniture is in a
mishmash of styles – good taste and the appalling are side by side.
A garish glassy cocktail bar, for instance, stands next to a great
Gothic-looking bookcase, without books. A suit of armour, and
animals' heads all around. A television screen set in an antique
case. Peach mirrors all around the room. The huge ugly table is set
for a wedding although it appears the wedding feast has almost
been finished. This castle is in Golders Green. Around the table
the people are eating furiously. SARAH SWARTZ is dressed as
a bride. She is attractive in a slightly overblown way. Beside
her is the groom ALAN FINK, a nervous slight boy, dressed in a
dinner jacket. Next to him his parents sit – HERBERT FINK,
in a flashy American get-up, and his intense wife. Next to them
sit ROMAINE SWARTZ – a buxom girl in late twenties – she
seems very hungry, as usual. And there is her brother MELVIN
– who wears a sports blazer and flannels – he is always slightly
aloof and seems to despise the surrounding people. Next to him
MILLIE SWARTZ, a rather attractive woman who tries to look
younger than her years, heavily made-up and wearing a lot of*

expensive jewellery. MORRY SWARTZ is not at the table but is feeding a bird in a cage – he too is dressed in a dinner jacket but he has his slippers on. There are streamers and balloons about. When the curtain goes up there is a silence for a while as we just see the spectacle of people stuffing themselves.

MILLIE: Morry, come back to the table, we're supposed to be celebrating.
    (*MORRY takes no notice but it swaying with a champagne glass in his hand.*)

HERBERT: Come on, Alan, make a speech.

ALAN: I've already made four.

HERBERT: Make another one.
    (*All except MELVIN and MORRY bang on the table with their forks.*)

ALL: Speech! Speech!

ALAN: (*He pulls SARAH to her feet and they cuddle.*) Mum and Dad! My dear Mother- and Father-in-law, Melvin, Romaine, my darling wife – I promise to be a loving husband, to bring you breakfast in bed for the first three months, to look after the shop and make lots of money.
    (*They all clap.*)

SARAH: I'm so happy, I could cry.

MILLIE: Don't do that, your eyeblack will run.

SARAH: I could eat him, he's so handsome.

SADIE: What a handsome couple, don't they look lovely together?

MILLIE: Yes, it's a good arrangement.

HERBERT: Your turn next, Romaine.

ROMAINE: Don't do me no favours. I don't trust men.

HERBERT: Alan, you've got a lovely girl there, cherish her. She's a lovely well-made girl and you're a lucky well-off boy. Look, he's blushing, you naughty boy. Bet you can't wait for tonight, eh? It's lovely to see young people coming together. Wish I had my time over again – that's the way I used to like them – well covered.

SADIE: Herbert!

MORRY: (*Sings.*)
    Here comes the bride, short, fat and wide,

See how she wobbles from side to side.
Here comes the groom, skinny as a broom,
If it wasn't for the bride he would have more room.
(*All laugh nervously.*)

SADIE: Aren't we having a lovely time? I love a party. This is the happiest day of my life, by my life. Don't they look lovely standing together? I could cry.

MILLIE: Why you?

SADIE: I don't know, brides always make me cry.

HERBERT: (*He is also very tipsy and holds a drink up.*) Please God by me – I'll sing a song now.
(*The others take it up.*)

ALL: For they are jolly good fellows, for they are jolly good fellows, for they are jolly good felel – ows –
(*At this moment SOLLY walks in and holds up a solitary chicken.*)

SOLLY: And so say all of us.
(*They are all astonished.*)
I rang the bell, but I heard singing so I came in.

MORRY: Please excuse us, we're all upside down.

SOLLY: That's alright, my son, it's good to see people happy. What a lovely house.

HERBERT: Isn't it marvellous? What do you think of it? Do you know it cost twenty thousand to build.

SADIE: It's just like a palace, you could eat off the floor.

MORRY: Excuse us, but we're right in the middle of a wedding.

SOLLY: Carry on, it's so nice to see such a nice happy family gathering.

HERBERT: This is a nice stroke of luck, a rabbi calling on our children's wedding day. Heaven's happy with this match.

SADIE: Who wouldn't be? Look at them, they're so lovely.

MILLIE: Well, Rabbi, what can we do for you? How much money do you want?

MELVIN: Mother! You do go on – money, money, that's all you talk about.

SOLLY: Business can wait.

MORRY: Have a drink with us, please.

SADIE: Drink the health of our children.

SOLLY: Some of that Three Star brandy please. No soda.

MILLIE: What charity do you represent?

SOLLY: (*Holds up his glass.*) *Lechaim.*

MELVIN: Can I go now? I have a game of squash booked.

HERBERT: (*Points to couple.*) So have they.

MILLIE: No, you can't go. What's the matter with you?
(*She pinches his cheek, he squirms.*)
He's so highly strung and sensitive. Are you feeling alright, darling? Let's feel your forehead. Spit out three times and go and eat some fruit. Well, Rabbi, it's nice to see you in this house.

SADIE: Perhaps he'd like to bless the house – believe me, it's worth it.

MILLIE: Alright, why not? We've got everything but it can't do no harm.

MORRY: We've got nothing, we kid ourselves.

ROMAINE: Oh, Daddy's getting all philosophical again.

MELVIN: Dad's right and we're a load of hypocrites.

HERBERT: It's a lovely party, isn't it? And soon our dear children will be pushing off on their honeymoon.

MORRY: Thank God.

MILLIE: I agree, it's good at last they'll almost stand on their own feet. After all, you push them out of you – into the world – and then it seems you have to push them right through life. And now at last they're gonna push off. It's not fair – they leave you so suddenly – look at her, she's only a baby.

HERBERT: Some baby.
(*SOLLY takes another drink, walks around the couple, digs ALAN in the ribs and kisses SARAH.*)

SOLLY: Have a nice time, don't be greedy – in life. Love thy neighbour as –
(*He starts kissing all the women on the forehead, lingers over ROMAINE.*)
Be fruitful and drink lots of malt and may you have peach mirrors in your house and apricots on your table.

MILLIE: They're not moving out yet, we've still got them for a little while – until the architects have finished their house. Then they'll move away; they grow up and leave you.

MORRY: What do you mean? Look, Rabbi, see that building next door? (*Shows SOLLY through the window.*) That's how far they're moving.

MILLIE: They've got the best of everything – I've seen to that. It cost a fortune, but who's complaining?

MELVIN: There she goes again. Must you always mention money?

MILLIE: I'd like to see you manage without it.

MORRY: For once I agree with your mother. I wouldn't care if you worked – you're supposed to look after the shop but what do you do all day? You're out playing golf and in the Turkish baths, trying to be like an English gentleman – Gandhi was more of an Englishman. Something for nothing, that's all you want. I had to work for it.

MILLIE: He's not that bad.

MELVIN: He's almost right, but can I help it if I don't belong?

ROMAINE: There he goes again, don't belong. Go out and don't belong – just fifty years or so.

MELVIN: Shut up you, you silly fat cow.

SOLLY: Children, children, remember the Sabbath day and keep it holy.

SARAH: But this isn't the Sabbath.

SOLLY: I never said it was. You must learn to respect your parents.

MILLIE: That's what I keep on telling him, he's killing me – killing me.

MELVIN: You're a long time dying.

SOLLY: Peace, peace, my children. We must forgive and love each other.

MILLIE: Alright, Mel darling, I'll buy you your glider.

ROMAINE: I want a car.

MORRY: Two years ago she bought him a sports car and last year she bought him a yacht, and now, a glider. We've had the ground and the water and now we'll have the air. What happens when we run out of elements?
I suppose next year it'll be a spaceship. Alright, let's change the subject. Rabbi, it's a great honour to have you

here; tell us the purpose for your visit to our humble – big house.

SOLLY: I'm Rabbi Solly Gold, at your service. I bring the word of God, I spread love and happiness. I'm on my usual pilgrimage through Golders Green and I pass this way but once – for today of all days is the day of days.

ALAN: You said it, today's my wedding day.

HERBERT: And tonight's the night.

SARAH: (*Pinching ALAN's cheek.*) Isn't he lovely? I could eat him.

SOLLY: Apart from that, it's still a very special day.

SADIE: It's a holiday or festival or something, isn't it?

HERBERT: No, I know them all.

MELVIN: It's the Amateur Gliding championship today.

ROMAINE: It's just another Sunday.

MORRY: And I've got heartburn as usual and a splitting headache.

MILLIE: And I've got heartache, and backache and stomach-ache –

SOLLY: I'm ashamed of you all. All of you. Look at you! Call yourself good Jews? And you didn't even know it was rabbinical chicken Sunday? I'm disgusted.

MILLIE: Rabbinical chicken what?

MORRY: Forgive me, Rabbi, but I don't follow religion – too many hypocrites.

SOLLY: You've all heard of Mother's Day? And Father's Day? And Doomsday? Well then, you surely must know that seven years ago the American Reform Orthodox Proxy Rabbi's Association proclaimed this Chicken Sunday. In the old days it used to be a great Hasidic feast. Don't you remember?

(*He dances around wildly and mumbles gibberish.*)

We revived it. Five times a year it falls. Surely someone must know the famous song?

(*Sings and dances again.*)

On the second Sunday of December,

Don't forget to remember,

Give, give and give some more,

To the Rabbi at your door.
The third Sunday that comes in May,
That most auspicious Rabbinical Day,
Give, give, and give your all,
To the Rabbi who comes to call.
On the fourth Sunday in July,
If a Rabbi passes by,
Give! give! Don't ask why
It's Rabbinical Chicken Sunday.

HERBERT: Of course, now I remember, I was only reading about it the other day.

SOLLY: Then as you know, the idea is for an esteemed rabbi, like yours truly, to go humbly from door to door, giving a chicken as a symbol of life and collecting a small amount for charity.

HERBERT: Ah, charity – what a lovely word that is. I'm a Mason, Rabbi, and that's the basis of our creed. Ever thought of going on the square? I'll propose you.

MILLIE: (*Takes out purse.*) We always give to charity. That should be my middle name – Millie Charity Swartz. What charity this time?

SOLLY: The Rabbinical Chicken Sunday fund for the prevention of cruelty.

MILLIE: Cruelty to who? Chickens?

SOLLY: Cruelty to anyone.

HERBERT: You're a man after my own heart. Here, let me give you something. (*Hands SOLLY a note.*) Honestly, I give, give and never think about it. (*Turns to the others.*) Just gave him a flyer. Why not?

MILLIE: But we don't want a chicken, we've just eaten half a dozen. I'm beginning to look like a chicken.

MORRY: You always did.

SADIE: I never get tired of chicken.

SARAH: Neither do I – I love them casseroled.

ROMAINE: I prefer them fricassee with breadcrumbs.

MORRY: Take no notice of any of them. Put the bird on the table. Go on, Millie, give the Rabbi some money. As a goy named Bacon once said –

MILLIE: Please don't mention that word, this is a kosher house. What will the Rabbi think? You give him the money, you want the bird.

MORRY: Who should I make it out to?

(*Takes out cheque book.*)

SOLLY: Please, please. I'm surprised with you – you must surely know that truly spiritual organisations don't believe in banks. It's unholy – it's usury, it cuts across the holy act of giving from one to the other.

MORRY: How much?

SOLLY: Shall we say ten pounds?

MILLIE: Expensive chicken!

SOLLY: (*Taking money from MORRY.*) Fine – wonderful. Now, let's forget all about money and get down to business, the business of blessing. (*To SARAH and ALAN.*) What kind do you want? The special super de luxe deep significant kind, or the simple blessing of the bedchamber?

SARAH: How much do they cost?

SOLLY: Let me see –

(*Takes out little book; consults it.*)

The significant, cabalistic eternal marriage blessing costs enough – mind you, it's worth it – two hundred and fifty pounds.

MORRY: The man who thinks up them charges should be in charge of my business.

SOLLY: It all goes to charity mind you.

HERBERT: Our children deserve special prayers. After all, God can't be expected to be tuned in everywhere – we must have a strong transmitter. And the money goes to charity after all, don't let's stint ourselves. Mr Swartz, you can afford it – if it was my house I'd give willingly.

SOLLY: Good, I'm glad you take that attitude. According to the law you must pay –

HERBERT: Me? Oh –

SADIE: But we –

HERBERT: How much does the cheaper blessing cost? You know, the bedchamber kind?

SOLLY: Only twenty-five pounds, and it's a pretty good

blessing. For as the good book says: When the bedroom is happy every room is happy.

HERBERT: We'll have to have that one then – I haven't got the loose change here and I've left my cheque book at home – I'll owe it to you, don't forget to remind me.

SOLLY: (*Points to MORRY.*) He'll lend it to you, won't you, Mr Swartz? Of course he will.

(*MORRY nods slowly and gives SOLLY more money.*)

That's twenty-five pounds this gentleman owes you. Now on with the blessing. Oh, what a wonderful couple they are – they take my breath away. All I can say is they deserve each other. How I envy them – wish I could get married.

MORRY: Why can't you? Rabbis can.

SOLLY: I was married once. She was beautiful. Miriam! She died in childbirth.

MILLIE: I'm so sorry.

SOLLY: That's alright – we have to get over these things. But no other girl will take her place; besides, now I've taken my vow of chastity… Right, now the – let me see – the bedroom all-purpose blessing…

(*He takes up wine and starts to mumble gibberish and sways backward and forward.*)

Mayyoulivelonganddiehappy. Pleasegodbyyouyou shouldlivesolongmayyougetwhatIwishyoufrompurimto shobosnochmaohgodunitetheminmorewaysthanonewhats onecanneverbeundonemazelmazelmazeltovmazel mazelmazeltov.

(*He now repeats this over and over again and claps his hands until he virtually hypnotises himself and starts dancing suggestively around the couple. He does this so completely and with such conviction that he has the others following him – going round and round in a circle, copying him. Seeing his power he dances around the room in conga-fashion and the others still follow him in and out of the rooms. The couple still stand where they were, completely oblivious to all this. When SOLLY stops dancing he shrugs, all the others seem rather stunned and dazed.*)

HERBERT: Your Hebrew was the funniest I ever heard.

SOLLY: That's the new semantic Semitic based on the
emetic antics of the yigdal incorporating the Aztectoltec
Ashkenazim. We're branching out.

HERBERT: Of course, I was only reading about it the other
day in the *Jewish Chronicle.*
(*SOLLY sits down at the table and eats a chicken leg with
great relish.*)

SOLLY: This is a lovely house.

SADIE: It's a palace. You could eat off the floor.

HERBERT: It's a castle. Believe me, a king could live here.
And Rabbi, come here, look at these peach mirrors – all
embossed – what do you think of them? I tell everyone
about them. They cost the earth.

MORRY: I hate them, they're designed to make you look
better than you are. Every day I feel lousy but the mirrors
make me look in the pink of health.

MELVIN: Mirror mirror on the wall – who is the peachiest of
us all?

HERBERT: Do you know how much this house cost?

SOLLY: You told me. But tell me, Mr Swartz, who are you
that you can afford such opulence?

HERBERT: You mean to say you never heard of him? Didn't
you see that full page ad in the *Jewish Chronicle* last week?
This is Morry Swartz – *the* Morry Swartz – the shoe king.
He's rich, he's famous – haven't you heard the jingle on
Tele? Swartz's Shoes – Swartz's Shoes are the shoes for
You. Get some, get some, for your wife, and your children
too. My son married his daughter. His shoes are the best.

MORRY: Don't you believe it, I never wear them – they
cripple me. Don't talk about business, it's a millstone round
my neck. Let's change the subject. What synagogue are
you from?

SOLLY: Synagogue? Oh no, I'm a peripatetic rabbi – I travel.
Of course I have many synagogues under me, for between
you and me – I don't want to boast, but I'm a fully fledged
Synog. Regalia and all. You should all be ashamed of
yourselves – don't you know your own religion?
(*They all look ashamed.*)
I have now renounced ceremony, severed myself from

paraphernalia and am having a Sabbatical year, for
the whole world is a place of worship. Every house is a
synagogue.

HERBERT: I think I read about you in the *Daily Express* and
the good work you are doing.

SOLLY: Of course you did, though I shun personal publicity.
I've just returned from the provinces where I've been
making fifty conversions daily.

ROMAINE: But Jews don't go in for conversion.

SOLLY: Don't be ridiculous, I've been converting the Jews
back to their own faith.

MORRY: You've got your work cut out.

SOLLY: I'm so ashamed, of all of you, everywhere I go
the same story – everyone only interested in money, no
thought for the spiritual.

MILLIE: What's the name of your organisation?

SOLLY: The Liberal Orthodox Hasidic Reform United Union
of Peripatetics.

SARAH: Well, Mummy, it's time we started on our
honeymoon.

MILLIE: Oh darling, I'll miss you.

SOLLY: Going somewhere nice? Bournemouth? Cliftonville?

ALAN: No, we're going to the Mount Royal Hotel at Marble
Arch.

SOLLY: Eh?

SARAH: What's wrong with that? All sorts of interesting
foreigners come and go and it's opposite the park and it's
not too far away.

ROMAINE: And the food's smashing.

MILLIE: Five miles away is far enough – she's never been
that far from me. Don't forget to phone me tonight,
darling. If there's anything you want or want to know, I'm
here at the other end of the phone. And remember I'm
always here and you've always got a home here.

MORRY: Alan, look after my baby and we'll look after you.

ALAN: Don't worry, Dad, she's in safe hands.

SARAH: You ready, Alan?

ALAN: What do you think?

MELVIN: Thank God for that. Now I can get to that game –
I'll drop you off in my car.

SARAH: No thanks, we're taking Daddy's Rolls.

(*There is now a lot of kissing and pinching and crying by the women and back slapping by the men, then all the people talk in a group near the door as ROMAINE and SARAH exchange a few words.*)

Don't worry, Romaine, it'll soon be your turn.

ROMAINE: Who's worried? Make sure you have their barbecued trout – it's out of this world.

SARAH: I wish it was you who got married today, really I do.

ROMAINE: I've got no time for men. But be careful of their horse-radish sauce.

SARAH: I know it's going to be lonely for you without me around but maybe I'll find a nice boy there for you.

ROMAINE: Men are horrible, they only want one thing. Of course, the speciality of the house is smoked salmon rolled up with capers and stuffed into cold Scotch salmon.

SARAH: Oh I do wish you could get married – you've got such lovely eyes.

ROMAINE: I told you I don't trust men. You going to cook for Alan or employ a cook?

SARAH: I want to cook myself – I can make omelettes. Oh look at him, he seems half-starved.

ROMAINE: What he needs is plenty of lockshen soup, gefilte fish, apple strudel, cheesecake.

SARAH: You're so clever, you must teach me.

ROMAINE: And steaks – lots of steaks, for breakfast. It's the latest rage – and salt beef always goes down well.

SARAH: You're so good, so good, you deserve a man.

ROMAINE: Don't do me no favours.

ALAN: Coming, darling?

HERBERT: Well, Kinderler, be happy, tonight we'll really be related, eh Morry? You know you haven't lost a daughter, you've gained a son.

MORRY: Looks like I've gained a family.

SADIE: My boy is a good boy and she's a good girl, don't they look lovely together?

MORRY: Alright, alright, go then – and if you need any more money, I know that you know where to come.

MILLIE: I'm so happy, so happy for both of you.

SOLLY: (*Blessing them.*) Eat plenty of fruitcake and may all your troubles be little ones.

MELVIN: Well, Sis, Alan, lots of splendid luck and all that sort of rot and play the game and all that kind of thing. (*He hurries out and he is followed by SARAH and ALAN.*)

MILLIE: (*Shouts after them.*) Wrap up warm – don't forget, phone me.

SADIE: Alan! Don't forget your tablets – well, they've gone now. Suppose we'll go also.

HERBERT: Can't we stay a little longer? Play cards or watch Tele or something, after all our families are now united? Come on, Romaine, put some records on, let's be lively.

MILLIE: Alright, let's all go to the other room and play canasta – I feel funny tonight.

SADIE: Believe me, Millie, I've also got the shivers – I know how you feel. My baby got married – (*They all start for the other room but SOLLY and MORRY don't move.*)

MILLIE: Coming, Morry?

MORRY: No, I don't feel well.

MILLIE: (*To the others.*) You all go, I'll be in in a moment. (*They all go in. SOLLY goes to the bar and drinks.*) You drive me mad you do. If you don't act a bit more sociable I'll brain you.

MORRY: I can't stand them.

MILLIE: You're ruining everything.

MORRY: Everything's ruined anyway. I wanted Alan for Romaine, you married off the wrong one.

MILLIE: Well, at least we got one of them off our hands. Alan's a good boy, he's a plodder.

MORRY: Can't stand his father!

MILLIE: Well at least he's not badly off – even if he is stupid.

MORRY: He's nothing, just nothing in trousers.

MILLIE: He's a turf accountant, rolling in it.

MORRY: Turf accountant? In my day they called it bookmaker. He hasn't got two pennies to rub together. Street corner spiv.

MILLIE: He's got an office with a typewriter and two girls working for him.

MORRY: I bet!

MILLIE: Besides, he must be respectable, he's a Mason.

MORRY: That explains everything.

MILLIE: He's got marvellous connections.

MORRY: I need unconnections. I've got too many. We'll
never get poor Romaine married now.

MILLIE: Why not? She's got nice eyes.

MORRY: Let's face it – she's fat and ugly and she's not a
chicken. I told you to tell that marriage broker that
I wanted a husband for her and not Sarah. Sarah could
always find a husband.

MILLIE: She'd have got swept off her feet for a lowlife who
only wanted her for her money.

MORRY: What about Alan? You think he's marrying her for
love? Every time he looks at me, cash registers ring in his
eyes.

MILLIE: I know, but this is different; we chose him, it's
respectable this way. Anyway, who wants Romaine
married? She's such a good girl around the house – no
romantic-shmantic nonsense about her.

MORRY: We sold the wrong one – the wrong one. Poor
Romaine, running to seed, well – hardly running –
hobbling. It's all your fault.

MILLIE: Do me a favour, go to sleep – you're uncouth. A rich
man with nothing. Look at him. At least I know how to
treat guests, even if I don't like them.
(*She goes into the other room and we can just see them in
there playing cards. ROMAINE is dancing rather sadly
around the card table.*)

SOLLY: (*Giving MORRY a drink.*) One thing I don't
understand, if you're so rich, why so few guests?

MORRY: Who do I need to impress? Anyway, I don't like
anyone, not even myself. I'm surrounded by enemies, all
after my money.

SOLLY: You're right, and listen, your enemies praise you but
your friends tell you the truth, and I'm telling you that
there's something missing in your life.

MORRY: I don't trust no one. I love my children but what's
the use, they're spoilt and take no notice of me. I love my

wife but we're miles apart – getting further away every minute. I'm finished.

SOLLY: They're sucking the life out of you. Bloodsuckers, that's what they all are.

MORRY: Riches? You can keep them. All my life I slaved. For what?

SOLLY: It's obvious to me you're a highly spiritually developed man. Ah well, it's time to be gone.

MORRY: (*Breaking away from his own thoughts.*) No, no, Rabbi! Please don't go. You give me a certain peace, when you sit beside me.

SOLLY: I've work to do, my son.

MORRY: Please spare me a little longer, I want to talk to you. I feel I could pour it all out, you have such a beautiful face. Please, please, just for a few minutes.

SOLLY: Oh well, if you insist, my son.
(*He helps himself to another drink.*)
Maybe I can help you, though I do want you to understand that my time is valuable.

MORRY: I'll make it worth your while. It's worth anything to me, just to get it all off my chest.

SOLLY: Alright then – just relax. Lie down.
(*Using the method of a psychoanalyst, he makes MORRY lie flat on a settee.*)
Tell me everything, confide in me, God is listening to you.

MORRY: I'm afraid of dying, I'm also afraid of living. Everyone fiddles. My accountant is a crook; so is my doctor and my solicitor. I don't trust my wife; she tries to look too beautiful – who for? Me? After all these years? So I hired a private detective to watch her and now I've had to hire another one to watch him.

SOLLY: That's right, tell me everything – unburden yourself.

MORRY: Yes, I can trust you. You radiate love and kindness. I'm a humble man, Rabbi. Not very intelligent, but a bit clever. You don't need brains to make money, you need knack. I don't believe in anything – what can I do? My son is a no-good snob, my wife nags, nags, grabs, grabs, and now I'm left with Romaine on my hands. Till the day I die I'll see her fat podgy fingers eating Turkish delight and marshmallow.

SOLLY: But surely anyone would marry her?

MORRY: You'd think money was good enough bait, but no, not with her – they fight shy of Romaine, and can you blame them?

SOLLY: But she's attractive! Lovely! A big girl, full of –

MORRY: Too bad you took that oath of chastity – still, once sworn never torn – besides, as you said, you loved your wife too much. You would have made a lovely husband for my Romaine. Too late now.

SOLLY: So what can I do for you?

MORRY: I'm useless, not going anywhere, not getting anywhere, except under the ground. I'm crippled with pain, so Rabbi, what can I do?

SOLLY: One minute! It just dawned on me – of course, now I remember you.

MORRY: Do the synagogue boys know me then? Am I that well known? Have I got a good name?
(*He gets up.*)

SOLLY: You started down the lane, didn't you, with a shoe stall?

MORRY: Yes, I started humble.

SOLLY: And you're still a humble man – God is pleased with you. Didn't you then start a small shoe shop in the Mile End Road?

MORRY: That's me.

SOLLY: Of course! And then you built up your shoe empire.

MORRY: Do you know, I'm shoemaker by appointment to the Queen of Tonga and the President of the USA. But between you and me – I wouldn't be seen dead in my shoes.

SOLLY: My mother once brought me to your shop in Mile End – you served me yourself, don't you remember?

MORRY: Does a prostitute remember all her customers?

SOLLY: You saw we were poor so you gave me the pair of shoes, for free. Providence has brought me to you to repay that debt – that wonderful gesture of a man with a soul, a man with such humanity – shush – don't talk – I'm trying to get in touch with the angels now. Marvellous things are going to happen to you.

MORRY: Rabbi, you're a wonderful man, I envy you. So

you're an East End boy – like myself. Well, you made good, maybe there's still a chance for me.

SOLLY: I'll see what I can do. I'll put a word in.

MORRY: I know you. I know I do – as if I've known you for years. What did your father do?

SOLLY: He was a great composer and my mother was a ballerina, she used to dance at the Palaseum, didn't you ever hear of Bertha Goldskya?

MORRY: Not off-hand.

SOLLY: Now, let's get down to hard facts – how much are you worth?

MORRY: Who knows? Between half a million and a million. It fluctuates. But what's the use? Has any single pound brought me a single ounce of happiness?

SOLLY: You could always give it away.

MORRY: You kidding? You're not married to my wife. Anyway, I don't really want to give it away. I mean I worked so hard for it. That's my dilemma.
(*They have been drinking continuously and both are staggering around, MORRY more so than SOLLY.*)
When I was a kid I was happy.
(*SOLLY puts his arm around him.*)

SOLLY: Tell me about it.

MORRY: Seven of us – happy kids, all sleeping in the same big bed.
(*He takes some cushions and lays them on the floor. SOLLY does the same.*)
The bedroom small, can't you see it? My father struggled and my mother worried and we played. I was rich then; caterpillars in boxes and conkers on strings and every day was an adventure. Mummeeeeeeee! Throw me down a peneneeeeeeee! And when the winter evening came we played hide-and-seek in a peasoup fog and went home to a bowl of peasoup... And don't you remember the pillow fights and feathers everywhere?

SOLLY: On guard!
(*He hits MORRY over the head with a pillow. MORRY is sent flying and feathers are flying everywhere.
MORRY gets up and hits SOLLY over the head. Soon*

they are fighting and laughing with everything they've got.)
MORRY: Hurray! Hurray! Charge! Confetti – Hiphip – Hip
– Hoooray –
(*MILLIE comes into the room followed by ROMAINE,
HERBERT AND SADIE.*)
MILLIE: Take no notice of him, Sadie, he never grew up.
(*Pushing the others back into the room; trying to suppress
her anger.*)
Strange games you're teaching my husband, Rabbi.
SOLLY: I'm illustrating a theme from the Bible. We got
carried away – such spirit your husband has.
MILLIE: Back inside, folks – he's a little unhinged tonight.
The trouble I have with that man; never mind, there are
worse fish in the sea, so they say.
MORRY: I wish you'd go fishing.
(*They all laugh as they go back into the room but MILLIE
turns on MORRY.*)
MILLIE: You wait till I get you alone, I'll give you what-for,
showing me up.
(*She goes in with the others.*)
MORRY: See what I mean? Who can I turn to? Child games
are over. My mother and father died and everyone grew
up.
(*He starts to tidy the mess and SOLLY helps him.*)
All the family have grown up and grown old – (*He groans.*)
Oh my back! It's like a knife. Everyone lives in Hendon
and Hampstead Garden suburb – but there's no garden
in the heart. We're all dead people in stuffy living rooms,
now, but then it was paradise.
SOLLY: With my help you can become happy again.
MORRY: Come on, let's have another drink, let's eat, drink
and be merry for tomorrow we die, please God.
(*They drink again and MORRY dances and sings to the
tune from 'Thieving Magpie' by Rossini.*)
I am a lobos, I am a lobos
I take the shicksers to pictures on shobos.
(*He suddenly stops and becomes doubled up with pain.*)
There it is – Oooooooohhhhhhhh – I've overdone it. I'm

finished. (*He gradually lies down.*) Ohhhhhhhohohoh – I'm
dying – I'm done for.

SOLLY: What can I get you?

MORRY: Stay here. Just speak to me, your voice soothes
me. Will God forgive me? I'm dying. Will he forgive me,
Rabbi?

SOLLY: He hasn't got much choice with me to help you.
Don't speak now – you're doing alright.

MORRY: Oh my stomach, Oh my back, Oh my God.

SOLLY: Listen – I want you to stand up.

MORRY: You crazy! If I stand up I'll fall over.

SOLLY: Stand up!

MORRY: Oh go away from me. Leave me alone.

SOLLY: If you stand up you won't fall over. I have spoken.

MORRY: Leave me to die in peace.

SOLLY: Have faith in God! Stand up – He will heal you.
Stand up. I promise you – you won't fall over.

MORRY: Alright, for His sake I'll chance it –
Oooooohohohooo. (*He gradually gets to his feet.*)

SOLLY: There you are – oh ye of little faith.
(*At this MORRY crumbles and falls over.*)

MORRY: I told you – oh let me die. I'm suffering from an
incurable disease.

SOLLY: Where's the pain now?

MORRY: Where isn't it! In my toes, in my head, in my
fingers, in my neck, in my back. (*He slowly crawls to his feet
by holding on to the settee.*)

SOLLY: You'll be fine – I'll cure you. Nothing to worry about.
Solly Gold will fix it.
(*Unintentionally SOLLY slaps the old man vigorously on
the back. MORRY is hurled to the floor again.*)

MORRY: Oh! You've killed me!
(*He writhes and moans and turns over and over in great
agony but suddenly he stops and stands up.*)
That's it! The pain's gone! You've done it!

SOLLY: Of course. What did I tell you?

MORRY: I'm cured! You don't understand – I can stand up
straight with no pain! It's a miracle! A miracle!
(*He kisses SOLLY resoundingly on the forehead.*)

For years I've suffered and now I'm well, thanks to you.

SOLLY: It's the work of God, I'm just His instrument.

MORRY: It's a miracle. And to think I doubted. He sent you to me – I can't believe it – how can I thank you? How can I repay you?

SOLLY: We'll find a way.

MORRY: Stay here with me – stay here for a time – for a few days. Please be my guest.

SOLLY: I told you my time is precious – there are others who need help…people starving… I'm the best collector this side of the Thames.

MORRY: I'll make it worth your while – I'll give you more than you'll collect in a month. But you must stay, I need you. You can help me.

SOLLY: Alright, if this is the will of God, who am I to argue? I'll stay for a while.

MORRY: Oh, we'll have a marvellous time, you and I together! I'm young again. I'm reborn. I can move, I walk, I can dance! It's a miracle. Thank you, thank you. Watch me dance – Kazatzka – I haven't done it for years. (*He dances wildly to the music that comes from the other room. SOLLY claps his hands and they make a terrific noise. The family and the Finks come in from the other room – stand around in amazement as MORRY dances into the other room followed by SOLLY clapping. The phone rings; everyone rushes for it but MILLIE gets there first.*)

MILLIE: Hullo! Oh – It's them! They've just arrived – they're in the room.

SADIE: What's it like?

MILLIE: What's the room like? Oh, it's all pink – and silver – overlooking the park… They can see the speakers on speakers' corner…how thrilling – what's the weather like? Oh yes, of course.

ROMAINE: What's the food like?

MILLIE: Did you hear that? They haven't eaten yet – the waiter's just taken their order.

HERBERT: Tell them to behave themselves – I mean they can do what they like but tomorrow is another day.

MILLIE: Alan, your father sends his love. Wrap up warm, darling – the nights are drawing in. I'm so happy for you, you naughty girl.

SADIE: Tell him to take his pills.

MILLIE: Take your pills, Alan.

(*MORRY comes dancing back into the room, SOLLY stops clapping.*)

What's that, darling? How's Dad? Morry? Morry? Did you hear that? Haven't you got a message for your daughter?

MORRY: Tell them, God is good. I'm cured at last and Rabbi Solly Gold did it. (*Carries on dancing.*)

MILLIE: How should I know, darling – he's round the bend – only more so. Says he's cured. Bye-bye – Dolly. Ring me later – Soon. If you want to know anything – I'm here all the time and don't forget… Alan, look after her, and if you can't be good, be careful…

(*She hangs up and they all once more turn to MORRY who continues his dance with SOLLY clapping his hands once more. They stand staring in amazement as the curtain falls.*)

Scene 3

The next day. The curtains are drawn and the lights are on. It seems like the middle of the night but in reality it is eleven thirty a.m. SOLLY enters in a very flamboyant-looking dressing gown, goes to the cocktail cabinet and drinks, goes to the peach mirror and smiles at himself.

SOLLY: This is the life for me, I was born for luxury.

(*He takes another drink and ROMAINE comes on – also in dressing gown. She touches him on the shoulder, he jumps.*)

ROMAINE: Talking to yourself, eh?

SOLLY: I was talking to God.

ROMAINE: Go away, you can't fool me. I'm not like my father.

SOLLY: Can I get you a drink?

ROMAINE: A bunny hug, please.

(*He quickly hugs her.*)

SOLLY: With pleasure.

ROMAINE: (*Struggling free.*) A bunny hug is Advocaat and cherry brandy.

SOLLY: Oh, I'm sorry, I'll get it. You must excuse me but I want to make people happy and I thought that was what you wanted.

ROMAINE: Wait till I tell my father.

SOLLY: Well, if you don't want it, at least you need it – that's obvious.

ROMAINE: Wait till my mother comes down.
(*She takes the drink and drinks it.*)

SOLLY: Your father knows what he's doing – he understands the intricacies of religion.

ROMAINE: He understands nothing, he's a fool.

SOLLY: He can't be a fool if he made a fortune.

ROMAINE: Most people who make money are mad – they're all a bit touched.

SOLLY: My aunt Sophie had a fortune and she was untouched.

ROMAINE: How long you staying?

SOLLY: How long do you want me?
(*He pinches her cheek.*)
I can help you.

ROMAINE: Don't need help.

SOLLY: We all need help. Come, my daughter, think of me as a friend.
(*He puts his hand on her shoulders.*)

ROMAINE: Not too close.

SOLLY: Confide in me. Tell me everything.

ROMAINE: There's nothing much to tell.

SOLLY: You're very deep, I can see it. I'm trained to search your inner depths. You're a restless spirit, I can see great fires raging in you soul. Oh, thou fairest of women –

ROMAINE: I'm starving.

SOLLY: Thine eyes are as a dove's.

ROMAINE: You been listening to Housewives' Choice?

SOLLY: They hair is a flock of goats.

ROMAINE: Cheek! I shampooed it last night.
(*He tries to cuddle her but she keeps on retreating from him.*)

SOLLY: Thy mouth is comely and they breasts are like two fawns –

ROMAINE: How dare you! You're a dirty old man.

SOLLY: I'm not, that's in the Bible – here read!

ROMAINE: You're still a dirty old man.

SOLLY: I'm not old.

ROMAINE: Wait till I see my father. He'll throw you out – Man of God!

SOLLY: Wishful thinking, my daughter. I have not behaved improperly. I will admit though to being human. Under this habit is the same old habit – the desire for a beautiful girl like you.

ROMAINE: Wonder what's in the fridge for breakfast? How about some steak?

SOLLY: You know how to please a man. Why is it that you're not appreciated in this house? Why do they always leave you out?

ROMAINE: How do you know?

SOLLY: God knows everything, and I've come to tell you that you deserve better for you're the most beautiful woman I've ever seen.

ROMAINE: You trying to get round me?

SOLLY: (*Soft.*) That would be hard – the angels are doing their nut over you. I'm going to help you get what's coming to you, get what you deserve. Your body is a poem conceived by the love of God and my imagination.

ROMAINE: Come off it, you know I'm fat.

SOLLY: Not fat, well built, a big girl – a real woman, with everything in its place and plenty of it. A wonderful sight – paradise, the promise of bliss.

ROMAINE: Of course, I'm reducing. At least I'm trying – I'm going to cut down on potatoes tomorrow.

SOLLY: Don't! Stay as you are – you're lovely. Beauty is in the eyes of the beholder and behold thou art fantastic – colossal – a double feature – I'm here to show you how much you're wanted.

ROMAINE: Some boys whistled me last July.

SOLLY: Oh if I wasn't a rabbi – if I hadn't taken my vow! My wife! God rest her soul, would understand, I'm crazy about you.

ROMAINE: How would you like your steak?

SOLLY: Overdone – almost burnt to a cinder.

ROMAINE: I like the opposite – very rare –

SOLLY: Go quickly before I forget that I'm a holy man.
> (*She smiles and goes into the kitchen. He rubs his hands and looks at reflection in mirror.*)
> Careful, Solly my boy. Careful, go slowly or you'll spoil everything.
> (*He reads the Bible.*)

ROMAINE: (*Calls from kitchen.*) Come and watch me cook!

SOLLY: You trying to lead me astray? (*He now fights with himself.*) Careful, boy – take it easy. Oh, what's worth more to me? A fortune or a fat girl? Nothing's ever easy, is it? Just my luck. (*He still fights with himself.*) No! Moneymoneymoneymoney! It all boils down to that in the end.

ROMAINE: Come on, come and watch me. I'm sorry I was cross with you before. I got you all wrong.

SOLLY: No, I can't come now, I'm reading.

ROMAINE: What?

SOLLY: The most stupendous, smashing, story of them all – rape, love, hate, war, sex, everything – the Bible.
> (*Now he flips through the book and gets really excited.*)
> Cooo, it's all here – everything. Now I know where everything comes from!
> (*Suddenly he gets wildly excited.*)
> This is it! Here it is! I've got it! Solly, you're marvellous! It's a cinch. A cinch, a winner! It's all here, in black and white – it can't fail.
> (*He can hardly contain his pleasure. He drinks to his reflection in the mirror. MORRY walks in briskly.*)

MORRY: Wonderful morning.

SOLLY: How do you feel?

MORRY: On top of the world, thanks to you.
> (*ROMAINE comes in.*)
> Hello, darling. (*He kisses her.*) How are you? Isn't it a lovely day?

ROMAINE: You feeling alright?

MORRY: Alright? I'm alive at last, aware – free! Make me some breakfast.

ROMAINE: But you never eat breakfast.

MORRY: This morning I feel hungry. Just something light, there's a good girl.

ROMAINE: Bit of toast?

MORRY: No, some grapefruit juice, some cereal and to follow, some fried kidneys and eggs.

ROMAINE: Something light? Oh, I see. Daddy, you kill me.

MORRY: Don't be saucy or I'll cut you off.

ROMAINE: Cut you off! Cut you off! That's all he knows. I feel like a water supply.

MORRY: Come on, there's a good girl – let's not argue anymore. I'll buy you a pound of marzipan whirls.

ROMAINE: With almonds inside? Daddy, I don't know what's come over you, but it makes a change.
(*She goes into the kitchen.*)

MORRY: I've got a good idea. Let's go to Brighton in my Rolls, lay on the sand, then maybe we'll go to the Wax Works. Or, I forgot – no sand at Brighton! How about coming to the East End and having a salt-beef sandwich?

SOLLY: No, there's important work to do. Now that you're healthy in body we've got to consolidate our position and then make you healthy in soul.

MORRY: But I'm happy now. I feel fine, thanks to you.

SOLLY: You only think you're happy, but the spiritual inertia will creep up on you if you're not careful and you'll have more than *angst* in your pants.

MORRY: Yes.

SOLLY: I want it louder than that – an affirmation, a total acceptance. Now listen, do you trust me? – Do you – place – yourself – in my – care?

MORRY: Absolutely! For some reason I trust you with my life. I dreamed and dreamed last night – wonderful dreams – you may be a stranger but you're not so strange as my own family.

SOLLY: Good! Now! Concentrate. I'm going to make a real *mensch* of you. First I've got a message for you.

MORRY: From the Stock Exchange?

SOLLY: Somewhere more important.

MORRY: (*Incredulous.*) More important than the Stock Exchange?

SOLLY: I've got a message from God – for you. He spoke to me last night.

MORRY: Go on – you're a liar.

SOLLY: Would God talk to a liar?

MORRY: I'm sorry, I didn't mean it. A message for me?

SOLLY: When I knocked on the door I had a vision. And when I saw your face I saw a purple light, and when you spoke I knew my search was over.

MORRY: Search? Purple light?

SOLLY: How can I tell him I said to myself – how? How can I prepare this humble man for the news – for his mission. The Almighty said – 'Speak, speak!'

MORRY: Don't leave me up in the air – for God's sake, spit it out.

SOLLY: All night I lay awake arguing with the angels telling them that you were not ready. There I was praying and weeping. All the stars in the sky burst into the room, a great halo covered the universe, and a golden rainbow stretched from Golders Green to Stamford Hill. Then, just at dawn, amongst a choir of assembled archangels the Holy One spoke again: 'Behold – I send you Elijah the Prophet – '

(*ROMAINE comes in and SOLLY quickly stops gesticulating.*)

ROMAINE: We haven't got any grapefruit juice.

MORRY: Grapefruit juice? What are you talking about? Go away!

ROMAINE: That's more like it. Now you're yourself again. (*She goes off.*)

SOLLY: (*Continues.*) 'And he shall turn the heart of the fathers to the children and the heart of the children to their fathers.'

MORRY: What does it all boil down to?

SOLLY: 'Behold nations shall come to thy light and kings to the brightness of thy rising... The fires –'

MORRY: Please tell me, don't beat about the burning bush.

SOLLY: I've come to proclaim you the messiah of the world.
  (*He kneels before him.*)
MORRY: Me? Don't make me la – – ugh.
SOLLY: It's no laughing matter but a time for jubilation. For
  you and me and the whole world.
  (*ROMAINE comes in to lay the table. SOLLY quickly gets
  up until she goes out again.*)
MORRY: Would it be alright if I had a cigarette?
  (*SOLLY nods.*)
  Like one?
SOLLY: What brand? (*Looks.*) Alright.
  (*Takes one and strikes a match.*)
  You'll catch the whole world alight.
  (*As he talks he forgets the lighted match and burns himself.*)
  It's hard to believe, I know, but you must believe.
MORRY: But Rabbi, you can't mean it. You're joking.
SOLLY: I never joke. Certainly not on matters like this. Would
  I jeopardise my immortal soul by such blasphemy?
  (*He keeps his fingers crossed and offers up a silent prayer
  for himself.*)
MORRY: Me? The messiah? Me? Little Morry Swartz? Go
  on, you're having me on. Me? The messiah?
  (*He looks at himself in the mirror.*)
  I've got bloodshot eyes.
SOLLY: You should have seen Moses. Look at me – listen
  – I've come to help you, Morry. Look – I'm telling the
  truth, by my life. Tell you what I'll do – want another
  miracle? Alright. Will that please you? Ye of little faith,
  I'm surprised at you – and you all ready to be the messiah.
  Didn't I perform a miracle on you last night?
MORRY: Yes, you did – but –
SOLLY: That was the first sign – to make you stand up and
  believe in me.
MORRY: But why me? Why do they have to pick on me?
SOLLY: Why not you? Morry, listen. Do me a favour. Do
  yourself a favour. You are not the messiah yet – Oh no –
  not by a long chalk. Hahahah. Did you think – no, there's
  a long way to go and I've come to take you there – to
  prepare you.

MORRY: But I'm a hypocrite.

SOLLY: Who but a good man would admit that?

MORRY: When I pray my words are empty. I can't get through.

SOLLY: I've got a direct line.

MORRY: I have no real love or reverence for anything –

SOLLY: That's because you haven't been alive till now.

MORRY: Would you swear on the Bible? That what you've said is the truth, so help you God?

SOLLY: Of course I would.

>   (*Puts his hand on the Bible while crossing the fingers of the other hand.*)

>   I swear on the Bible that you Morry Swartz are destined to become the messiah.

MORRY: It must be true – no one would swear like that without meaning it. I feel marvellous. Know what I'm going to do?

SOLLY: What? Pray?

MORRY: No, I'm going out in the garden – something I haven't done in years. (*He goes out.*)

SOLLY: Please, God – you there? If you are there, forgive me, *feinlights* – I'm doing it for your good. You see – alright, so I'm a bad boy. To forgive is human – I'll make it up to you... I'll make a bit of cash and make myself happy, and if I'm happy – well, we're all sailing – So listen, do me a favour – and if you're not there – and don't exist – what am I talking for anyway?

>   (*ROMAINE comes in with MORRY's breakfast.*)

ROMAINE: Where is he?

SOLLY: In the garden.

ROMAINE: (*Shouts from door.*) Dad! You're breakfast is ready!

>   (*She puts it on table then brings SOLLY's breakfast and SOLLY starts eating. MORRY comes back in.*)

>   This the way you like your kidneys, Dad?

MORRY: You mad? You know I never eat a big breakfast – who feels like eating anyway at a time like this? Now leave us alone, we're having a business discussion.

ROMAINE: Suppose I'll have to eat my steak in the kitchen. Business discussion! First he wants breakfast then he doesn't. Drives you mad, he does.

(*She goes back into kitchen.*)

MORRY: How we going to do this, Rabbi? How will we convince others?

SOLLY: (*He furiously cuts into his meat.*) You'll convince others not by magic but by logic, by example, by the lights that radiate from you – the light of wisdom, the light of knowledge. There, I will guide you. You'll bring people to God by your simplicity, by being humble. No miracles. Do they have to have miracles – disappearing tricks and rigmarole in order to believe? Oh, ye of little faith, you will say, isn't life a miracle?

MORRY: But why me? Surely there are others more worthy.

SOLLY: It happens that way sometimes. Look at Gautama Mohammed, and Izzy Totenspielgle. Listen, you are the new messiah – the everyday messiah – the ordinary fellow – the average bloke. Good common or garden messiah – a simple, humble, kind and worthy example – a heart of gold and an upholder of charity. This steak is tough, change your butcher – with you being ordinary you become extraordinary. It is the specific, the specimen, that makes the generalisation pointed. The microcosm proves the macrocosm – simple! To cut a long story sideways, you are an honest man.

MORRY: Me? Honest? How do you suppose I made a fortune?

SOLLY: Silence. I cannot tolerate your scepticism – your self-criticism. You must learn to love yourself. It's not how you made your money that matters anymore – it's what you do with it! The millions you made in money we will now make in souls. Making money was an exercise God set you.

(*He stands up and exclaims.*)

The nation is ready – the Commonwealth is linked – the world is watching and with my help you'll come into your kingdom and heaven will reign on earth. Cats and dogs will lick your feet – people will be nice. God watched you from the start – He helped you make a fortune and found a shoe empire! And now it's no longer Morry Swartz the King of the Shoes, but Morry Saviour Swartz the King of the Jews!

(*He sits down again and cuts more meat.*)

MORRY: (*Looks at mirror – gestures and poses.*) Do you think it's possible? Why? But why not? Sure! I got a scholarship as a kid when nobody else did.

SOLLY: You'll follow me and I'll follow you.

(*He walks round and round in a small circle and is followed by MORRY.*)

Morry Swartz the King of the Jews

Have you heard the latest news?

He saved the soles upon your feet

And now He'll save your soul – complete.

I'll help you, Morry, don't worry.

MORRY: Who'll help you?

SOLLY: God help me, I mean God'll help me. Now get on with your breakfast, you need to build up your energy for the election campaign.

MORRY: Look at me – haha – the messiah! And I'm only a small man.

SOLLY: So was Napoleon.

MORRY: Look what happened to him.

SOLLY: Well, what about my father? Look what happened to him, and he was only a small man.

MORRY: What happened to him?

SOLLY: He was the first man to swim the Atlantic, wasn't he?

MORRY: You said he was a composer.

SOLLY: Can't a crazy composer go swimming?

MORRY: Rabbi, I only hope I prove worthy of my task. This is the happiest day of my life. I want to tell everyone. At last I've got something to live for.

SOLLY: Now listen, be a diplomat – not a word to anyone, not yet. It's too soon – they're not ready yet for the shock. They're not so spiritually advanced. This must stay our secret until God says otherwise – otherwise you'll be a laughing stock. You know how people are.

(*ROMAINE enters.*)

ROMAINE: I've finished my breakfast. The steak was like butter.

SOLLY: Mine was like leather.

(*MILLIE enters in her dressing gown, looking like death.*)

MILLIE: Did the phone ring?

ROMAINE: No!

MILLIE: Why not? What's the time?

ROMAINE: Getting on for twelve.

MILLIE: What? Why didn't someone call me? Why doesn't someone draw the curtains? I feel terrible. Oh, oh, what a night I had – and I've got such a day in front of me.

SOLLY: Maybe I can help you.

MILLIE: No one can help me – you can only help yourself. I didn't sleep a wink.

SOLLY: Is it the international situation that's worrying you, my daughter?

MILLIE: International? What? What are you going on about? And stop calling me your daughter – I'm old enough to be your mother. It's the servant situation that's worrying me. Other people's worries don't keep me awake, I've got enough of my own: my baby got married, my son's driving me to the grave and my husband to the workhouse – and she's (*Points at ROMAINE.*) driving me to the madhouse.

SOLLY: If you go to all those places at once it should be very interesting.

ROMAINE: Would you like some breakfast, Mummy?

MILLIE: Couldn't touch a thing. I've got the shivers, and I've got daggers in my head, and my heart is pal –

ROMAINE: Made some lovely kidneys for Dad, who doesn't want them now.

(*She puts the plate in front of her mother.*)

MILLIE: No, I couldn't. Do me a favour, you know I never eat break...

(*She sniffs plate and starts eating very ravenously.*)

Such a day in front of me – an appointment with the hairdresser at two, the dressmaker at three, and the chiropodist at four, and the dentist at four thirty, and I told Sandra I'd go with her to a tea dance at five, and then this evening to the theatre with Estelle to see that wonderful play about homosexual-ality, and on top of all that I've got to find a new maid.

MORRY: What's wrong with the one we've got?

MILLIE: Nothing, except we haven't got her anymore. He didn't even notice she left.

MORRY: The German girl gone? Where?

MILLIE: Back to Germany. The German girl was three girls ago – we've had French, Italian and Irish since then.

ROMAINE: I'll have to do all the washing and the washing-up now, I suppose.

MORRY: About time you did something – it's all piling up in the kitchen. You can't blame the girls for not staying in this house. Who'd want to cope with us? But I'm going to change all that. From now on we're going to be a family again – all sitting down to meals at the same time. One happy family.

(*The phone rings. ROMAINE and MILLIE dash for it. ROMAINE gets there first.*)

ROMAINE: Sarah! Darling, how are you?

MILLIE: Give me that phone – I'm your mother! (*She snatches it away.*) Hello, Dolly – Sweetheart. How are you, darling? Did you sleep well? What? You poor girl, never mind, you'll get used to it. (*She turns to tell the others.*) He likes to sleep with the window open. Had breakfast yet? Was it nice? Bed comfy? How's Alan? Send him my love. Tell him not to worry and remember this is your honeymoon. What's that? Oh, I'm so pleased. Bye-bye, Dolly, see you soon, then – see you – Tata – as quick as you like. Good-bye. (*She puts down the phone.*) They're coming to lunch. She misses us.

MORRY: But she's only just left.

MILLIE: It was last night. She's homesick. Blood is thicker than water.

(*MELVIN comes in dressed in blazer and white trousers.*)

MELVIN: Lovely day. Seen the papers? What's it going to do?

MORRY: We're on the brink of another war.

MELVIN: I didn't mean that. Is it going to rain? What's the forecast?

(*Takes a newspaper, reads the back page.*)

MORRY: The back page – that's all he knows – and on the front page the world's doing its nut. Look at him, the English Sportsman, the Cricket Fixtures, the rugger scores –

MILLIE: You hungry, darling? Some nice fried fish in the fridge.

MORRY: I know what he needs, and I don't mean lockshen soup.

MELVIN: Think I'll have a bash in on the tennis court this morning, a nice brisk game to start the day. Has Derek phoned?

MORRY: Aren't you going to work?

MELVIN: Aren't you?

MORRY: How dare you talk to me that way – who paid for everything – who poured out his heart?

MILLIE: Melvin's not too strong, don't nag him.

MORRY: Look at him – the Sportsman. Tallyho Moishe. He's always on holiday. It's either winter sports or summer holidays. Climbing he goes, and all that horrible nonsense. What's wrong with Shoot-up Hill? All the year he's on holiday, and then he needs another year's rest to get over it.

MILLIE: How dare you chastise my child like that?

MORRY: He's a stuck-up snob, a delinquent with cash, a Teddy boy of the tennis court. Well, I'm telling you.

MELVIN: Really, this is all rather beneath me. He does go on. I'm going in the garden, can't stand the atmosphere here. (*He goes.*)

SOLLY: Morry, remember all will change by your attitude – by love and understanding – don't excite yourself, let's go for a nice drive and look at trees.

MORRY: Yes, you're right, you're so right. Melvin, forgive me.

MILLIE: Now something is really up. Morry, I'm worried about you.

MORRY: I'm in good hands.

SOLLY: As I told your husband, you must learn to love everyone – or how will you love yourself and if you don't love yourself, who will love you?

MORRY: He's so tight. Well, Rabbi, what about our drive?

MILLIE: (*Fussing with breakfast things.*) Come on, Romaine, don't leave it all to me.

(*She and ROMAINE go into kitchen.*)

SOLLY: Morry, if only you could get rid of your family
for a little while. They clutter up the place so – I can't
concentrate.

MORRY: Now you know how I've suffered all these years.

SOLLY: Can't you send them on holiday? I must have peace
to work. They inhibit me. I don't mind Melvin around –
he's a fool – but the others must go.

MORRY: But how? How? If only I knew a way.

SOLLY: I'll fix it.

MORRY: You'll be lucky. She'll never leave me, never. Never
let me out of her sight.

SOLLY: You leave it to me – I guarantee by tonight we'll
have the place to ourselves. Let's go now and plan our
campaign. (*He calls to MILLIE.*) Don't worry, Mrs Swartz,
I'm taking care of your husband.
(*He and MORRY leave. MELVIN comes back in and then
MILLIE and ROMAINE follow.*)

ROMAINE: He's going mad.

MILLIE: Going? Going? He's gone. Went years ago.

ROMAINE: I don't trust that Rabbi.

MILLIE: Where was I? What was I doing? Must get a maid,
number one. There's ice cream in the fridge. Melvin, have
some and be a good boy. I must get dressed.
(*Doorbell rings.*)
Oh, who can that be?
(*MELVIN goes and voices are heard outside.*)
It's them Finks again, they make me sick.
(*The Finks enter.*)
Hello, Sadie, I was just speaking about you.

HERBERT: Only good I hope. You didn't mind us dropping
in, did you, Millie? After all, we are related now.

MELVIN: Someone once said, 'God gives us our relatives.
Thank God we can choose our friends.'

HERBERT: Heard from the children, Millie?
(*He sits down, smokes one of MORRY's cigars and takes
a lot of drink.*)

MILLIE: They just phoned me.

SADIE: How are they?

MILLIE: They sounded so happy.

SADIE: I know, they were the same when they phoned me an hour ago.

MILLIE: They're coming to lunch.

SADIE: What a coincidence, I'm dying to see them.

HERBERT: It will be so nice – a happy family gathering! What's nice for lunch? Eh, Romaine?

SADIE: Can I help, Millie?

MILLIE: Yes, get a chicken in the pressure cooker as quickly as possible. Now you must excuse me for a few moments – I must get dressed and I've got a thousand and one things to do. (*She goes.*)

HERBERT: Well, Romaine, it's your turn next. Who's going to be the lucky man –

ROMAINE: I'm not getting married – I like laying in bed in the morning. Anyway, men are all the same – only after one thing…

HERBERT: Good thing, otherwise where would we be? Still, I don't know why you can't get off. Nice, well built girl like you. Wish I had my time again.

SADIE: I'm sure she's going to make someone very happy; meanwhile come and help me make lunch.

ROMAINE: Lunch, lunch – We've only just had breakfast! That's all they think about in this house – food! Food! (*She follows SADIE into kitchen.*)

HERBERT: You're a sportsman, aren't you, Melvin? Do you ever shoot any nice wild – er, birds, on your travels?

MELVIN: I've bagged some grouse, and a partridge once.

HERBERT: You're a dark horse, you know what I mean? You're a sport and I'm a sport – couldn't we go out together and perhaps you could show me some highlife in some low dives. Ain't that clever?

MELVIN: You're drunk.

HERBERT: I'm an outdoor type like you, but I love indoor sports. Anything between eighteen years and twenty-five, and female of course –

MELVIN: What do you take me for? Please, Mr Fink, I think I've heard enough.

HERBERT: (*Digs him in the ribs.*) Come on, tell me, we're both men of the world –

MELVIN: You should be ashamed of yourself.

HERBERT: I'm only human, out for a bit of a skylark in the dark –

MELVIN: Have you no morals? What about your wedding vows? Play the game, for God's sake.

HERBERT: I was only kidding. I'm a sportsman like yourself – live only for dogs and horses. I love 'em. My wife's a girl in a million. What do you take me for? I've got a son as old as you! Never mind, Melvin – no offence, no harm meant – I won't hold it against you that you got me all wrong. I have these jokes. I understand you. Course I study a bit cycle-logy myself; what you need is a bit of this and that and one must never forget the other. Would you like to be a Mason? I'll propose you. Marvellous – the little case and the badge and the lovely apron – it's a brotherhood…a real brotherhood…

(*He almost slumps forward as he drinks and drinks. ALAN and SARAH appear.*)

ALAN: Hello, Dad, been celebrating?

(*HERBERT jumps up, kisses SARAH and slaps his son on the back.*)

HERBERT: Sadie! Sadie! They're here. Hello, my boy. Yes! You've got that grown-up look.

SADIE: (*Rushing in.*) Alan! How are you? Did you take your pills? Sarah darling, how are you?

SARAH: Ecstatic.

ROMAINE: Enjoying your honeymoon?

SARAH: Smashing! Where's Mum?

ROMAINE: Upstairs. Well, how's married life?

SARAH: Smashing. Where's Dad?

ROMAINE: Out. What's the hotel like?

SARAH: Smashing. Where's Dad gone?

ROMAINE: For a drive. What's the food like?

SARAH: Sma – Not so hot.

ALAN: She's marvellous to me, Mum – she thinks of everything. I married an angel.

SARAH: Oh, isn't he lovely, I could eat him. (*Pinches his cheek.*)

ROMAINE: Save your appetite, there's chicken for lunch.

(*MILLIE enters dressed up with lots of very expensive but garish jewellery.*)

MILLIE: You're here! And no one told me, darling! You look
lovely.

SADIE: They make such a lovely couple.

MILLIE: Taking care of her Alan? Good. Dolly, you look
pale.

SARAH: I feel fabulous, Mummy. That hotel is out of this
world.

MILLIE: You're thinner.

SARAH: Mummy, I only left yesterday.

MILLIE: I don't care, I've got eyes, haven't I? I'm so happy
for you, you bad girl. It's not fair, you're only a baby. Oh
darling, you looked lovely yesterday, now your worries
will begin. I wish you every happiness. So, how do you like
married life?

SARAH: Terrific.

MILLIE: Anyone seen my silver nail varnish? Can't find a
thing in this house. Look, I'm going mad – it's in my hand
all the time. Come over here, Dolly, and tell me all about
it.

(*SARAH and the other women sit on the settee chattering
quietly while MILLIE paints her nails.*)

HERBERT: Melvin, come here, have you got to know my boy
yet? I think you've got a lot in common. Have a chat – be
friends – it's nice to be happy. (*He drinks some more.*) Oh, this
is the life for me... I'm so sleepy. (*Dozes off.*)

MELVIN: Do you like sport?

ALAN: Who don't? Like a nice game of football, myself.

MELVIN: Cricket?

ALAN: No, it's a bit slow for me. Now football –

MELVIN: Rugger? No! Ever been yachting? Skiing?

ALAN: It's all a bit hard on the old calf muscles, ain't it?
I have a flutter on the pools each week.

MELVIN: Well, what do you play?

ALAN: I like a nice game of football, myself.

MELVIN: I loathe soccer; what about swimming?

ALAN: I'm afraid of water.

MELVIN: Do you ride?

ALAN: Sure, but only on buses, hate the underground,
I like a nice game of football, myself.

MELVIN: There must be some other sport you like. What about running? Or tennis?

ALAN: I don't mind a game of ping-pong.

MELVIN: Ah! Table tennis, not a bad little game. As a matter of fact, I'm the champion player of Hampstead Garden Suburb. Care for a game?

ALAN: Well, I'm not so hot, you know –

MELVIN: Be a sport, come on – I have a table in the other room. Don't worry, I shan't play my best game.

ALAN: You'll lick me hollow.

MELVIN: It's the spirit that matters – don't worry, just relax.
(*MELVIN leads ALAN into the other room and now we can see them playing in there – ALAN wildly rushing to catch the ball with his bat and MELVIN being very calm.*)

ROMAINE: The chicken must be ready; come and help me, Sarah.
(*Off they go.*)

MILLIE: I wonder where that man is?

SADIE: They're all the same. I'll lay the table.
(*She and MILLIE start laying the table.*)

HERBERT: (*In his sleep.*) Come on, boy – come on – Silver Flash – Silver Flash – you're there, you're almost there – come on – all my money's on you.

SADIE: Wake up, Herbert. (*She shakes him.*) Look, he's sweating. Wake up – you're dreaming.

HERBERT: Where am I? Where? What did you wake me up for? I had twenty-five on that dog! And he was winning –

SADIE: It was a nightmare. You look worried.

HERBERT: Hello, Millie, my ship was just coming in. Me worried? I never worry.
(*In the other room, MELVIN is now frantic and rushing around while ALAN is calmly lobbing the balls. ROMAINE and SARAH enter the living room with the chicken and some vegetables, and everyone sits down. MELVIN comes in sadly followed by the beaming ALAN.*)

MELVIN: I wasn't doing my best today, on purpose of course.

ALAN: I won, what about that, Sarah? I won. Can I join your club, Melvin?

MELVIN: I let you win, to encourage you. Who cares about

stupid ping-pong anyway?

ALAN: I won! I won! Since I've been married I feel like a new man. Did you see that, Dad? Did you see me win?

(*MELVIN sits down.*)

HERBERT: What? You won? Bravo! I'm proud of you! What did I tell you, Melvin?

(*When he sees MELVIN's attitude he speaks more harshly to ALAN but much softer in tone.*)

You bloody fool! Trust you, what did you go and win for? We don't want enemies in this house – now play him again, and lose next time.

(*Now they are all seated and all are eating. MORRY and SOLLY enter.*

SOLLY goes around inspecting the plates. He whistles.)

Did you have some birdseed for breakfast, Rabbi?

SOLLY: Stop! All of you. Stop eating!

(*Some are shocked and some splutter.*)

MILLIE: Oh my God – what's the matter?

SOLLY: There must be no more flesh eaten in this house.

MORRY: That's right. No more meat.

SOLLY: From now on this is a vegetarian house. (*He says a few words of gibberish – as if praying.*)

MILLIE: No more meat?

MELVIN: You gone potty?

SARAH: Mummy, what's the matter with him?

SOLLY: He has decided. No more steak, no more liver, no more fish, and no more chicken.

ROMAINE: I'll die without meat.

MILLIE: I don't mind you coming to this house – I don't even mind you hanging around for a few days – but when you tell me that I must become a vegetarian, that's the last straw.

HERBERT: I'm sure there's some perfectly reasonable explanation.

ROMAINE: But yesterday was Chicken Sunday, you said so yourself.

SOLLY: Don't you people realise that we're in the last equinox of the solstice? We were just sitting near Highgate Pond contemplating the nature of things when suddenly it came to us in revelation –

147

MORRY: Honestly, by my life, a duck swam up to me and seemed to want to communicate. The Rabbi translated.

SOLLY: It said, 'The souls of innocent animals cry out in bondage. Save us from the knife; no longer must our blood be shed.'

(*He and MORRY seem to be enjoying themselves.*)

MILLIE: A joke's a joke, but we've had enough. Eat up everyone, take no notice.

SOLLY: Don't move! This is God's word. The next one to eat flesh will be banished from this house.

(*MILLIE and ROMAINE eat.*)

Alright, you brought this on yourself.

MILLIE: Isn't it time you were going, Rabbi?

MORRY: Show them a miracle – teach them a big lesson.

SOLLY: No, why should I waste miracles upon them? Would they believe it if they saw? Clear them all out of the room – all of them – they offend my eyes.

MILLIE: Right, now I've heard enough. I must ask you to leave. Mr Fink, please help me – Alan, Melvin!

MELVIN: Be a good chap, go quietly.

HERBERT: Can't we talk this over quietly?

ALAN: (*Hiding behind SARAH.*) Sarah, what shall I do?

MILLIE: Call yourself men? Look at you!

MORRY: I'm the boss in this house, and I'm taking over. I'm wearing the trousers from now on and the Rabbi is my guest if you don't like it you can lump it – and Mr Fink, please don't come so often.

MILLIE: How can you talk to our guests in this way? What's come over you?

MORRY: For once I'm saying the things I believe.

SOLLY: You've all strayed from the path of righteousness, there must be a change before God can enter.

MELVIN: Yes, it is rather stuffy in here. Toodleloo, have fun.

(*He goes.*)

MILLIE: Morry, shall I send for the doctor? Do you want a rest?

MORRY: I've had a rest too long. Carry on, Rabbi – the house is yours.

SOLLY: Let's all be calm, my children, and remember the wise words of the Kama Sutra. Now I want you all to go

onto your knees, and think sensuously about life – become
ecstatic, at one with the pulsing beat of the throbbing
universe. The fast begins tomorrow.

MILLIE: Fast?

ROMAINE: I'll die.

MILLIE: Look, what do you want? Just tell us. For charity? A
bit more money? Here you are – just take it and go –
(*MILLIE takes money from her purse.*)

SOLLY: You don't understand. I'm staying until the new
heaven on earth is proclaimed – but don't worry, we're
preparing for it right away – for Morry Swartz is to be the
first acolyte.

MILLIE: Morry, listen, this is me – Millie, your wife. This will
break our marriage.

MORRY: This will make our marriage.

MILLIE: This man is dangerous.

SOLLY: Of course I am. Because I'm going to wipe out pride,
to drive out greed and hate, and place in its place love.
And then there'll be a new heaven on earth.

MILLIE: Oh, how much will it cost us? I can't have a Rabbi
in the house – what will the neighbours say?

SOLLY: Halleluiah, eventually.

MORRY: Darling, don't upset yourself – don't cry. How lucky
we are to have this illustrious saint in our own living room.

MILLIE: If he doesn't leave this house right now, I will.

MORRY: You can't leave me.

MILLIE: That's what you think.

MORRY: But I need you.

MILLIE: It's him or me.

MORRY: He must stay.

MILLIE: (*Cries.*) I've never been so insulted in my life.
Romaine, pack your bags, we'll show him. I'm going as far
away as possible.

SARAH: Where to, Mum?

MILLIE: Bournemouth! He'll see, he doesn't think I'll do it!
Romaine, I said pack the bags.

MORRY: Good luck to you, my love – you deserve a holiday.
We both need a rest from each other.

MILLIE: What? How could you? After all these years? That

settles it. Romaine! Will you go and pack those bags?
(*She punches her daughter.*)
It's all your fault.

ROMAINE: It always is. Mummy, don't leave them alone, who knows what will happen.

MORRY: Millie, please don't go – I need you.

MILLIE: You just said –

MORRY: I've changed my mind.

MILLIE: Well I haven't. I'm going to teach you a lesson once and for all. Come!
(*She is about to stomp out and she pushes ROMAINE.*)
Sarah, don't stay in this house, it may be catching. (*She goes out.*)

HERBERT: You're overwrought, Morry, I understand.

MORRY: Good-bye, Mr Fink.
(*HERBERT goes out after SADIE. MORRY speaks to SARAH and ALAN.*)
You going to Bournemouth with your mother?

SARAH: What, and break my honeymoon? Not on your life. We're going back to Marble Arch. Bye-bye, Daddy, I wish you better.
(*She kisses her father and leaves with ALAN.*)

SOLLY: Well, it worked.
(*They shake hands.*)
Am I not a great psychologist? Now we're in business.
(*HERBERT furtively appears as he puts on his coat.*)

HERBERT: Did I hear someone mention business? Can you cut me in, gentlemen? I've got connections.

SOLLY: We're going to be a very limited company.

HERBERT: Too bad. I want you to understand, Morry, that I sympathise with you completely. We men should demand equality. I love the way you stood up to her.

SOLLY: Good-bye, you old hypocrite.

HERBERT: Good-bye, Rabbi, I love your sense of humour – they need putting in their place – they need a firm hand.

SADIE: (*Off.*) Herbert? Where are you?

HERBERT: Coming, love. (*He hurries out.*)

MORRY: Peace at last; all my life, for fifty years I've had screaming people around me, and you pulled it off.

SOLLY: But be careful, they'll try and turn you against me – people are afraid of purity.

MORRY: Just let them try. Oh well, I'll miss Millie, you know.

SOLLY: You won't have time. You'll be busy becoming the great messiah. Oh, I can see you now – virgins dancing around you and children, dressed in white, pelting you with rose petals.

MORRY: I don't want to show off, I want to be a quiet messiah. I don't want them to laugh at me.

SOLLY: They'll cry as you pass, cry for joy. I'll do all the talking and you do all the hand waving. (*Waves like an old queen.*) You know, just like politicians at election time – (*MILLIE comes in having hastily packed. She is followed by ROMAINE.*)

MILLIE: Right, I'm all ready. I'll be staying at the Atlantic Hotel, Bournemouth. When you get rid of the Rabbi telephone me and I may consider coming home. You'll see, my boy, you'll learn.

MORRY: Get sunburnt and don't eat too much candy floss, and remember you're a vegetarian.

MILLIE: Right, that settles it. Good-bye! Come on, Romaine – what are you dawdling for?

(*She pulls ROMAINE off.*)

MORRY: This calls for a celebration. I can't believe it! (*Looks out of window.*) Yes, they're really going.

SOLLY: Now we must plan, prepare, organise.

MORRY: What can I do to help?

SOLLY: At the moment nothing but just give me a few hundred quid or so to start with, for petty cash.

MORRY: Sure. How much, exactly?

SOLLY: Eight hundred and fifty should see us through to the week-end.

MORRY: I'll get it for you.

(*MORRY goes out of the room.*)

SOLLY: Here's to Morry Swartz, the saviour – certainly saved me. Give us your money, we know what to do with it. Empty your pockets. Pop goes your sadness! Oh, I'll never go hungry again – not that I ever did. But this time I've hit the jackpot. (*To the mirror.*) Well, and don't you deserve it?

Ain't you working hard enough? Believe me, I like to see a Yiddisher feller getting on. You're looking well, take care of yourself. It does my heart good – so-long for now.

(*He hears MORRY returning and returns to a pious posture.*)

Give me the money.

(*He snatches it and puts it away quickly.*)

Shush! Don't move – hold your breath.

(*MORRY obliges.*)

I'm getting a message. Turn off the light – I mean, pull the curtains.

(*MORRY does so.*)

Ohyesohyesohyesohyes.

(*He mumbles very fast some gibberish and moves backward and forward in typical Jewish praying style.*)

MORRY: What is it?

SOLLY: A revelation. Shush – go on – I can hear you.

MORRY: Is it the Lord?

SOLLY: Shush! Yes sir, I've got that clear! We will do what you say – but my mother in the grave – yes sir. I understand – whatever you say. I've got the message and I'll pass it on! (*He turns to MORRY.*) See them go? Radiant angels, look at them, what charm they have, did you ever... Oh what do you think of those purple cloaks and those golden clouds like chariots –

(*Sings.*) Bring me my bow of burning gold...

Look! – just look at their halos – Good-bye. (*He waves at space.*)

MORRY: Who are they?

SOLLY: Gabriel, Michael, and Raphael, of course. Didn't you see them?

MORRY: I'm not sure.

SOLLY: What, you didn't even see them?

MORRY: I – think I did.

SOLLY: I should think so too. Did you get the message? Surely you got the message –

MORRY: Almost – but it was a little blurred – please repeat it for me again.

SOLLY: It said that we must search for your throne –

MORRY: Yes, yes, I got that – where?

SOLLY: In the West End – it was plain enough. It once belonged to King Solomon and now it's going to be yours.

MORRY: What have I done to deserve all this? Why should I be chosen? I'm not worthy. How much will it be?

SOLLY: We must pay the earth if necessary. Don't worry, we'll beat them down. What's the matter, you worried about money all of a sudden?

MORRY: Of course not. Do you want it now? Shall we get it now?

SOLLY: No, plenty of time. We'll go tomorrow and we'll search all over Soho. That's where I'm sure it'll be, and do you know – I bet it won't cost more than three or four thousand.

MORRY: That cheap. What shall we do now?

SOLLY: Well, there's so much – lots of things, to buy – bills to get printed, clothes and everything, jewellery – ceremonial of course – but that can all wait till tomorrow. For the moment how about you and me going Morrie Bloom's and having some salt beef?

MORRY: But I thought we are vegetarians?

SOLLY: Don't be silly, that's for them, not for us. We must set the example but that doesn't mean we must follow it.

MORRY: I don't like that. I want to be pure. What's good for my Millie and everyone is good enough for me. Besides, I really feel now for the souls of little animals. It started as a joke but now I believe it.

SOLLY: Have it your own way but don't you see, how can we convert people to vegetables unless we go amongst the meat eaters? And where will we find meat eaters? Why, Bloom's, of course. And how can we go to Bloom's and not eat salt beef? Do me a favour. Use your head – don't worry – you'll lead the world, and I'll lead you.

(*He puts MORRY's hat on and slaps him on the back and when MORRY smiles as if he understands, SOLLY leads him off. MORRY still seems slightly confused but SOLLY's smiling face seems finally to convince him.*
The curtain falls.)

Scene 4

A few days later. The contrast is amazing, for although it is the same room, all the furniture has been moved out. The room is completely transformed and now only contains a little table with a telephone on it, two chairs and a seductive couch. The peach mirrors remain. The interior, however, does not look bereft but rather like a throne room. MELVIN comes in, looks at himself in the mirrors, studies his nose, teeth and then starts exercising and then weight lifting. He is dressed in a swimming costume. SOLLY and MORRY enter, struggling under the weight of a grand looking throne. MELVIN doesn't notice them and comes on. SOLLY visually instructs MORRY of the exact place to centre the throne.

SOLLY: There! Not bad for five thousand.

(*He sits on it and smokes a cigar. MORRY sits on the floor.*)

MORRY: Please let me smoke.

SOLLY: Please don't be so childish – you must practice frugality and economy. Self-denial is the way to sainthood.

MORRY: (*Peers at the throne.*) He said it was solid gold – I can't see it.

SOLLY: It's spirit gold. Can't you see the aura? It looks like wood but it has a spiritual inner tube.

MORRY: When is the coronation?

SOLLY: Be patient. Aren't you happy with the day drawing near?

MORRY: I miss Millie.

SOLLY: Look, sit down here and realise your true responsibilities.

MORRY: (*Rising.*) I must phone her. I want her to know that I want her to be happy – that I want her to be Queen Millie.

SOLLY: No, sit down. She must come to you, in her own time.

MORRY: It's the first time we've been apart.

SOLLY: Now, listen. For a few days now you've been worried. Well, it just won't do. It's not easy being messiah. You've just got to grow up and stand on your own feet. You're not allowed to worry, you've got to radiate happiness and calm.

MORRY: Look, have a heart, I'm only just indentured, don't

expect me to be a fully fledged graduate. You're sure she didn't phone, Melvin?

MELVIN: Dad, leave me alone. I'm practising for the Maccabee games this evening.

SOLLY: I shall walk out on you if you continue like this.

MORRY: Please be patient with me. I'll be alright.

SOLLY: Now I must phone Rabbi Teitlebaum to tell him the latest news. You go to your room and stare at the sky. I want you to study cloud formations – add up the large ones, then add up the little ones and take one from the other and take away the first number you thought of.

MORRY: Thank you. There are moments when I lost heart. Thank you for being so firm and nice to me
(*He goes out counting on his fingers, trying to remember SOLLY's instructions. SOLLY picks up phone and dials.*)

SOLLY: Hello? International? Get me Washington, America – Central one-nine-six-eight-four. This is Speedwell four-seven-five-six. Who? (*He looks at MELVIN and whispers.*) Joe Bloom – Yes, Joseph Bloom. What? Half an hour delay? What are you doing at that exchange? Exchanging dirty stories? Alright, you do that. (*He puts down phone.*) They're going to ring back.
(*MELVIN is standing on his head.*)
Isn't it a miracle? Do you know you can phone anywhere? Australia! Japan! Solomon Islands! I used to think they belonged to me. Who do I know in India? Good job I'm not rich, I'd spend it all on trunk calls. What are you doing standing like that? You hoping to become the Premier of Israel? Why do you waste all your time with muscle stuff?

MELVIN: (*Stands upright.*) Look, I don't tell you how to pray. So don't tell me how to play.

SOLLY: At your age you should be having a good time with girls.

MELVIN: Not interested.

SOLLY: All this sport is a cover up for the things you're really longing for.

MELVIN: Nice advice, coming from you.

SOLLY: Sex is nice, it's here to stay. You can't get away from it, it follows you everywhere. Don't swallow it, wallow in it – find yourself a nice girl, not too nice. When I was a young man I knew my onions.

MELVIN: *You?*

SOLLY: Girls were my downfall before I picked myself up. It was the fat girls – oh, fat girls were the ruin of me and the making of me. I still have a soft spot for them.

MELVIN: You surprise me.

SOLLY: Listen, a dog collar doesn't stop a man being a dirty dog. Mind you, I don't mean myself – I'm finished with all that now.

(*He puts on a record. The majestic choir of 'The Messiah' by Handel is heard.*)

Do yourself a favour – sow your wild oats on fertile feminine ground. Throw away your discus, take up the challenge.

MELVIN: But I'm shy – how do I start?

SOLLY: If you see a skirt, follow it. You're a man now – follow your natural instincts. Forget all about games, that sort of game – and play the game of life. A woman is the prey and you are the beast – and do they love it. Follow your natural inclinations – haven't you got any? You must have. Look at yourself – all them pimples; disgusting! Put some brilliantine on your hair, a smile on your face. (*He illustrates all this for MELVIN.*) Then saunter amongst them, looking supercilious, debonair, aggressive, like a lion, like a peacock –

MELVIN: All at the same time?

SOLLY: Like this: Inscrutable – slinky. Pout your nostril all the while and clench your jaw.

(*MELVIN tries it.*)

And you'll be a wow. Go amongst them boy – there are masses of waiting virgins – go and break their…hearts.

(*He puts up the volume of the record and he leads MELVIN out.*)

Come, I'll help you choose the right suit.

(*The music blares out. ROMAINE and MILLIE appear. They enter, gasp, and rush out of the room again after screaming. Then they stealthily creep back in again and ROMAINE turns the record off.*)

MILLIE: It must be the wrong house.

ROMAINE: No, this is my record player but not my record. Oh, Mummy –

MILLIE: Oh, Dolly – what can we do? We're ruined! I'll kill him – kill him – Where's everything? (*She weeps.*) I'm finished, finished.

ROMAINE: Mummy, don't cry, pull yourself together – (*She cries.*) Ohohohohohohohohoho!

MILLIE: Romaine, I'm ashamed of you, always going to pieces in a crisis. Stop crying and be a big girl. (*She looks round the room.*) Oh my lovely television set – where is it?
(*She cries again and now they lean on each other and both weep.*)
This is the end. I'll pull my hair out, I'll scream – I'll faint, I'll kill myself. Have you got a cigarette?
(*ROMAINE gives her one.*)
Turn your back for five minutes – I'll kill him.

ROMAINE: I told you not to go. I warned you against that rabbi.

MILLIE: If we didn't go you'd have been head over heels in love with him.

ROMAINE: Me? Bloody cheek.

MILLIE: I saw you falling for that snake in the grass.

ROMAINE: *Me?* You think I'd throw myself away on that low-life?

MILLIE: That swine.

ROMAINE: A villain!

MILLIE: Crook. Rogue.

ROMAINE: Monster. Maybe it wasn't him.

MILLIE: Who else? Oh, we're ruined. My Sheraton! My cocktail cabinet, my virginals! He's taken everything, and your father's gone off his rocker. That's where you get it from.

ROMAINE: What are we going to do?

MILLIE: (*Goes to phone.*) The police, that's the only thing. (*Dials.*)

ROMAINE: (*Stopping her.*) You out of your mind? Find out

first who's taken the furniture. Who you going to accuse?

MILLIE: That terrible man! Don't you see, we've got to get him out. He's after our money.

ROMAINE: Who isn't? Listen, if you call the police, it will get into the papers and we'll be the laughing stock of the neighbourhood.

MILLIE: Better a laughing stock with money than being respectable and broke. Your father's mad – stone bonks. I must call the police.

ROMAINE: Alright, if he's mad they'll take him away, then there'll be a whole legal rigmarole. Meanwhile we'll all be starving.

MILLIE: Sometimes you use that stupid brain of yours. You're right. But I still say you've fallen for him.

ROMAINE: Fallen? May I drop down dead on this spot if I have! Oh, I feel wobbly at the knees – (*She collapses on the small settee.*)

MILLIE: Darling, don't swear your life away, it's precious to me. Love is blind. You've done nothing else but talk about him since we left. I'm not a fool – you make me so mad. Feeling better, Dolly? My whole family's turning against me.

ROMAINE: Do you honestly think I'd fall for a rat like that?

MILLIE: Yes. Never mind, he's enticed you the way he has Morry. He's hypnotic – you know, like Rasputin.

ROMAINE: I never met him.

MILLIE: What have I done? Am I bad? Haven't I given to charity? Why should it happen to me?

MELVIN: (*Breezes in.*) Lo, Mum. Lo, Roroe. Back already?

MILLIE: (*Falls on him.*) Melvin! Darling! What's happening?

MELVIN: (*Releasing himself.*) You're smothering me.

MILLIE: What's been happening here?

MELVIN: Oh, I don't know. Something or other. Must dash now – I'm late as it is.

ROMAINE: But where's the furniture?

MELVIN: Oh yes, it's gone, isn't it? And about time too – it was simply gasters. Now, Mummy, please – later. I'll be late for the games.

MILLIE: Where's your father?

MELVIN: Your husband is contemplating or some such thing
– somewhere or other. Well, tata for now.
(*She won't let him go yet.*)

MILLIE: And where's that snake of a Rabbi?

MELVIN: He's a very nice chap and I won't hear a word
against him. Since he's been here the house has been
tolerable.

MILLIE: What's he doing to your father?

MELVIN: I don't know and I don't care. I'm off now, please
keep your fingers crossed for me. (*He goes.*)

MILLIE: When I see that Morry I'll kill him.
(*MORRY wanders on, looking very happy and very far
away. He sees MILLIE and kisses her.*)

MORRY: Hello, Millie – how are you darling? Two weeks
passed already?

MILLIE: (*She stifles her anger.*) I only stayed away two days.
Do you think I'd trust you here any longer? Look what's
happened already. What have you been doing?

MORRY: Looking at the clouds. I never knew they were so
beautiful. Have you ever looked at clouds, Millie? Shall we
both do it together now? And there are birds in London –
and trees. I've never seen them before.

MILLIE: He's gone cuckoo. Listen Morry, come to your
senses.

MORRY: All my senses are working overtime. I can smell
and hear and see and touch.

MILLIE: This Rabbi is a phoney. Did you see his credentials?

MORRY: Do I ask for the credentials of God? He is honest
and beautiful. The most trustworthy person I ever met.

MILLIE: How do you know?

MORRY: I know because I know.

MILLIE: How do you know you know?

MORRY: Because I'm happy. Really happy.

MILLIE: How do you know you're happy? You're not happy.
You only think you are. He's taking you for a ride – I feel it
in my water.

MORRY: It's a lovely journey and at the end of it I shall be
the messiah.

ROMAINE: Messiah?

MILLIE: Messiah? Romaine, shut up – don't interfere. Listen Morry – carefully – take it easy. Did you say messiah?

MORRY: Yes, very soon now I shall be ready, when I reach perfection.

MILLIE: He won't make a messiah of you, you bloody fool. He'll make a mess of you. You're sinning – do you know you're sinning?

MORRY: Thought you didn't believe in God. Sinning against who?

MILLIE: Sinning against me – against you – against everything. Listen, Morry, look at me – I'm your wife, your other half. How can you be a messiah? You're overwrought. I understand. There ain't no such person as God and thank God there isn't, because if he existed you'd really go to hell, and please God, soon you realise all this and come to your senses.

MORRY: All I want is for you and everyone to be happy. Don't get angry with me. I'm so happy.

MILLIE: I could ki –

(*Turns to ROMAINE as if to show her they must bear with him for the moment.*)

It's just that you're getting old, Morry, old and scared.

MORRY: I'm not old. I'm as young as the world, and happy and free. I must go now and see the new moon rise. (*He sails off.*)

ROMAINE: Poor Daddy. Isn't it funny, he's happy and we're sorry for him. Poor Daddy.

MILLIE: We'll have to humour him. I'll even become vegetarian to please him now. How could he change so quick? He wouldn't trust a fly till that Rabbi came along.

ROMAINE: Everybody believes what he wants to believe, believe me.

MILLIE: Oh shut up you! It's all your fault.

ROMAINE: But I told you I didn't trust him.

MILLIE: Now be quiet will you, and stop bickering. We've got to think of a way. To make Daddy see, somehow. But we mustn't let the Rabbi know that we suspect he's a phoney. (*The phone rings and they both dash for it but SOLLY enters the room briskly and while they are struggling for the receiver he takes it from them.)*

SOLLY: If it's from America, it's for me. Would you mind, please? This call is confidential – please leave the room.

MILLIE: From America? What do you think we are – millionaires?

ROMAINE: He wouldn't be far out.

SOLLY: Now leave the room, please. You shouldn't be here anyway, but in Bournemouth. This is urgent. Rabbi Teitlebaum!

(They go but stand in the doorway. He is aware of this fact and has to modulate his conversation accordingly. Every time he looks at the door they pretend not to be there.)

'Lo! State Department? I want Joe Cohen in the visa section. Hurry, this is costing a bomb. *(Pretends now to pray.)* I'll hold on, yes I'll hold on – oh God in heaven, give me the strength to hold on. Extension five-nine-one, so be it. Hurry up, for St. Peter's sake. Wrong testament? Sorry. Hurry up, oh Lord – Hello! Joe? You old bastard, this is me! Who, he says! Solly Gold – Don't hang up – listen! I've got money! M – o – Money – Money for a change. Listen, I need a visa urgently – I'm loaded, loaded man, and I'm all ready to blow. What's that? But I tell ya I've got loot. So make me a visa and be a sport. Who picked you up when you were on the floor? *(He sees the women coming closer.)* Do you mind? No? Not you – GOooo – For he will bring the wicked down to the ground! I'm loaded – would I lie? What do you mean? Gone respectable? Gone straight? Don't give me that! Joe, Joe – you can't do that to me. Listen! *(Sees the women again.)* Thou shalt not covet thy neighbour's daughter nor his peach mirrors – Joe! Don't do this to me – remember the old days when we were both crooked and keep it holy. Joe, you're a lousy swine – you're my only hope! Joe! Joe! Joe… *(Realises the women are there once more.)* And Joseph brought the evil report of them unto his father… *(Pretends to quote from Bible – then enraged again.)* Oh, you rotten – lousy – stinking – good-for-nothing… *(He sees the women*

again.) Bye-bye, Rabbi Teitlebaum... Let the wicked be no
more. I'll let you know – He hung up! You can't trust no
one. (*He puts the receiver down*.) Hello, my daughters, how
was Bournemouth? Still kosher and godless?

MILLIE: Hello, Rabbi, glad to see you looking so well, and
I'm glad to see you looked after Morry.

SOLLY: Where is he?

ROMAINE: In the garden watching the moon.

SOLLY: Good. I'll find him. Well, welcome home. Are you
thoroughly cleansed and vegetarian now?

(*ROMAINE is about to protest when her mother shuts
her up*.)

MILLIE: What else? It's wonderful! Nuts and raisins for
breakfast, turnips and lettuce for lunch, and carrots for supper.

SOLLY: Good! Good! You've got a glow in your face. (*He goes
off*.)

MILLIE: May he rot, may he burn – may he get run over and
smashed – may he drown.

ROMAINE: And all at once.

(*HERBERT, SADIE, ALAN and SARAH enter*.)

SARAH: Mummy! You're back.

(*They kiss*.)

ALAN: What's the matter, where's the furniture?

MILLIE: Sarah darling, we're in terrible trouble.

SARAH: I know, I've been having nightmares.

MILLIE: The Rabbi is a charlatan – what can we do?

ROMAINE: He's fleecing us – taking us for a ride.

HERBERT: I told you so.

MILLIE: No you didn't.

HERBERT: I could have told you so.

SADIE: Shut up. It was a palace here, a real palace. Where's
the furniture? Where?

HERBERT: The woodworm run away with it.

(*Nobody laughs*.)

Hahahahahaha! I'm only trying to cheer everyone up.

ALAN: What's it all add up to?

MILLIE: My Morry thinks he's the new messiah no less. (*She
weeps*.)

ROMAINE: And that Solly Gold is getting all our money and Daddy won't hear a word against him.

HERBERT: I knew it. I can smell a crook a mile off.

SADIE: What will the neighbours say?

(*She cuddles ALAN.*)

Oh my poor boy.

SARAH: To hell with the neighbours – what about us?

HERBERT: Open and shut case. Leave it to me, let Fink think – Simple – the police! (*Goes to phone.*)

MILLIE: What? And let my Morry be the laughing stock of all the world?

ROMAINE: They'll take him off in a strait jacket.

SARAH: And we'll be starving while the lawyers argue.

HERBERT: Poor Morry – what can we do?

ALAN: We must think of something.

(*MORRY wanders in.*)

MORRY: Hello everyone. Lovely evening. I just saw Sirius and Orion, and heard the music of the spheres. I'm no longer just Morry Swartz of Golders Green – I'm Morris Swartz of the Universe. I'll see you all on the great day. Toodleloo.

(*He wanders out again and the women cry and the men shake their heads.*)

SARAH: He overtaxed his brain.

MILLIE: He never had a brain – only an adding machine up there.

ALAN: Hold it – I've got an idea coming up! Shush…

SARAH: Isn't he marvellous? I could eat him.

ROMAINE: Not yet, wait till he comes out with it.

ALAN: Got it! (*Claps his hand.*) That Rabbi Whatyoumaycallit, must confess directly to your father, must say that he's a complete phoney, now how? How can we get him to confess?

(*They all walk backward and forward thinking.*)

Who would he tell the truth to? Who has he got a weakness for?

(*ROMAINE is somehow now in the centre of a circle of walking people, they all stop together, turn and stare at her.*)

ROMAINE: What's up? What have I done?

SARAH: It's not what you've done, it's what you're going to do.

ALAN: I've seen the way he stares at you. You'll have to do it.

ROMAINE: Do what? I'm getting out of here.

(*She tries to go but MILLIE stops her.*)

MILLIE: Dolly, do you love me? Do you love your father? Do you love luxury? Well, then you'll have to help us all.

HERBERT: Only you could make him confess.

ROMAINE: But I don't trust him.

SADIE: This time you don't need to.

SARAH: Lead him on a little, get him hot under the collar –

ALAN: Tell him you're passionately in love with him but unfortunately you couldn't give yourself to a Rabbi –

HERBERT: Tell him it's against your principles, and you could make love to a layman –

ROMAINE: Are you all mad or something? What do you take me for?

MILLIE: A good girl. And when he confesses that he isn't a rabbi, lead him on a bit more – tell him you don't like good boys –

ALAN: And when he confesses that he's a crook… (*Thinks for the next move.*)

SARAH: You'll switch on Melvin's tape recorder that we'll hide under the couch.

MILLIE: And when Daddy hears the tape, we'll be rid of that worm.

ROMAINE: I won't be left alone with him.

MILLIE: You'll be alright, don't worry.

ROMAINE: Do you think I'm gonna sacrifice my purity for rotten money?

HERBERT: You've got to lose it sooner or later.

SADIE: Herbert, shut up. Listen, Romaine, we all have to take chances –

ROMAINE: You're all against me.

ALAN: Whatever happens, we'll sympathise and understand. We're depending on you. I expect you'll pull it off.

ROMAINE: Nobody cares for my feelings. (*She almost weeps.*) I'll be expecting, alright, with that snake in the grass.

Mummy, look at me! I'm your daughter. Your own flesh
and blood. Don't leave me alone with that monster.

MILLIE: Listen, your purity, my darling, is worth all the tea
in China, all the gold in Hatton Garden. Don't worry, we
won't let it go too far. If you scream we'll break the door
down – but don't scream unless you can help it, they cost
enough. He'll confess. After all aren't you a lovely girl?
And why not, why be ashamed of what you've got?

ROMAINE: Oh go on then, go, leave me alone. What do
I care? (*She does a great tragedy act and falls on the sofa.*)

MILLIE: Good luck, Dolly – a lot's at stake.

ROMAINE: Telling me!

HERBERT: We'll wait in there and be as quiet as little mice.

ROMAINE: Don't look through the keyholes – I'll be
embarrassed. Promise?

ALL: Promise.

MILLIE: Where's the tape machine? Melvin's room?

SARAH: No, it's in here.

(*SARAH gets it from the other room and brings it in and
places it under the sofa.*)

It's all ready. At the crucial moment just switch on, like
this –

(*She demonstrates and then they all troop into the other
room and shut the door.*)

ROMAINE: (*Overplaying.*) What do they care? Do they
consider my feelings? I shall run away!

(*She overweeps and then stops as she sees herself in the
mirror.*)

How marvellous. I looked like Anna Magnani just then.

(*She smiles and poses in front of the mirror as if to make
herself look enticing, then she weeps again.*)

Oh, what do they care – leaving me with that shark.

(*She switches off the main lighting and the indirect lighting,
now makes the room look seductive. She sprays perfume
upon herself and then puts on a soft tango. She settles down
and starts to eat Turkish delight but changes her mind and
then, fixing her dress to look more sexy, she dances to the
music seductively. Then we see SOLLY. He comes on like
a furtive fly, in quick, sharp jerking angular movements,*)

as if drawn by an irresistible impulse. He is about to go directly to her, but goes to the adjoining door, where the family are, and locks that door on this side. When she sees this she starts to get panicky, but carries on – dancing. Suavely he pours two drinks and goes to her. As she drinks, he pinches her on the bottom.)

Stop pinching me – I'll go black and blue.

SOLLY: I don't care what colour you go – I like you anyway. I don't hold with the colour bar.

ROMAINE: It's not nice, not decent, getting fresh like that.

SOLLY: I'm sorry but you see I'm homesick and my fingers twitch. Care for another drink?

ROMAINE: I'd like a bunny hug.

(He hugs her passionately. She struggles to get free.)

I didn't mean that. I meant the drink. Cherry brandy and Advocaat.

(He pours her a vast glass full.)

Eh! When! When!

SOLLY: Anytime you want to.

ROMAINE: I didn't mean that! I meant – that's enough in the glass.

(SOLLY gives her the drink and then takes her arms and pushes her into a dance.)

SOLLY: May I have this dance? Do you come here often? What a smashing bit of overtime you are.

ROMAINE: I think you're crude.

SOLLY: Sorry, I get carried away by your beauty – what I mean is, God worked overtime when he created you.

ROMAINE: Never knew that rabbis drink, and dance, and pinch girls.

SOLLY: What else? All work and no play makes Jacob a very miserable geezer. Haven't you read the Songs of Solomon? But anyway – you are so marvellous I could even leave my religious world for you. Let's sit down.

I want to give you some spiritual instruction.

ROMAINE: No, no, I'm afraid.

SOLLY: Foolish lady, I'll look after you. Sit down, I'll make it worth your while.

ROMAINE: I shouldn't really.

(*She sits down.*)

SOLLY: Doing what we shouldn't is one way of finding out the mysteries of creation.

(*She leans down to switch on the machine and as she does so he kisses her. First she struggles but then she subsides into his arms and while doing so, she switches off the machine again.*)

ROMAINE: You're free with your kisses. But what about your dead wife and your vow of chastity?

SOLLY: I know Sophie wouldn't mind.

ROMAINE: You said her name was Miriam.

SOLLY: Don't change the subject, I'm doing my nut over you. When the ape is king dance before him – and desire is ruling my soul right now. Shall we dance?

ROMAINE: Please come down to earth, I've got something to tell you.

SOLLY: You are as pure as the moon, as passionate as the sun, my dove.

ROMAINE: Make up your mind.

SOLLY: My undefiled one.

ROMAINE: And I intend to stay that way. Now listen! I don't know who you are or what you're after, but I'm giving you a chance to get away.

SOLLY: How beautiful are thy feet in sandals –

ROMAINE: I've got corns.

SOLLY: The joints of thy thighs are like jewels.

ROMAINE: And they're staying in the safe because you're a thief. But I like you, so I'm giving you a chance to run. Run, before you're caught.

SOLLY: What are you talking about? I've got nothing to be ashamed of.

ROMAINE: I don't know why I'm telling you, but I don't trust you, so don't try and get round me. You're a bad boy and you know it.

SOLLY: Me? I'm a – angel, a saint. Ask anyone.

ROMAINE: Listen, you can trust me. There's no time to lose.

SOLLY: Enough of this.

ROMAINE: You're no good.

SOLLY: What's good? What's bad? Relative terms, my daughter. Thy navel is like a round goblet.

ROMAINE: Cheek! How dare you, you've never seen me! Oh don't you see I'm on to your game? You're a fraud.

SOLLY: Enough of this, let's get down to something serious – let me kiss you, let me love you!

(*He tries furiously to embrace her, but she keeps freeing herself. It's almost a chase.*)

ROMAINE: It's because I like you that I won't go along with them – let them do their own dirty work.

SOLLY: Thy belly is like a heap of wheat.

ROMAINE: That's the last straw.

SOLLY: Forgive me, I get carried away. I was only quoting from the Bible.

ROMAINE: Then it should be banned.

SOLLY: Nonsense, it's beautiful – have you ever read it?

ROMAINE: No, but I've seen the film. Please, listen, there's no time to waste.

SOLLY: Alright, spit it out, what's it all about?

ROMAINE: Now he hears. Solly, my family are on to your game, they are trying to get me to make you confess. I'm the decoy.

SOLLY: On to my game? Confess? Confess to what?

ROMAINE: You can trust me, I'm on your side. I must be mad, but I am.

SOLLY: Why should I trust you all of a sudden?

ROMAINE: Because here's the tape machine that I was supposed to switch on when you started confessing.

SOLLY: (*As she shows him the machine.*) Tape machine? What are you talking about? I'm a servant of the Lord.

ROMAINE: I must be mad – I'm out of my little mind. Fancy telling you, but you've turned my head – turned it against my own family. I'll never live it down. I'm no good.

SOLLY: (*Embracing her.*) We make a fine pair.

ROMAINE: So you own up that you're a crook?

SOLLY: Not on your life. I'm straight – straight up – strait as a jacket.

ROMAINE: Solly, Solly, oh Solly boy, you can trust me. (*She cuddles him.*)

SOLLY: Why should I?

ROMAINE: Cos I want to see you get away – I don't want them to catch you. Because you're romantic. Take what you want and go.

SOLLY: I want you. But why are you doing this for me? I can't believe it.

ROMAINE: Look! They're waiting in there, waiting for me to entice a confession out of you – I swear on my soul, on my purity, that I'm on your side and speaking the truth. By my Aunt Sadie's life.

SOLLY: Alright then, if that's the case I'll be on my merry way. Good-bye, maybe we'll meet in the desert.

ROMAINE: Not so fast. Just one little thing before you go. Please tell me everything – tell me why a nice boy like you should be such a bad boy.

SOLLY: Why? You want to redeem me? Sorry, I pawned myself ages ago and lost the ticket.

ROMAINE: Oh Solly, what can I do? I've fallen for you, for a tyke like you. My mum always told me I was no class. I've fallen right down.

SOLLY: Don't believe you.
(*She kisses him.*)
Well, maybe I believe you a bit – kiss me again.
(*She does.*)
Yeah! Oh, Romaine – I could feel your whole heart pouring into that kiss.

ROMAINE: I want to help you. Can't you see that? Tell me about yourself.

SOLLY: Alright, I admit I'm not a Rabbi. I'm a liar, a lobos, a gonif. You know – I take things from people who can afford to do without. But I'm the best con man in the business – the world's not much to write home about is it?

ROMAINE: Maybe, but fancy doing your tricks on my father, he's such a good man.

SOLLY: Alright, so now you know. Happy? I'm a lowlife. I'm a thief. That let's me out.
(*He turns his back and is about to go when he turns back and smiles.*)

Run away with me.

ROMAINE: Where?

SOLLY: Anywhere.

ROMAINE: Run away? No, I couldn't.

SOLLY: Why not?

ROMAINE: Why not? Why not? I love my luxury.

SOLLY: Now's your chance to really live.

ROMAINE: I couldn't run fast enough to keep up with you. Besides I'm too selfish – I've got so much to give that I need a lot in return.

MILLIE: (*Off.*) You alright, Dolly?

ROMAINE: Fine – fine! Hurry, hurry – Solly, Solly, time is pressing.

SOLLY: Nobody here understands you – how deeply romantic you are. Just like me. Chasing the stars, looking for kicks and only getting kicked in the teeth. Look at you – you're a child of the sun, a victim of circumstance holding on to your chastity – saving it all for a rainy day. But why be a pessimist? No one can love you like me. You're fat and I love you that way.

ROMAINE: I'm not fat, I'm well built. Besides, I'm starting to diet tomorrow.

SOLLY: No! No! No! You mustn't do that. I'm crazy about you the way you are. I'll take you to the life of luxury you dream about – a life of romance in the best hotels, as much Turkish Delight as you want, we'll go to Rome, Miami, Glasgow.

ROMAINE: But you're a liar, Solly, how can I believe you?

SOLLY: What's truth? Ask philosophers, they're all in the dark –

ROMAINE: But you've committed crimes, I know it. You're on the run.

SOLLY: Who isn't on the run? I'm not bad darling, I'm just not good.

ROMAINE: How can I do this to my family after all they did for me?

SOLLY: Such as?

ROMAINE: Offhand I can't remember.

SOLLY: With me you'll come first – after me. No more dull
life. I'm your man from now on and you'll hide with me.
Hiding and flying – romance on the run. Snatched hours of
passion in hotel bedrooms; different places, different faces.
Romaine, your humdrum life is almost over for Solly Gold
is taking over. Give me another kiss.
(*They kiss.*)
There's plenty more in store where that came from, and
so much more – oh so much more. Why have I told you
everything? You know more than anyone now! It's the first
time I've told anyone anything. I must love you –
I must really love.

ROMAINE: That settles it. I'll get my things.

SOLLY: Don't bother, I'll buy you everything new on
Broadway next week.

ROMAINE: With what? On peanuts and prayers?

SOLLY: With the money I've got from your father already
and the money I'm getting from him in a minute or two.

ROMAINE: Oh Solly, I was forgetting that. It's so dishonest.

SOLLY: Is it dishonest to make him happy for the first time in
years? You'll help me.

ROMAINE: I'll never forgive myself.

SOLLY: You don't have to – Good will. We'll fill a suitcase full
of fivers and be on our merry way.

ROMAINE: It is true, he *is* much happier. That can't be bad,
can it? What about the police?

SOLLY: (*He jumps.*) Please, I don't like bad language. That
word makes my blood run cold. We'll go to the docks
tonight and get a boat. Let's call your father now.

ROMAINE: One minute, I'm not coming with you unless you
marry me.

SOLLY: Don't you relish sin? Silly girl – alright! I'll marry
you, on the other side.

ROMAINE: Other side of where?

SOLLY: Tell you when we get there.

ROMAINE: Just one thing more – are you sure you're not
married?

SOLLY: Absolutely, definitely not – I cross my heart, that's
the truth so help me God. Come on –

ROMAINE: There's just one other thing –

SOLLY: I love the way you're so concise. What is it?

ROMAINE: Where did you get the Rabbi's clothes?

SOLLY: From an old lady in the East End.

ROMAINE: You must take them back, I'm superstitious.

SOLLY: Let me burn them, let me chuck them away.

ROMAINE: No! We'll take them back to her on our way to the docks.

SOLLY: It's too risky.

ROMAINE: If you love me you'll do it – just this once, for me.

SOLLY: I must learn the art of blackmail from you. Alright, and now I'll find your father. Wait here for me.

(*He pretends to go but hides and watches ROMAINE.*)

MILLIE: (*Off.*) You alright, Dolly?

ROMAINE: Sure.

MILLIE: (*Off.*) How's it going?

ROMAINE: Perfect.

SARAH: (*Off.*) Got the recording yet?

ROMAINE: Not yet, be patient.

(*SOLLY is obviously satisfied with her, and goes before she sees him. Now she poses herself in front of the mirror, and obviously she thinks she is stunningly beautiful.*)

Oh God forgive me, but I must grab the opportunity. Why not? Eh? Oh romance, Romaine – romance at last!

(*SOLLY brings MORRY on.*)

SOLLY: Well Morry, the great day approacheth and verily I say unto you that a purple light surrounds you. Sit on your throne.

MORRY: How we doing, Solly? What's the score?

SOLLY: Great news. We're almost there – I saw half a dozen angels at Golders Green Station today – they're assembling and all roads converge here and now rejoice even more so, for your blessed daughter Romaine has become an acolyte. She is our very latest and brightest disciple. She has repented from her evil ways and stands before us, devoting herself to the cause.

MORRY: About time too.

ROMAINE: Daddy darling, how you feeling?

MORRY: Never felt better in my life.

ROMAINE: Solly, let's go now.

SOLLY: Yes. Now listen Morry, Romaine and I are going on a pilgrimage.

MORRY: I want to come with you.

SOLLY: I'm afraid that's impossible.

MORRY: It's so lonely becoming the messiah sometimes. Please!

SOLLY: Not tonight. We must go to sordid places to spread the word, to the docks to get love and give love. You must be unsullied – think only of higher things. And then we're going to Westcliffe-on-the-Sea where we'll distribute charities to the Jewish Society for the prevention of cruelty to dead poets and to the Sisters of Nathaniel Greenbaum. We'll need a little money for this purpose.

MORRY: How much?

SOLLY: Don't want to bother you with sordid details, tell me the combination of the safe and I'll save you the trouble.

MORRY: No, no, the secret of the combination dies with me. Not that I don't trust you. How much will you need?

SOLLY: Not too much, a few to begin with – about – erm – forty thousand?

MORRY: That's a lot of money.

SOLLY: It's to help the needy, the lonely, the sick, the lost, the sad dreamers and happy destitutes.

MORRY: Well that includes practically everyone alive. I'll get it. You going to give all this away tonight?

SOLLY: If I can. That's why I'm taking Romaine with me.

MORRY: Good. Money must go to those who need it. As for me, what else is it but bits of metal and paper around an idea? Forty thousand. Hope I've got that much loose laying around…

(*MORRY goes off.*)

ROMAINE: I don't like it; Daddy's out of his mind.

SOLLY: We've burnt our boats now and we're in this together – sink or swim. Don't worry. (*He calls out.*) Morry! There'll be plaques up to you all over London 'Morry Swartz, the saviour, saved our hospital' –

'Morry Swartz, the messiah, got us out of a mess' – 'Morry Swartz lived here' – 'Morry Swartz ate here' –
(*MORRY enters with some packets of money and tosses them to SOLLY.*)

MORRY: Don't want no plaques, just a plain bit of marble when I die, saying: 'He tried to do good.' Hope that keeps you busy.
(*As SOLLY stuffs it into the suitcase.*)

ROMAINE: Daddy, Daddy, are you happy giving this away?

MORRY: The more that goes the happier I am.

ROMAINE: What about your life's work? You worked so hard?

MORRY: My life's work is just beginning. Listen darling, in this world you own nothing but your bones and even they let you down in the end. You come in with nothing and go out with nothing – and you're nothing unless you realise this, at least, now and again.

ROMAINE: Come on, Solly, time's getting on.

SOLLY: Rest now, Morry. Contemplate. Count the stars and lose yourself in the cosmos. Pray for us all, especially me, just in case – with all this money. We'll see you in the morning.

ROMAINE: Forgive me for everything.

MORRY: There's nothing to forgive. Go in peace. The way you both look so lovely, I could kiss you. As a matter of fact I will. (*He does so.*) I'm so happy because before I only thought I was rich, now I know I am. Goodbye.

ROMAINE: Good-bye, come, Solly.

SOLLY: Good-bye, Morry – you're a lucky man. I'm carrying all your worries from now on.
(*He holds up the case and follows ROMAINE off. MORRY picks up the Bible that SOLLY has left behind, sits down and reads from it.*)

MILLIE: (*Off.*) Romaine! You ready yet? Romaine? Are you there?

SARAH: (*Off.*) Romaine? Did you do it? Why don't she answer?
(*The door is tried and they furiously push it from the other side.*)

MILLIE: (*Off.*) Romaine! Stop playing about. It's locked on the other side. Romaine! You alright? Darling, where are you?

HERBERT: (*Off.*) I'll have to break the door down.
(*MORRY goes to the door and unlocks it just as HERBERT has flung himself against it. They all fall into the room. MORRY goes from them and sits on his throne.*)

MILLIE: What are you doing?

MORRY: Isn't it obvious? Just sitting down.

SARAH: Where's Romaine?

MORRY: Gone with the Rabbi.

ALAN: Gone?

SARAH: Gone where?

MILLIE: What do you mean? Oh my poor baby.

MORRY: They've gone on a pilgrimage. She's in safe hands. Don't worry.

SARAH: Daddy, don't you realise, he's a crook! A no-good good-for-nothing. He's not a Rabbi!

HERBERT: I'm afraid you've been taken for a ride, Morry; it happens to the best of us.

MORRY: Don't worry about me, Fink. Go home and settle your own problems.

MILLIE: Take no notice, Herbert. Morry, you ought to be ashamed of yourself. Listen! Just listen to his confession.
(*She switches on the tape recorder and 'The Messiah' blares out.*)

MORRY: They're playing my music again.
(*MILLIE switches it off.*)

MILLIE: Oh, my daughter! He's carried her off.

SARAH: That would have been difficult –

MILLIE: What's going to happen to her? I knew it.

SADIE: Call the police, Millie, call the police.

MILLIE: What? And have her dragged through the Sunday papers? I'll never live through it.

MORRY: (*Reads from the Bible.*) Praise him with the sound of trumpets, with the stringed instruments and the pipe. Praise him upon the loud cymbals –
(*MILLIE crashes two metal trays together. Everyone jumps except MORRY. MILLIE also jumps.*)

MILLIE: Will you shut up! He reads the Bible. Will that bring your sanity back? Don't you see? He's taken your furniture, your sanity, your money and your daughter.

I suppose you won't be happy till he takes me!

MORRY: That's an interesting thought. (*Returns to the Bible.*)

MILLIE: I knew all along, I knew it.

SARAH: What?

MILLIE: That he was a crook and she was no good. I knew it.

HERBERT: I knew you knew. So did I.

SADIE: What did you know?

HERBERT: I knew that I knew. You didn't know – but I did. I told you so.

ALAN: I knew all along – he couldn't kid me.

SARAH: I didn't know then that I knew, but now I do.

SADIE: I knew. I don't say much but I see all. I could tell from his face. I knew. Mark my words, I said, he's up to no good.

MILLIE: I knew it. I knew it. Serves them right. They deserve each other. What do you think of it, eh? Your own daughter. Please God, she should be safe, the lousy bitch. I knew it. I knew it would happen. I knew it.

(*MORRY sits quietly reading and they all walk around his throne. Round and around they go, talking to themselves and trying to convince each other. Then suddenly they all come into one group and carry on with the above dialogue all over again and far more quickly. It seems they are about to come to blows, when the curtain falls.*)

Scene 5

We are back in the East End. Scene is exactly the same as in the Prologue. It is early morning. The tailor is seen working away in his house, sewing frantically; he reacts – looks up, and soon we realise he has heard something. SOLLY comes on followed by ROMAINE who carries lots of cases. She seems all in. SOLLY is dressed in very American-looking clothes and he carries the Rabbi's clothes in a small bundle. The tailor comes to the window and hides as soon as he sees SOLLY but watches them all the time.

ROMAINE: Why did we have to get up so early?

SOLLY: The boat leaves in an hour.

ROMAINE: I'm still asleep.

SOLLY: Here's the house. I'll dump it on the doorstep.

ROMAINE: Oh no you're not. You're giving it to the lady in person and apologise.

SOLLY: She won't be up this early.

ROMAINE: We'll wake her up.

SOLLY: You're very cruel. Look, the door's open. Obviously she still trusts people…let's go inside. (*He calls.*) Yoohoo
– yoohoo –
(*Soon they are inside and now we cannot see them. JOE, the tailor, jumps up and goes to a door in his house and calls his wife.*)

JOE: Rita! Rita! Get up – get up quick! Rita, for God's sake get up –
(*RITA rushes in in her nightclothes, she is distraught and almost panicking.*)

RITA: Joe, what is it? Is it bombs?
(*She tries to dress hurriedly and gets everything in the wrong place.*)

JOE: Shush! That blaggard who got that money from us and the lady next door has returned.

RITA: Thank the lord. I thought the world had come to an end.

JOE: And guess what? – he's got with him that missing heiress, what's her name – Rona Swarb or something –

RITA: Missing heiress?

JOE: Wake up. The one who was in the papers. The one that reward's for. You phone her mother quickly while I keep them here. The number's in the paper.

RITA: All night he works. All night. I just want to get some sleep. I'm fed up with you and the whole business.

JOE: Do as I say. We'll make a few hundred and I'll take you on a cruise. Quick!
(*She quickly runs for the newspaper and then goes into a backroom. JOE comes out of his house and creeps towards the next house just as SOLLY comes running out with ROMAINE; they are chased by the old woman who is throwing things at them.*)

WOMAN: A fire on you! Get out of my sight!

SOLLY: I've come to pay you back – to make it worth your while.

WOMAN: What do you take me for? Think you can buy me after what you did?

(*She hits him with a stick and he takes shelter under his coat. He brings out several pound notes and waves them about.*)

SOLLY: Truce! Truce! Is this flag the right colour?

WOMAN: Thief! Liar! Rogue! Crook – police. (*She suddenly stops and takes the money.*) Get out of my sight! (*She is about to go inside.*)

SOLLY: (*To ROMAINE.*) See darling, anything can be bought with money, especially people. When pound notes flash, principles crash.

WOMAN: I can't afford principles. They won't buy my husband's tombstone.

(*She is about to go in and SOLLY is about to go off with ROMAINE when he sees JOE. He is about to run when:*)

SOLLY: Must you be so passionate?

JOE: So, you've returned to the scene of the crime?

SOLLY: Can't we talk this over like English gentlemen?

ROMAINE: Leave my Solly alone or I'll murder you.

(*As JOE gets off him SOLLY gets up.*)

SOLLY: I'll explain and settle everything.

JOE: Wish there was a copper about; they're never around when you want one.

SOLLY: I agree with you. And it all comes out of the taxpayer's pocket.

(*RITA comes out.*)

JOE: Well, what have you got to say for yourself?

SOLLY: Help.

JOE: You're a lousy rat.

SOLLY: Let me go and I'll make it worth your while.

JOE: You can't buy me.

SOLLY: I actually came to give you your money back.

RITA: There you are, Joe – I knew he was an honest feller.

SOLLY: Look, here's the money. I'll give you twice as much.

JOE: Nothing doing, I won't be bought. I demand justice.

SOLLY: You're living in the wrong world.

(*The PROSTITUTE comes from her room.*)

PROSTITUTE: What's all the noise? Can't a nightworker get some decent sleep?

(*JOE is holding SOLLY by the arm and ROMAINE is trying to pull him in the other direction. The PROSTITUTE walks around SOLLY.*)

Haven't we met before?

SOLLY: Perhaps in some previous incarnation.

PROSTITUTE: I've heard it called some things. Why are you holding him?

JOE: He owes me money.

SOLLY: I've offered to pay him back, twofold.

ROMAINE: It's the truth, honestly it is.

JOE: I don't want to be paid back, I want justice.

SOLLY: There he goes again, using horrible words, makes me shudder. Just think of that poor old bitch, Justice – blind, deaf, dumb, crippled, and no hands.

WOMAN: He's a thief. He got money out of me, my poor husband's clothes, and chickens.

PROSTITUTE: Come on, Joe, let the poor blighter go, the law will be around if you're not careful.

RITA: Let him go, Joe, we don't want no trouble.

SOLLY: Lady, I admire your common sense. Joe, do what your wife says.

JOE: I'm thinking about this poor girl here. He's a deceiver, leading her up the garden.

SOLLY: It ain't half pretty.

JOE: Don't you see he's no good? (*To ROMAINE.*) How can you fall for a type like this?

SOLLY: I'm not a type, I'm a specie.

ROMAINE: Soll's a good boy, I've changed him. Leave him alone.

RITA: Come on, Joe, let's go to bed. Poor girl, I pity her running off with a type like that.

JOE: I'm not going to let this happen. I'm going to save her.

RITA: I know what you're after – the reward.

JOE: Shush. Yesyesyes, yes. Quite, for her own good.

PROSTITUTE: Go on, let them go. You were young once.

RITA: Never. He never was young.

JOE: Will you shut up?

SOLLY: (*As they argue.*) I think you're all marvellous and here's a token of my appreciation –

(*He throws a small packet of pound notes in the air. Everyone starts scrambling for them; at this SOLLY pulls ROMAINE and starts to rush off. The attaché case, however, comes undone and pound notes are flying everywhere. SOLLY rushes about like a madman and ROMAINE sits down and cries. Everyone else desperately fights each other for the money.*)

JOE: He's robbed the bank of England.

SOLLY: Have you no respect for private property?

PROSTITUTE: Someone's been working overtime.

RITA: Joe, Joe, come inside.

(*As she pulls JOE she is stuffing pound notes into her dressing gown.*)

WOMAN: Now my husband can have a marvellous memorial.

POLICEMAN: (*Enters.*) Hello, hello, what's all the fuss?

(*They all try to shield SOLLY but POLICEMAN walks into the centre and sees him.*

SOLLY is sitting on the pound notes now like a chicken sits on an egg.)

SOLLY: We're discussing the political situation.

POLICEMAN: Looks like a mother's meeting – what's it all in aid of? Eh? I remember you. Didn't I run you in? Wasn't your mug in the *Police Gazette?*

SOLLY: The only *Gazette* I was in was the *London Gazette* when I was mentioned in despatches, and the *Hackney Gazette* when I was born.

POLICEMAN: I remember you now. You're the loud-mouth spiv I spoke to last week. What are you sitting on?

SOLLY: Lettuce leaves.

(*POLICEMAN tries to drag him up.*)

ROMAINE: Leave him alone.

SOLLY: (*In a gibberish codding way.*) Lettuce alone – leave us alone – they're my lettuce leaves.

POLICEMAN: Stand up.

SOLLY: Oh alright. Bloody law has to interfere.

POLICEMAN: Where did you half-inch these from? Whew!
Quite a fortune – talk yourself out of this!

SOLLY: I talked myself into this. This is my personal fortune.
I can explain. I won it.

POLICEMAN: What? On tiddlewinks?

SOLLY: No, on Pontoon.

WOMAN: He's a liar. He's a villain.

POLICEMAN: Alright, come along with me. We'll sort it out
down at the station.

SOLLY: Come on, Romaine. Whither I goest thou must go.

ROMAINE: I've never been in a police station before.

SOLLY: Better get used to it.

JOE: One minute, Officer, may I have a word with you?

ROMAINE: Solly, tell him the truth. The fact is we're running
away, we're madly in love.

POLICEMAN: Just you two wait there and don't move (*To
JOE.*) Now what is it?

JOE: Don't you recognise her? She's the missing heiress. Don't
you read your Express?

POLICEMAN: What do you mean – heiress?

JOE: Listen, just keep them here for a while. Her old man's on
his way to claim his daughter and to pay me the reward.

POLICEMAN: (*Loudly to all.*) I've got my duty to perform.
There's some dirty business going on with all this money.
I'm taking them into custody.

PROSTITUTE: What's the matter with you this morning,
George? Why are you so narked? Didn't you get your
dropsy from the girls last night?

POLICEMAN: Now you shut up – or I'll run you in also.

SOLLY: Please, Constable – a word in your ear.
(*He leads POLICEMAN to one side.*)
This is not a bribe, it's just a present or a loan. Just turn the
other way, will you? I've got a boat to catch.
(*SOLLY offers him a wad.*)

POLICEMAN: Right! Bribery and corruption as well! You're
for it, my lad.
(*The POLICEMAN takes the money, puts it in his pocket
and takes SOLLY by the scruff of his neck.*)

SOLLY: In that case give me my money back.

POLICEMAN: What money?

(*MORRY, MILLIE, SARAH, ALAN, HERBERT, SADIE and MELVIN enter hurriedly.*)

MILLIE: Oh darling! (*She rushes to ROMAINE.*) How are you? Where have you been, you bad girl? I could murder you. You alright darling?

ROMAINE: I'm so pleased to see you, Mummy.

MORRY: Hello, Solly. How's tricks?

SOLLY: Complicated.

MILLIE: Fancy running away like that, where have you been?

ROMAINE: Lying low.

MILLIE: Naughty girl.

SOLLY: You said it.

ROMAINE: (*Sings.*) 'Ah, sweet mystery of life, at last I found you.' (*She kisses all the family on the cheek.*)

MILLIE: You'll have to marry him now. You're ruined otherwise. (*To SOLLY.*) You'll have to marry her.

(*SOLLY kisses MILLIE, who smiles.*)

SOLLY: Who's disagreeing? Mother.

MORRY: Congratulations.

(*General back slapping.*)

ALAN: Wish you joy.

HERBERT: Please God, by you.

SADIE: May we only meet on holidays.

SARAH: I'm so happy for both of you.

MILLIE: Isn't it wonderful?

PROSTITUTE: Here comes the bride.

WOMAN: I love a wedding!

(*Everyone is joyful except the POLICEMAN.*)

SOLLY: Ladies and gentlemen: I'm delighted to announce my betrothal to Romaine and I'm going to make it all worth your while. I'm marrying a fortune – I mean I'm so fortunate. A priceless beauty. A jewel. A gem.

(*Everyone cheers and JOE brings out some drinks and everyone drinks.*)

POLICEMAN: Hold on! What is all this? Is all that money his legal property? Didn't he steal it from you?

MORRY: Steal from me? He'd have a hard job.

POLICEMAN: There's something fishy here.

SOLLY: Probably your socks.

POLICEMAN: I'm not letting you get away with this. There's some conspiracy somewhere – abduction, seduction, larceny – Come on, I'll get to the bottom of this if it kills me.

SOLLY: Now listen, what have you got against me?

POLICEMAN: You're guilty. You're a common crook. Society ain't safe with you around.

SOLLY: We'll hear what society has to say. Nobody has anything against me. Now listen folks – (*He addresses the people around him.*) You judge me dispassionately. I'll make it worth your while. You stick by me and I'll stick by you. Be my tribunal. Roll up, roll up one and all – am I guilty or not guilty?

WOMAN: Not guilty – a nice boy. Look at his eyes, so kind.

RITA: Not guilty. I hope you'll come and visit us sometime.

JOE: Not guilty. I'll make you a nice suit. Saville Row cut – Mile-End Road cost.

HERBERT: Not guilty. A potential Mason of the highest order – an influential custodian of property.

SADIE: Not guilty – a nice boy. Thoughtful.

ALAN: Not guilty. Blood is thicker than water.

SARAH: Not guilty. He makes my sister happy.

MELVIN: Not guilty. He's a sportsman.

MILLIE: Not guilty. How could he be? He's my future son-in-law.

MORRY: Not guilty. Officer, you haven't a leg to stand on.

SOLLY: You're wasting your time, Constable. Back to your beat now, my good man.

POLICEMAN: Alright, but I'm keeping my eye on you. (*He goes off and everyone cheers.*)

SOLLY: Whenever you want to get the better of them call them Constable or my good man. (*To MORRY.*) How can you forgive me?

MORRY: You showed me the way.

SOLLY: But I must confess to you now, I'm not a rabbi.

MORRY: I've known that for days now.

SOLLY: You know?

MORRY: Suddenly I came to my senses but in such a way

that I see more clearly now than ever before.

SOLLY: But you did believe that I was a rabbi, admit it. I'm a bloody marvellous actor.

MORRY: Yes, I believed. You see, I'm a simple man and you swore on the Bible.

SOLLY: Aren't you disappointed that you're not the messiah?

MORRY: In a way; I just wanted to make people happy. But now maybe I can be a saviour in another way. I was bored with life until you came, but now I can feel a miracle working inside me. I'm going to travel and relax from now on and try and do some good with my money.

SOLLY: And what about my money? This money?

MORRY: It's yours. Call it my dowry for Romaine. Besides, you earned it. You cured my backache. Hundreds of doctors treated me for years and fleeced me blind and still I suffered. You worked a miracle.

SARAH: It was an accident.

MORRY: Call it what you like. The point is the pain is gone.

SOLLY: But I must admit, Morry – I've been a bad boy. Can you forgive me for my past?

MORRY: Easily. What about my financial advisers? My solicitor and accountant? And my branch managers? They've been diddling me for years. You're an amateur compared to them.

SOLLY: I'm not an amateur – I won't have you say that.

MILLIE: Relax, Solly, let's all be friends. You're one of the family now. (*She kisses him.*)

SOLLY: I'm so glad you like me now. You had me worried at first.

MILLIE: No, I admit that I didn't understand you but I feel so much better since you came into our lives. I'm a vegetarian now – on your advice, and it's working wonders. I've lost two pounds in three days – I look so young, don't I? Besides you've got such a big dowry from Morry, we must keep it in the family – so welcome.

SOLLY: Mother! At last I've got a Mum of my own. My Mum took one look at me and ran away.

MILLIE: No more lies now. We want you to look after the business – to take complete charge.

SOLLY: What?

MORRY: It's true. If you can't lick them, make them join you. With you in the business nothing can stop us.

SOLLY: You said it. You're very smart. I'll make it the greatest shoe concern in the universe! I can sell anything, even your shoes. 'Swartzes everlasting immortal soles.' I can sell binoculars to a blind man, roller skates to a cripple. Romaine, Romaine, I'm the happiest guy in the world.
(*He cuddles her but she doesn't react.*)

SARAH: Solly, you're as good as gold.
(*Everyone slaps him on the back.*)

MELVIN: I would like to thank you, Solly, for helping me so much.

SOLLY: You as well? I'm so glad I helped. But tell me how?

MELVIN: I took your advice. The other evening at the Maccabee games I took the plunge and spoke to a girl, and now we're mad about each other. We're going to Israel next week – going to get married. And then we're going to start a new Kibbutz – devoted entirely to the propagation of sports and English sportsmanship. You know, cricket, polo, and badminton. She's lovely. What a figure, and can she throw the discus!

MORRY: Come on then, let's all go home and prepare for more weddings.

SOLLY: I feel like dancing.
(*He dances with MILLIE and soon everyone is dancing round and round as JOE plays the mouth organ.*)
Come on Romaine, back to Golders Green, back to a life of luxury and love.
(*She was the only one not dancing.*)

ROMAINE: I'm not going back.
(*SOLLY leaves MILLIE. He wonders if he heard right. Meanwhile the rest of the cast dances around – in and out of the houses – where they drink and eat.*)

SOLLY: What do you mean, not going back?

ROMAINE: I love you, Solly. I want to go forward with you.

SOLLY: But everything's arranged, everything's marvellous. Your family approve of me.

ROMAINE: Well, I don't approve of them. I want us to start

185

afresh – without their lousy money. For you and I to go off
into the world with nothing except our love.

SOLLY: Oh God, you've been reading *True Romances*.

ROMAINE: Darling, I want us to start from scratch.

SOLLY: I've been scratching all my life. Sweetheart, I want us
to have a little money to start with.

ROMAINE: I want you to work for me – to prove you love
me.

SOLLY: Work? That's something I've done without for thirty
years and I'm damned if I'm going to start now. You're
mad. I agree let's not go back with them – we'll just go as
we are – take the money and ourselves, that's all.

ROMAINE: It's the money or me.

SOLLY: Why do you see everything in black or white?

ROMAINE: What do you want – the money or me?

SOLLY: I want both. Don't you see I was born for luxury?

ROMAINE: Well I've had enough of it.

SOLLY: Come on, darling, I love you, you know I do.

ROMAINE: You work so hard at not working, you may as
well work and have a holiday. It's goodbye then.

SOLLY: Goodbye? What? What about last night and the night
before? What about the things you whispered in the Three
Nuns Hotel?

ROMAINE: No! No! No! I don't trust you – I never should. I
should have listened to my Mum.

SOLLY: Alright darling, come with me, now.

ROMAINE: No, it's too late, you're hoping to get that money
later on. I don't want you any more.

SOLLY: Alright then, I'll take the money.

(*The family have now stopped dancing.*)

ROMAINE: I'm not going with him.

SOLLY: She's mad.

ROMAINE: He doesn't love me for myself.

MILLIE: Oh darling, you sure?

ROMAINE: Oh Mummy, I don't want a life of poverty,
I want to come home with you – (*She weeps.*) He just
wanted, that was all – after he ruined me.

MILLIE: I don't like my Dolly unhappy, and on such a happy
day.

SOLLY: But it's all crazy. I do want her! Morry, please try and
persuade her –

MORRY: Do you want him, Romaine? Make up your mind.

ROMAINE: No! I never want to see him again. I don't want
him or any man – you can't trust them.

SOLLY: Morry, as her father it's your duty to make her see
sense. You know I'm right for her.

MORRY: Sorry, my boy. She must make her own decisions
– I'm not going to interfere. I learned from you how to be
tolerant. Thanks.

SOLLY: Alright then, I'll go – I'll take my money and go.

MILLIE: Oh no you don't! That's my money – Romaine's
money, for her dowry, and as she's not getting married, I'll
keep it for her.

ROMAINE: I don't want it.

SOLLY: Well I do. I earned it, you said so.

MILLIE: Well, it's mine now.

SOLLY: But I made you all so happy – you said so.

MORRY: I know, but women – what can you do with them?
Tell you what I'll do – to save any arguments – I'll send
it to Israel when Melvin goes, and with it, maybe they'll
plant avenues of orange trees. I might even live to see
them grow – the way they work out there. Well, that's that.
Goodbye, my boy – thanks for everything. If you're ever
passing, drop in for a chat.

SOLLY: A chat! A chat! I say, can you lend me a fiver?

MORRY: Sorry, I don't keep any loose change on me. Come
on, everyone. Come on, Fink.
(*They start to move off.*)

HERBERT: I told you, Morry, never to trust that man.

SADIE: Herbert, shut up.

MILLIE: Feeling better, darling?

ROMAINE: Smashing; what's for lunch?

SARAH: Chicken, casserolled, and Neapolitan ice cream to
follow.

MELVIN: Goodbye, Solly. If you ever want to become a
pioneer – and play hockey in the Holy Land, look me up.

MORRY: Come on, everyone – liven up. Goodbye, Solly – all
the best…

(*They are gone and now the other people go in.*)

SOLLY: (*Forlorn. Looks around, picks up a cigar butt.*) I made them all happy and I didn't earn a bean and I let a fortune and a fat girl slip through my fingers at the same time. What am I going to do for cash? There you are, you try and help and that's the thanks you get. What a life. The world's nothing to write home about. Believe me, if we can't help ourselves how are we going to help others? One thing I'm sure of, I'm not going to work. No, work's too much like an occupation – work's

alright for the working class, but for me – it's got to be something better. I must think of something – something really spectacular this time... I've got it! No, no – (*He walks around the stage.*) One minute – No. I'm bloody fed up. You can't con an honest coin these days...

(*He sits down, picks up some fag ends, rolls a cigarette and becomes deep in thought as the curtain falls.*)

The End.

WHO SHALL I BE TOMORROW?

Characters

ROSALIND FRASER

GERALD

Who Shall I Be Tomorrow? was first perfomed at the Greenwich Theatre, London on 24 September 1992, with the following cast:

ROSALIND, Joanna Lumley

GERALD, Harry Landis

Director, Matthew Francis
Designer, Stephen Brimson Lewis
Lighting Designer, Kevin Sleep
Sound, Steve Huttly
Theme Composer, Steve Brown

ACT ONE

Scene 1

Setting: a bedsit ground floor room in Belsize Rark Gardens, North West London. The occupant, ROSALIND FRASER is an actress and everything that she has collected, the bric-a-brac of several years on the stage, is crowded into this space. ROSALIND has never been able to throw anything out. Once these objects furnished a house, then they furnished a spacious studio flat, now ROSALIND's possessions clutter this room. Her world has become smaller and smaller. Theatrical posters cover the walls. There is an upright piano. ROSALIND sleeps on a divan, but there is also a settee that opens up to become a spare bed. An alcove provides a small kitchen. The room is one of many that are rented in a large, run-down, but once elegant stuccoed house. It is night. ROSALIND is lying in bed. Bach's 'Double Violin Concerto' is playing on the stereo. At first everything seems serene, but then we suddenly hear the far-off throb of 'Led Zeppelin'. Someone is playing heavy metal in an upstairs room.

ROSALIND: (*Suddenly sitting up.*) 'Sleep no more.'
    (*A quick glance at her watch, then she tries to settle again but the throb seems louder. She gets out of bed and gets a broom, stands on a chair and bangs the broom several times against the ceiling. The music is turned down.*)
    Thank you.
    (*She is about to return to bed but changes her mind and decides to get herself some milk. She pours some into a mug and then settles down into a deep armchair and sips the drink. She sits thoughtfully, as if trying to calm herself, but then she notices that her clothes cupboard door is slightly open.*)
    I closed that.
    (*She gets up to close the door, but instead she peers inside.*)
    (*Very quickly, as a child would in a game.*) The bogey man will get you!

(She closes the door and stands against it, smiling. But then the throb of heavy metal starts again, though not quite as loud as before. ROSALIND is about to bang the broom again, but decides against it as another disturbing thought enters her mind.)

Where did I put it?

(She immediately searches through papers on the writing desk.)

It's got to be somewhere!

(She goes to the mantlepiece, looks behind photos, searching through hap-hazard documents.)

Damn! Bookcase!

(On her way to the bookcase she catches her reflection in the full-length mirror.)

If you had been second-rate at least you could have earned a living.

(She now goes to the bookcase and searches between books. Again she has no success. She opens a book as if to search through the pages. But then is diverted by the words.)

How beautiful.

(The magic of the words immediately cause her to go to the telephone where she dials half a number, then hangs up.)

No. Ben needs his beauty sleep.

(She dials again.)

Poor Gerald. I shall just have to wake him. Gerald? This is Lois... Lois Lane. How fortunate to find you in.

(He obviously is not amused this time of night.)

Gerald! That's meant to be a joke, Gerald. Sorry, darling I had no choice. I'm fine but I just couldn't sleep. I've lost something rather important...well, mislaid. Not to worry. I hope I'm not being too selfish. If it had rung more than three times I would have strangled it. Listen, I must read you this poem. It's by Vladimir Mayakovsky. It's his Last Poem. Listen! 'Past one o'clock. You must have gone to bed. The Milky Way streams silver through the dark. I am in no hurry; I do not wish to wake you with telegrams or thunder. Let us say the incident is closed. Love's boat has been smashed against the daily grind. Behold, how quiet the world. Night wraps the sky in a tribute of stars...' Isn't that indescribably beautiful? And

a few moments later the wretched man killed himself.
Gerald? Gerald! Are you awake? What?
I disagree. I love this poem. I am not obsessed with
suicide. I'm just scared. You know what about. Tomorrow
morning. Have you forgotten? I'm so sorry Gerald,
I shouldn't get angry. I do need you. Always. I am
perfectly alright. I just needed a human voice. How's your
cold darling? Good. I shall be very cross if you neglect
yourself. And how's Desmond? Oh! Oh dear! Never mind
darling. I'm sure he'll come back tomorrow. (*She coos, as
if to a baby.*) Be good. Love you. Don't worry. It'll turn up.
Goodnight.
(*She hangs up, then sees the cupboard door has come open
again.*)
'Then is it sin to rush into the secret house of death, 'ere
death dare come to us?' Roz! The bogey man doesn't exist.
Good girl. Go to bed. Nothing to worry about. People
always reassure that everything will be alright. You thank
them then you close the door –
(*She closes the cupboard door. The music throbs louder.*)
– and lay awake all night.
(*She gets some pills.*)
Sweet Oblivion. Thank you.
(*She gets back into bed.*)
'Stand on the highest pavement of the stair…
lean on a garden urn…
weave, weave the sunlight in your hair…'
Mother. '*La Figlia che piange.*' Very nice. Feel much better
now. Surrounded with a sleep.
(*She is about to take the pills when there is a ring on the
doorbell. She jumps out of bed.*)
(*Quietly, to herself.*) Ben? (*But then she freezes.*) No. He rings
three times.
(*The bell rings again. She is very scared.*)
Who? Who is it?
(*She takes up the broom.*)
GERALD: (*Tentative voice from outside.*) It's Gerald.
ROSALIND: (*Disappointed, yet relieved.*) Gerald?
(*She opens the door carefully. It is secured with a chain.
GERALD is there, wearing pyjamas.*)
Gerald! Why did you come down?

GERALD: I was worried.

ROSALIND: Worried? What on earth for?

GERALD: May I come in?

ROSALIND: Honestly. I wish you wouldn't worry about me. Gerald, you poor love. You have a black eye.

GERALD: (*Cultured and fastidious. He is in his late fifties or early sixties.*) I have not got a black eye. I am tired. I –

ROSALIND: Desmond!

GERALD: It was not Desmond. I slipped and fell against the edge of the door.

ROSALIND: Liar! It was that bastard. It's just as well he's gone off. Come on, I'll bathe it.

GERALD: Rosalind. Please do not fuss. I am not concerned about me. I am concerned about you. So, you've mislaid it again.

ROSALIND: It'll turn up.

GERALD: Of course it will. So why are you depressed?

ROSALIND: I am not depressed. I am perfectly alright. Rest assured I am not going to kill myself. Know why?
I want to live long enough to become famous again; to see my obituary in *The Times* before I die. Oh, look at your poor face. It's a terrible bruise. How can you put up with that swine?

GERALD: I am a fool or a saint. He has been with me for two years. Two months of heaven. Twenty-two months of hell. If I never see him again that's too soon. If he comes back begging I shall not be here. I shall move to British West Hampstead, the last outpost of civilisation. (*He yawns.*) I'm tired of the love game. I'm giving it up.

ROSALIND: I shouldn't have woken you. I am so unbelievably selfish.

GERALD: But I need to be needed. Sleep comes too soon.

ROSALIND: Give me a big hug.
(*They both cling to each other with their eyes closed.*)
MMMMMMmmmmmmm!

GERALD: Roz, could I possibly make myself a nice hot cup of Ovaltine?

ROSALIND: Of course. And make yourself some Marmite soldiers while you're about it.

GERALD: Goodie. A midnight feast.

(*They both now seem mightily relieved. He goes to kitchen alcove to do the deed.*)

The same for you?

ROSALIND: No thanks. But I would love a cup of tea.

GERALD: You relax. I shall do everything.

ROSALIND: I almost phoned Ben before I phoned you.

GERALD: (*Humouring.*) Yes darling.

ROSALIND: I know you sometimes have doubts about my relationship with him.

GERALD: I do?

ROSALIND: I love him and he loves me.

GERALD: (*Still in kitchen he mumbles a little song.*) 'Some day he'll come along, the man I love –

ROSALIND: What did you say?

GERALD: I said 'Smarvellous. Swunderful. You should care for me'.

ROSALIND: He's coming to dinner tomorrow.

GERALD: How nice.

ROSALIND: And this time you really must meet him.

GERALD: Wonderbar! I am in all day tomorrow. I shall be delighted to meet him.

ROSALIND: So, Desmond's gone walkies.

GERALD: And I am delighted and desperate. Why do we put up with heartless lovers?

ROSALIND: My lover is not heartless. He's just thoughtless. Nevertheless I just adore him.

GERALD: Exactly. Needs must. Fall in love with a bicycle, as long as it makes you both happy.

ROSALIND: (*Ignoring him.*) And you'll love Ben. He's so overworked, poor darling. The two great growth areas in the world today are cancer and psychotherapy. Everyone's going insane. But Ben remains so cool, so in control. He has such beautifully long eyelashes, such innocent cornflower blue eyes, such incredibly long fingers, such vibrant yet gentle hands.

GERALD: (*Sings an advert.*) 'The hands that do dishes can be soft on your face with mild green fairy liquid.'

ROSALIND: That first time! It was incredible. Did I tell you?

GERALD: Yes.

ROSALIND: It was my second or third session. I suddenly had this uncontrollable urge to touch him.

GERALD: Thrilling.

ROSALIND: I told him. But he didn't say anything either way. 'Doctor Harris, I really must touch your penis,' I said. Again he didn't respond.

GERALD: What happened?

ROSALIND: I leaned across and touched it. Clutched it.

GERALD: So? What happened?

ROSALIND: Nothing. He just carried on, writing notes. But two weeks later there was an imperceptible change. As soon as I entered his room our eyes locked. Not a word was spoken. Next moment he gently pushed me backwards onto the carpet. Then he brought a cushion. 'Please raise yourself,' he said, placing it beneath me. But I've told you all this, haven't I?

GERALD: Yes. But it's so pleasant hearing it again.

ROSALIND: 'What goes on inside your brain?
'The man asked his lover, again, again.
But then he decided to look inside.'
And at once committed suicide.' Gerald. He was so gentle, yet so savage, so overwhelming. Ethics and logic were swept aside by magic. And he entered me and crossed that great divide; placing himself and his entire career and life in jeopardy. And all because of that sudden mutual compulsion that took possession of us.
It was wonderful.
(*GERALD laughs.*)

GERALD: Sorry.

ROSALIND: You don't believe me.

GERALD: (*Protesting.*) Rosalind! (*He doesn't.*)

ROSALIND: Of course, it meant that I stopped being his patient to become his lover.

GERALD: A wise move. Sex is cheaper than therapy. And so much better for you.

ROSALIND: Gerald, he really does love me. He'll ditch his bitch. You'll see.

GERALD: Would you want that?

ROSALIND: Ah yes. That old chestnut. My deep need to be the other woman.

GERALD: Cosmopollution. Last month. I too wouldn't miss an issue.

ROSALIND: Gerald, why are you going on like this?

GERALD: (*He goes to the piano and sings 'I Slept Last Night in an English Garden' but changes the words.*) 'I slept last night with a Grenadier Guardsman.' I love the old romantic songs.

ROSALIND: How's the job?

GERALD: Mustn't grumble. I jog along in my own way, you know, tinkling twice a week in that chintzy bohemian caff in the Finchley Road. I'm sure the boss, you know, him of the fifty twenty-two carat gold rings must fancy me. But I mustn't complain. It does keep me in Misty Whore.

ROSALIND: So what's going to happen now?

GERALD: About what?

ROSALIND: About you.

GERALD: I don't want to talk about me.

ROSALIND: Seriously. Gerald. Desmond has done you a favour. Now you must think about the future. Have you anyone else lined up?

GERALD: Yes darling, thousands are hammering to get in. They're crawling over Paul Newman to get to me. Seriously. There is someone on the horizon. What did I do right? What has this naughty boy done to deserve such rewards? Here. Your Jasmine Tea.

ROSALIND: (*Sipping the tea.*) Delicious.

GERALD: Drink me and cheer up. (*He drinks and eats.*) Delicious. (*He allows himself a moment of sweet reflection.*) Did I ever tell you that mother –

ROSALIND/GERALD: Was born in Sofia, Bulgaria? She used to sing these wonderful strange lullabies. '*Tu madre cuando te pario. Y te quito al mundo. Coracon ella no te dio. Para amar segundo. Adio. Adio querida. No quero la vida. Mel amargates tu –*' I don't know what it means, but it always moves me so much.

ROSALIND: (*Breaking a possibly tearful mood.*) Please play to me.

GERALD: (*He plays some romantic Viennese song as he speaks.*)
Who doesn't need love? I need it three times a night and
more incessantly during the waking hours. A love song. (*He
sings as Tauber.*) 'You are my heart's delight and where you
are I long to be. You make my darkness light when like a
star you shine on me –'

ROSALIND: Gerald, I haven't been able to contact Ben all
day. I just get his answerphone. I don't understand it.

GERALD: There must be a perfectly simple explanation.
He's fallen under a tube train. On the Victoria Line. Good
riddance to both of them.

ROSALIND: Yes. Let's concentrate on us.

GERALD: On you darling. Not on me. Have you decided on
your piece?

ROSALIND: I think so.

GERALD: You think so! Darling, you've had two weeks.

ROSALIND: I mean who's going to come to see me at that
little pokey place? Anyway, who wants anyone to see
me? Have you seen the script? I mean, my part's not bad,
but who the hell is interested in some diatribe about a
mendacious ex social worker who aspires to the shires.

GERALD: Look Rosalind. It's work. And you haven't worked
since –

ROSALIND: I know. Don't rub it in. I'm scared. The streets
stink.

GERALD: I thought you were over all that.

ROSALIND: I am. But like everyone else, I don't like coming
home late. (*She sees the cupboard door is open, and closes
it again.*) This place. Must get this damned door fixed.
Gerald, we are living in very dark times.

GERALD: Then enliven it with your shining light. Be honest
Roz, you hate going out, day or night.

ROSALIND: That's not true. And you know it.

GERALD: I'm sorry. It's just that I love you and I'm very
concerned about you. Please don't get angry with me. (*He
shivers.*)

ROSALIND: Poor darling. (*She gets him a huge duvet.*) There
we are. I'll tuck you in. (*She does.*) There! You look so sweet.

GERALD: Did I ever tell you that my father was a famous painter?

ROSALIND: Three hundred times. At least.

GERALD: (*Not listening.*) My father was such a character, an outrageous Bohemian. A monster but lovable, in his beautiful green hat. He and my mother were inseparable. They loved each other; in those days they went in for that sort of stuff. Anyway, to cut a long story sideways his family nagged him incessantly. Get a proper job. Be respectable. Settle down. He was truly *avant garde*. Whilst the others were singing and dancing he had nightmares. He watched and listened and took the devil at his word. And he smelt the smoke of the incinerators long before the first match was struck. That's how I didn't die before I was born. Therefore they did not waltz into the oven eating chocolate eclairs. They caught an early train to Paris. Why did I think of my parents out of the blue? They had such high hopes for me; such dreams. They thought I would become the second Horovitz. Roz, seriously, I desperately want you to get this part and return to the stage. To once more achieve the recognition you deserve. And I could take all my friends and boast about you endlessly.

ROSALIND: Friends? Anyway, I wouldn't want you bringing anyone to that place. It stinks of sweat and stale fag ends. And it's run by a bunch of pimply, snotty nosed kids who have barely learned to wipe their arse. They mumble such mumbo jumbo. Grotofsky. Artaud. Theatre of Cruelty. How cruel. They call that theatre? I do not see the virtue of consorting with pygmies. And they are so arrogant. Nothing existed before they arrived; they invented sex, drama. Anyway, what the hell. I hate them. Hate them. The pavements should open and they should all hurtle into a bottomless pit.

GERALD: Bravo. That's the performance I want from Rosalind Fraser. Burning anger.

ROSALIND: That wasn't a performance, Gerald. That's true bile. My deep bitterness.

GERALD: No genius is expected to assess their own value.

It was the spirit of true anger. The real you. I want more.
More.

ROSALIND: I'm tired.

GERALD: I want Rosalind Fraser to be seen again.

ROSALIND: I want to disappear. To be swallowed up.
Annihilated.

GERALD: I want you to be seen. To be loved. I want people
to talk about you again. I've read the play.

ROSALIND: It's crap.

GERALD: It's not bad and I just know you will be noticed. I
know you're going to strike it big, Roz. It is only a question
of time. Please Roz! Let me hear you now. Then we'll
decide.

ROSALIND: Really? Shall? Now? Alright. You decide. Listen!
Remember that incredible part I played almost at the start
of my career? Leah, in –

GERALD: *The Dybbuk*, in the West End. Do I remember? Are
you kidding? Even though of course it was before my time.

ROSALIND: Of course.

GERALD: As I remember it's deeply psychological. It's
surely about the duality that pervades all mortals. The two
hemispheres of the mind and soul.

ROSALIND: I don't understand what the hell you're talking
about. It was just a remarkable play.

GERALD: Yes my sweet. Actors are not meant to be clever.
Drama means doing. So do it.

ROSALIND: Right. That incredible young girl is possessed by
the spirit of her dead lover.

GERALD: Roz. Do it.

ROSALIND: Please close that cursed cupboard door first.
(*He does.*)
Alright. If you insist. Just listen. (*As LEAH.*) I remember
now. Your hair was soft and it glistened as though with
tears. And –

GERALD: And your eyes –

ROSALIND: And your eyes were sad and gentle. Your fingers
were long and slender. Day and night I – I – thought of you.
But you went away and my light was put out and my soul
was wizened. (*She is struggling.*)

GERALD: Withered! And I was like a desolate widow when a strange man approached. Why have you forsaken me again?

ROSALIND: Gerald. Shut up. I know. I know. (*Now the deep voice of Kronnon her dead lover.*) I broke all barriers. I surmounted death. I defied the laws of the ages and generations. And when the last spark of my strength was burned out I departed from your body to return to your soul. (*Now tenderly as LEAH again.*) Return to me my bridegroom. I will carry you in death, in my heart, and we will together rock to sleep our unborn children. (*She cries.*) We will sew them clothes to wear and sing them lullabies.

GERALD: (*Sings a few words.*) 'Tum Bala, Tum Bala, Tum Balalaika... Tum bala, Tum bala, Tum Balalaika. –'

ROSALIND: Gerald!

GERALD: Sorry. Sorry.

ROSALIND: So, what did you think of my Dybbuk?

GERALD: Do you want my honest opinion or the truth?

ROSALIND: I can't take honesty. Give me the truth. Was it awful?

GERALD: Roz. It – doesn't have the ring of truth. Try something else.

ROSALIND: I don't want to go anyway. I'm sick of it. It's absurd. Where did I put that bloody thing? I can't bear the world anymore. What is an actress? It is a nothing covered over nothing. With platitudes. Attitudes. Bathos. Beatitudes. If only Ben wasn't such a bastard. I'm no bloody good. I was once. But I lost it. Where did I put it? My father was a shit. A real shit and I loved him. My mother was a saint. And I loathed her. Ben, help me.

GERALD: Rosalind! (*Helpless.*) Let me make you some passion fruit tea.

ROSALIND: He took me to the swimming baths.

GERALD: Who? Ben?

ROSALIND: No. My father. Don't be a bastard. I was five. I couldn't swim. He said, Rosalind, I promise before the morning is out you will be a swimmer. He told me to stand on the edge of the pool. I was afraid. He said Rosalind,

trust me. And then he pushed me. It was like dying. I
screamed and choked as I went down, down. It was the
worst moment of my life. It was worse than dying. When
they dragged me out I was silent. He laughed and rubbed
my hair and dried me with a huge towel and cuddled me.
I love you Rosalind. That morning is seared into my soul.
I have never been able to able to enter a swimming pool,
or take a dip in the ocean. But I sometimes dare myself
to paddle. Swimming without water. Now that would be
wonderful.

GERALD: Oh my god. (*He is distressed.*) Why you talking
about your father suddenly?

ROSALIND: (*She laughs.*) Ever been had?

GERALD: You bitch. (*He throws a cushion at her.*)

ROSALIND: I'm a wonderful swimmer. I love swimming.

GERALD: And I hate you. And I am even more convinced
that you have not lost one iota of your talent. I who was
weaned on Schnitzler and Molnar! I who experienced
the great Sybil Thorndike and Lotte Lenya! Rosalind!
Remember your beginning? Was that all an illusion? Your
St Joan? And the way you were discovered by that brilliant
director – George – No – Frank! Frank! Yes – What was his
name?

ROSALIND: I forget.

GERALD: And then a few months later, the West End.

ROSALIND: Yes. A few years of fame then all down the
drain.

GERALD: And the reviews! I didn't know you then but you
dazzled me.

ROSALIND: My auspicious, romantic past. Dorothy
Evans, a music teacher from Maesteg in the Rhondda
valley opened her legs and surrendered to Henry Fraser,
chartered surveyor, in a field north of Rickmansworth and
subsequently Rosalind Fraser was born.

GERALD: Rosalind –

ROSALIND: They were quite well off. Middle class,
Middlesex. It was a nothing place. He smoked *De Reske*
cigarettes, Dorothy played the Cello, believed that people

were nice. One night Henry Fraser carefully trimmed his moustache, pecked his daughter on the cheek, winked, went out and never returned. The girl's questions were never answered; his photos were taken down and Henry was never mentioned again. Dorothy was devoted to Rosalind; lived for her, doted on her every whim. And never even argued when the girl announced she was going on the stage. Then a stroke of luck. She was in the right place at the right time. Otherwise her life might have taken another direction. And that might have been – wonderful. A better life.

A proper life. This brilliant young director, Mr whatsisname, saw this green innocent child with high cheek bones. And bob's your uncle. She landed St Joan. She was fantastic, even if she does say so herself. Quote: 'Her poignant performance touched everyone!' I believe even two critics cried. But she was still a kid so it is hardly surprising that her head started to expand. Very soon she owned the world. And basked in the warm cocoon of love and adulation. Everybody loved her. For two years she bathed in the warmth of her success and every face smiled when she appeared. People stopped in their tracks. In the stores they whispered, smiled, as if by noticing her they too would be touched by magic. Her mother Dorothy just lived long enough to enjoy a few months of her daughter's meteoric success. But there was a price to pay. Rosalind started to lose all sense of self; felt herself disintegrating. Then – one day in the middle of the night, just as she was leaving the theatre, faces coagulated and Rosalind floated away.

GERALD: Roz! Please! You know this sort of talk is no good.

ROSALIND: You mean it threatens you. The phone rang and rang but she didn't answer. The phone stopped. As soon as Rosalind left her street door chasms opened up before her; pavements cavorted. Don't tread on the crack, face will turn black. Applause slowed down; slower and slower. Grunts, growls. She hated going out, so she went in. And in. They drove her to the Halfway House, nice friends who fell away. And so there was a period of convalescence. Tranquility pills. And soon she was almost normal. She could negotiate with the streets again, was quite pleased with herself. Days drag, but years fly. Waiting for the phone to ring. Counting out coins at the check-out. Making ends meet. Rosalind is almost well now, almost her old self. She should be grateful for small mercies, but she cannot think of any off hand. She can still hear her mother's cry when he penetrated her in that field near the trunk road near Rickmansworth, all those years ago. And she still finds it difficult to enter supermarkets, and she certainly cannot afford to visit the swimming baths. She is glad that she is now never recognised in the streets. She is still afraid of the bogey man. Watch out. Watch out. One day soon, Bogey man will come out, and he will say, no time to delay. Come on Roz you're on your way. Wait! Wait! Can't I say goodbye? Rosalind, I'm waiting, he'll reply. Thank you. Thank you. Goodnight.

GERALD: That's wonderful. That's your audition piece.

ROSALIND: Thank God I don't ever think about it.

GERALD: (*An idea strikes.*) Pretend it's lesser known Rattigan. A play he excised from his cannon. I know. Call it *Out of Season.*

ROSALIND: All I want to be is a working actress.

GERALD: Is that all?

ROSALIND: I used to stuff cotton wool into my ears and dive under the bedclothes. But that night the sound penetrated. So she listened, her ear flat against the wall. Henry. Yes. Yes. Nice. Nice. Be quick. Please be quick. Then the symphony of the bedspring. But there was another sound. Henry was punching her. Thudding into the dreary lump. At first the child thought mother was laughing. 'Help me! Please help me.' I rushed into the room. Blood was oozing out of her mouth, her nose. Her vagina. I dug my finger nails into his flesh. Pulled them all down his back. He turned. The wild dog smiled. His face came kissing close. He lit his breath. Flames spurted out and everything was shooting stars. The house burst into flames. Her charred heart shrivelled that night Gerald. Her childhood shuffled away. And I was left hurting too much to pick up the pieces.

GERALD: But you loved him?

ROSALIND: Since when has life been fair?

(*GERALD bursts out crying.*)

Gerald! Gerald! What's the matter? Gerald!

(*He sobs uncontrollably.*)

Gerald!

GERALD: Leave me alone. Just leave me alone.

ROSALIND: Gerald. I am furious with you. Gerald! I am extremely cross with you.

GERALD: Oh please. Rosalind, help me. Help me.

ROSALIND: Gerald, what is it my darling?

GERALD: Oh, I'm so wretched, so desperate.

ROSALIND: My darling. I'm so sorry. Please tell Roz all about it.

(*She cradles him and they gently sway together.*)

Is it Desmond?

GERALD: (*He sobs.*) That boy. I love him. He's not so bad deep down. He's got some very nice ways. Though off-hand I can't think of any. It's amazing Roz, some monsters have a facility that make them almost human. They enter smiling and contrite, and your anger subsides and you forgive them anything. Whenever Desmond enters a room it lights up.

ROSALIND: He'll come back.

GERALD: I don't want him back. I love him but I'm scared. He's been coming home late recently; later and later. I'm frightened. Who knows what he'll bring back with him?

ROSALIND: Gerald darling, you are careful?

GERALD: I try to be. But he's so headstrong and emotional and free. He trusts everyone, loves everyone. So I really must take care and hope that luck is kind and he doesn't come home offering a lethal gift. That would be extremely fatal, would it not?

ROSALIND: Darling. You'll be alright. Believe me.

GERALD: Will I? Are you sure?

ROSALIND: Absolutely. I promise.

GERALD: You don't think I'm dying?

ROSALIND: No. You're not the dying sort.

GERALD: Oh Roz, I will survive, won't I? Oh, thank you.
I owe you so much.

ROSALIND: You must survive. How would I manage without you?

GERALD: Please do Rita for me.

ROSALIND: (*She complies, making herself look sexy, posturing, holding her hair up, wriggling, trying to emulate Rita Hayworth.*) 'Put the blame on Mame boys, put the blame on Mame. One night Mame did the itchy coo. That's the thing that slew magroo. Put the blame on Mame boys. Put the blame on Mame –'
(*GERALD laughs and claps.*)

GERALD: Wonderful! Darling. Wonderful! I feel much better now. If I never see him again that's too soon. It's over. Finito. Caput. I shall now gird my golden loins, and go to my little cave up on the third floor where
I shall sleep the sleep of the unjust. And I shall see you in the morning light to wish you all the luck in the world, before you brave the environs of Camden Town. (*He kisses her.*) Thank you. I feel much better now.

ROSALIND: Goodnight Gerald my love. Sleep tight.

GERALD: I shall come and tidy up in the morning.

ROSALIND: No. You're not my servant.

GERALD: I am. And it's my pleasure. And please, do practice your own private Rattigan. You will be stupendoloso perfecto. Sweet dreams. (*He goes.*)

ROSALIND: (*She leans against the door, sighing with relief. Then she pours herself a drink.*) Now my nightcap needs a nightcap. Down the hatch.
(*She gulps it down, she ponders again about the lost item.*)
Where is it? Where the hell is it? It's got to be somewhere. I give up. Ben! You bastard! Where are you? Please come and fuck me to sleep. Please. Here I am, so where are you? So there I was, I was fast asleep. In that beautiful oblivion of amorphous dreams. Then someone was playing a mouth organ. I opened my eyes into this room. There was total darkness but someone was still playing that mouth organ. It was 'Greensleeves', played fast, over and over again. It was coming from that cupboard. I crept over, entered.

'Let's play games', my father whispered. 'Night games.' It was my father's voice. 'Daddy! Daddy! Where are you?' Suddenly his face lit up. He just sat there in the corner, laughing, rocking backwards and forwards. 'Over here darling. Our secret.' His arms reached out and pulled me towards him, pulled me down. I know what you're thinking and you'd be wrong. He didn't molest me. He just cuddled me into him, rocking backwards and forwards. 'I love you, love you. You're the only thing I love. Please don't ever leave me.' The next day he pecked me on the cheek, winked, went out and never returned. My questions were never answered; his photos were taken down and Henry Fraser was never mentioned again.

That bloody door!

(*She kicks the cupboard door closed, gets into bed and pulls the bedclothes right over her.*)

Goodnight.

(*Blackout.*)

Scene 2

It is morning. Sun streaming into the room. ROSALIND, dressed for the audition, is brushing her hair before the mirror. She goes to the phone, dials. Then furiously she slams the receiver down again.

ROSALIND: Ben! I need you to need me.

(*She hears the postman deliver the post. Then quickly going to the door she gets the letters and opens them.*)

What am I going to do? Drowning under a wave of bills.

(*Again she considers searching for the lost object.*)

Where the hell could I have put it? Damn! Damn! Damn!

(*She goes to the phone and dials. While she is on the phone GERALD enters quietly, hears her.*)

Yes please. Extension one – five – nine – if you don't mind. Yes. I'll hold on. I've been holding on all my life. Listen dear, listen carefully. This is Rosalind Fraser. Do you want my National Insurance number? Yes. Good. You found me. I do exist. That's right. Look! I am the person who called you yesterday. Yes. Good. You will recall that I informed

you that I've lost my Giro. I don't know. If
I knew I wouldn't need to speak to you. It gives me no
pleasure to telephone your offices. I mislaid it. Possibly
here, in my flat. The fact is I am desperate. I am falling
apart. I have no fuel, no food. There is no way I can
survive beyond this morning. Yes. Rosalind Fraser. Are
you an idiot? Do I have to repeat everything five times? I
need you to send me another one. Urgently. Yes!! My Giro
is not there. I have an audition, do you understand? How
the hell am I expected to get there? My shoes let in water
and it is pelting down. Yes. I am an actress. You wouldn't
understand this but I fulfil people's dreams;
I allow them to live beyond their means. Ah! You
remember me now! Miracle! Listen! Please help me.
I have no one to turn to. No family to borrow from.
I have eighty pence to my name.
(*GERALD quietly slips out again.*)
No savings. You must help me. I don't know how I'm
going to manage. Look at these shoes. I assure you I've
looked everywhere. How can I be expected to get
work unless I look decent? You do want me to work
I presume? How am I going to keep up appearances?
I must keep up appearances.
(*She puts down the phone and cries. There is a knock on the
door. She quickly dries her eyes, opens the door. GERALD
is there.*)
(*She snaps at him.*) Why did you knock? You have a key.
Come in. I'm late. What do you want?
GERALD: I've come to tidy up and wish you luck.
ROSALIND: Why do you insist on tidying up for me? You're
    not my slave.
GERALD: Am I not? It's the least I can do for someone so
    beautiful.
ROSALIND: Thank you. I'm sorry I snapped.
GERALD: Just be a good girl. Go and break a leg.
    (*They kiss.*)
I'm so glad you're doing the Rattigan.
ROSALIND: Gerald, I decided on *Come Back Little Sheba*. Is

that alright? It's more me. Goodbye precious. (*She is almost out of the door.*)

GERALD: Rosalind. A little gift for you. (*He takes out a twenty pound note.*)

ROSALIND: Gerald! I couldn't.

GERALD: Spend it on something frivolous.

ROSALIND: Gerald. You are impossible. Alright. But on one condition. That I pay you back next week. I am owed oodles of money.

GERALD: I must get on with my housework. Please go.

ROSALIND: Gerald, how would I manage without you? (*She goes.*)

GERALD: How would I manage without you?

(*He puts on an apron, takes up a duster and starts to dust. He also sings, from 'Mahoghany'.*)

'Oh moon of Alabama, we now must say goodbye. We've lost our good old mamma and must boys, oh you know why. Oh show me the way to the next pretty boy, we must have boys. We must have boys. If we don't find the next pretty boy, I tell you we must die. I tell you we must die –'

(*He continues humming, tidying the flat. Then he puts Tchaikovski's 'Pathetique' on the stereo and for a few moments he enjoys himself, conducting an invisible orchestra, then he looks out of the window and lights up.*)

Desmond! You've come back!

(*He rushes out of the room. The sixth symphony continues. A passage of time.*

It is now late afternoon. GERALD re-enters.)

Roz! You home yet?

(*He looks at himself in the mirror and sighs.*)

Is it worth it? Why do you put up with it? Because he lets you. Because he doesn't mind.

(*He inspects his skin then quickly rushes around, finishing the tidying when he hears her key in the door. He quickly goes to a sideboard, pours himself a drink, drapes himself into an armchair. ROSALIND enters.*)

ROSALIND: (*Her expression does not tell GERALD how the audition went.*) Gerald! You still here?

GERALD: I finished hours ago. I've been and come back.

I poured myself a *Tio Pepe*. I hope you don't mind.

ROSALIND: Why should I mind? You are funny.

GERALD: Well?

ROSALIND: Very well.

GERALD: Roz! How did you get on?

ROSALIND: One foot after the other. (*She sings in croaky voice.*)
'We must face the consequence; that ole devil consequence
–'

GERALD: Rosalind. I'm on tenterhooks. Stop playing.

ROSALIND: I get there, right. I walk onto the postage stamp
they call a stage. They file in, not just one or two, but a
whole phalanx, a committee of them, humourless boys and
girls. They all wear John Lennon spectacles. Shaven heads.
They look like an execution squad. 'We are democratic
here; we do things collectively, we discuss everything,'
they nod, in unison, superciliously.
I say 'Fine. You want me to read. Who am I to stand on
my dignity? Even though you must know I have had years
and years of wide experience, and normally one would
not expect an actress of my calibre to audition.' They look
up at me, smirking, sneering, as if to say, 'How dare you
have an opinion?' I tell them a story. 'Shelly Winters was
called to an audition for a production on Broadway. She
walks in with a shopping bag. She says, 'You want me to
read gentlemen. Okay, I'll read. But in my bag I have
two very good reasons why I consider your request quite
impertinent.' She reaches into her carrier bag and pulls
out one Oscar, and then another.' Gerald, I don't have two
Oscars to rub together. I don't even have a decent carrier
bag. But I do have an awlful lot of anger. The fact is, young
people in this game are arrogant, stupid and blinkered.
Worse, they have no sense of humour. My god, theatre is
the one democracy that cries out for a dictator.

GERALD: So, don't keep me in suspense. What happened?

ROSALIND: (*She smiles.*) Oh, they loved me.

GERALD: Good. What did they say?

ROSALIND: They said I read splendidly. Afterwards I had
the mechanical poofy little dears eating out of my hands.
I believe I've got the part. They said they were going to
phone Archie Woolf this evening.

GERALD: Roz! Dushinka! Habibi! (*He cuddles and kisses her.*)
This calls for Australian Champagne.

ROSALIND: Wait! I ain't officially got the part yet.

GERALD: You will. Your luck has changed. I am just popping
to the corner off licence, and we shall imbibe a naughty
bottle of Antipodean bubbly. Just the two of us.

ROSALIND: Perfect. But do remember that Ben may be
coming tonight.

GERALD: Oh nice. You've been in touch. (*He doesn't believe
her but maintains the deception.*)

ROSALIND: Poor love. He's buried in work, but hopes
he can make it. I'm going to cook him something really
special. Roast duck. Pomme Parmentier. Red cabbage. And
sherry trifle.

GERALD: Roz! You're broke.

ROSALIND: Gerald! I wish you would be nice about him.

GERALD: I can only love living flesh.

ROSALIND: (*Pause.*) What does that mean?

GERALD: (*Pause.*) Let's face it, if he came round tonight and
said, 'I'm all yours,' you'd panic.

ROSALIND: Gerald. I've been on my own so long. And
I don't want to wake up alone anymore. Enough is enough.
This place is damp. Spores are floating everywhere. It's
so cramped and the stench from the cellar. You must have
noticed it. I can't find anything. We must start painting
next week. Everything Magnolia. You promised. I don't
want to end up talking to myself.

GERALD: Roz, tonight we are going to defer the crisis. That's
my new philosophy. After all, why bother to solve the
crisis? A new one will only come and take it's place, and
it's certain to be far worse.

ROSALIND: You are the only permanent feature in my life. I
mean it.

GERALD: Good. Well, you've got Ben coming. And I hope
to be coming many times. So we both seem to have what's
coming to us. It promises to be a long and ravishing
evening.

ROSALIND: Oh? Is there someone new on the scene so
soon?

GERALD: Desmond.

ROSALIND: Oh no. He's back?

GERALD: Please do not hate me.

ROSALIND: Gerald, buy that bottle.

GERALD: Your command is my wish. I'm on my way. (*He goes to the door.*)

ROSALIND: Could I have misread their faces? I'm absolutely sure I clinched it.

(*She thinks he's gone and quickly gets some tablets from her handbag. GERALD at the door, sees.*)

GERALD: Roz! What are you doing? (*He takes the bottle.*) You don't need those.

ROSALIND: Please Gerald. I'm feeling great. I need a boost.

GERALD: Sorry. I'm not going to let you.

ROSALIND: You're right. Thank you.

GERALD: Speed kills. And I don't want to be left in this world alone, with Desmond.

ROSALIND: Alright! I'm sorry. Just get the champagne.

GERALD: (*At the door he suddenly gets an idea.*) Do you know, I think we ought to think about decorating this flat.

ROSALIND: Darling, this place doesn't need decorating. It needs pulling down.

GERALD: We'll start tomorrow. Just the two of us.

ROSALIND: Great! Tomorrow starts a new era. Don't be long.

(*He goes and she quickly takes the tablets, then she makes a phone call.*)

Hello. Is Doctor Benjamin Harris there please? Canada? Really? Oh, I didn't know. Rosalind Fraser, I'm an ex patient. No, no message. Thank you.

(*She puts down the phone, laughs.*)

She lied. She did see him again. Daddy. Years later. She had already embarked on the ocean of success. He appeared. Out of the blue. Come to the hospital. See your mother before she goes. The skin was yellow parchment. You could probably just rip it away from the skull. The creature stared up at her daughter without comprehension, but tried to open her mouth, emitting animal sounds. The

girl backed away. This obscene animal was not her mother.
Daddy was up to his old tricks. The woman disintegrated
that afternoon. They siphoned off her liquids, took it home
in two plastic milk cartons to make tea. They had egg rolls,
with cress. She left, she had to get to the theatre, for the
performance that evening. She got back to the theatre in
time for the half hour. Ben. Ben. Ben. You've done it again.
But she is not going to be your victim anymore. *Deus ex
Machina.* Success may have intervened, in the nick of time.
(*GERALD enters.*)

GERALD: (*Holding up the bottle.*) There you are me old Sheila.
Straight from the Billabong. What's wrong?

ROSALIND: Ben's not coming.

GERALD: (*Quiet and knowingly.*) Oh.

ROSALIND: His secretary just phoned. She said he's gone to
Canada.

GERALD: Having it off with a Moose.

ROSALIND: Gerald, is he with someone else?

GERALD: Roz, I'm sorry, what can I say?

ROSALIND: I'm thinking of taking a holiday.

GERALD: With what? Sorry.

ROSALIND: You're right. I must get that part; I must get
something.
(*He opens wine, pours two glasses.*)
I must phone my agent. (*She phones.*) Hello! May I speak to
Mr Woolfe please. Yes. Rosalind Fraser. Am I a client? You
must be a temp. Just put me through, there's a good girl.
Archie! They loved me. I was fantastic. I'm sure I've got it.
Oh? (*Her excitement suddenly abates. Her voice goes cold.*) Oh.
I see. I understand. Typical! Thank you Archie. (*But now
a sudden change of tone.*) Really? Really? You have? When?
BBC? Mmmmmm. Something to think about. Will you
post it? Bike it! Tomorrow. Great. One door closes, another
door closes. Joking. Of course. Thank you Archie for being
so patient with me. Love to Loretta. (*She puts the phone
down.*)

GERALD: You didn't get the part.

ROSALIND: No. The little theatre turned me down. What a
joke! I need a shower.

GERALD: This is absurd. They turned you down? Brush it
aside. It's inconsequential.

ROSALIND: Gerald, shut up.

GERALD: Sorry.

ROSALIND: But there is a new possibility.

GERALD: Really? Fabulous. Tell me.

ROSALIND: It's faint. So faint. I really was so good, Gerald.
I told you I did Lola. (*American southern accent.*) 'Then it
started to rain. And I couldn't find little Sheba. I almost
went crazy looking for her and there were so many people.
I didn't even know where to look and you were waiting to
take me home. And we walked and walked through the
slush and mud, and people were hurrying all around us…
and… (*Tears come to her eyes. She sits down.*) But this part is
sad Daddy. All of a sudden
I saw Little Sheba… She was lying in the middle of a
field…dead… It made me cry, Doc. No one paid any
attention. I cried and cried –'
(*GERALD is crying. She laughs.*)
Big deal baby. Cheer up, and down the hatch.

GERALD: Wonderful. Wonderful. Rosalind, don't be cruel.
Tell me about the new possibility?

ROSALIND: Archie's put me up for twenty episodes. It's a
Soap Opera.

GERALD: (*Immediately lighting up.*) What?

ROSALIND: They want to see me next Monday. Archie's
biking round the first script tomorrow.

GERALD: A Soap Opera! I want you to be a star in Soap. It's
everything I ever wanted, for you.

ROSALIND: I'm not very hopeful.

GERALD: Are you out of your mind? You've got to go in
there as if you are the only person that is absolutely right
for the part. And you are. No-one else stands a chance
against you. Rosalind, I will be so proud of you.
I will tell everyone.

ROSALIND: You will tell no-one.

GERALD: Look. Forget those kids. What do they know?
This is a great chance. Everything can turn around. And
it will. And all the Bens will be knocking on your door.

ROSALIND: Gerald, I'm trying to be honest with myself.
I do not think I can do this. I must phone Archie.

GERALD: First sign of real success, real hope and you run
away. What's the matter? Can't face a life of fame and
fortune?

ROSALIND: Tell me about Soap Opera. I never watch
anything.

GERALD: I never watch anything else. Soap opera is
glamour, is true art. It numbs me. It's hypnotic. So potent.
It's life, without the pain.

ROSALIND: It's junk food. I am an actress. I aspire.

GERALD: Listen! Think of this. More people will see you in
one night, than saw Sarah Bernhardt in a lifetime.

ROSALIND: Really? What a dizzying thought. Gerald, I'm so
tired.

GERALD: Of course. It's been one hell of a day. Come
upstairs and dine with us.

ROSALIND: No. I have the most splitting headache.

GERALD: Rosalind. Famous, or on the floor. Fabulously rich
or poor. Whatever you are and whatever you do it makes
no difference to me. I love you.

ROSALIND: I know. Thank you.

GERALD: And now, out of the frying pan and into the fiery
delectable, unpredictable Desmond. The primal poke!
Goodnight, sweet princess. I'll be so proud of you.

ROSALIND: Goodnight.

(*He goes. She turns down the light and changes into
night-things and plays soft blues music. She sings softly,
automatically, staring into space, quietly.*)

'My mother done tole me, when I was in knee pants, my
mother done tole me, hon, a man is a two face who gives
you the sweet talk and when the sweet talking's done, a
man is a two face, a worrysome thing that leads you to sing
– the blues in the night – Whooeee der wooeeeee –'

(*A soft plaintive train sound. She sits up.*)

Who am I? Please Ben. What can I do with the rest of
my life. You've got me where I want you. Please don't
leave me, now that I need you. Please Ben. You bastard.

Death! He's dead. I know he's dead. They're hiding it from me. No. Not quite dead. He's been smashed in a car-crash, he's on life support. There is a chance he may pull through. Ben, I'll look after you. I'll devote the rest of my days to you. (*She giggles. Now she assumes deep voice, as Ben.*) Rosalind! You're going to stop dramatising practically everything and you're going to bed; and you're going to sleep. (*Childish voice.*) Oh, am I? Oh, thank you Ben. (*As herself.*) My mind's slipping. Gerald, please believe me. He does exist. Alright, I believe you. Look, the cupboard has stayed closed. Even the bogey man needs his beauty sleep. Sleep now, even for you. Thank you. What a good idea. She's going to bed now. And she's going to sleep. And she's going to wake up.
(*She gets into bed and pulls the covers right over her head.*)
Thank you. Goodnight. Don't let the worms bite.

End of Act One.

ACT TWO

Hours later. GERALD is on the couch asleep. Again it is early in the morning and it is obvious ROSALIND cannot sleep. The last movement of Tchaikovski's 'Pathetique' plays softly.

ROSALIND: I know you're there. But you don't scare me anymore. 'How wonderful is death, death and his brother sleep –'

GERALD: (*Through his snoring and from the depth of sleep he utters quietly.*) Shut up. Shut up.

ROSALIND: Where? Where did I put it? Gerald. You're things are everywhere.

(*Lotte Lenya sings 'Mac the Knife' from 'The Threepenny Opera'. GERALD snores extra loud.*)

Gerald sends love to his Lotte. This room! It comes alive at night. It's a thing, watching me. Sometimes I even get homesick for Rickmansworth. Where did I put it? It must be somewhere in this Junk on the Yangtze.

(*She goes close to GERALD and laughs gently.*)

Damn you for not being Ben. Gerald! Wake up. I need you. Gerald!

(*She shakes him. He mumbles and moves.*)

GERALD: Des – !

ROSALIND: Would you like a cup of tea?

GERALD: What's happening?

ROSALIND: You were having a bad dream.

GERALD: Yes please.

ROSALIND: Yes please what?

GERALD: I would love a cup of tea.

(*She goes to kitchen to make tea.*)

What's the time? (*Looks at wristwatch.*) Don't you ever sleep?

ROSALIND: Not much. It's merely rehearsing for you know what. And I think I have learned my part quite adequately. I hate this room.

GERALD: I love it. I feel so much nicer down here. The atmosphere. It's so good to get away from his eyes. They scare me.

ROSALIND: Lapsang Souchong?

GERALD: Bliss. I'm so grateful. If I had stayed up there I'd end up dead. Tell you what. I'll never get out of life alive. He's dead jealous of you. He's fuming up there.

ROSALIND: We should grow up, Gerald.

GERALD: People don't grow up. They just cover up. Are you sure I'm not in the way?

ROSALIND: On the contrary. I'm glad of the company. Night whispers 'Rosalind! There's no hope. What's the point?' And morning comes round with the old flannel, 'Another day. Wakey! Wakey! Rise and shine.' Why don't you just throw him out?

GERALD: Easier said than done. He melts me when he wants to.

ROSALIND: Yeah. I know the feeling.

GERALD: Fancy needing protection from a child. 'Here's a soldier of the South who loves you, Scarlett, wants to feel your arms around him, wants to carry the memory of your kisses into battle with him.' Oh darling, wouldn't it have been marvellous if you and I could make love twice a night? And we could get married. You all in white and gold, with daffodils cascading from your hair and me all formal, basking in your beauty. And we could have five brilliant beautiful children. 'You're a woman sending a soldier to his death with a beautiful memory. Scarlett, kiss me. Kiss me once.'

ROSALIND: (*She kisses him.*) Poor Vivien. I love her. She visits me often in this room, at night. You hungry?

GERALD: Mmmm. Ravenous.

ROSALIND: I've got the very thing. Canadian Cheddar with pickled onions and crackers.

GERALD: Yummy!

(*He goes to piano as she goes to the kitchen. He sings like Alice Faye.*)

'You'll never know just how much I miss you. You'll never know just how much I care; and if I cried I still wouldn't hide my love for you –' I loved Alice Faye. Didn't you? She was vulnerable without being a victim. She was

fabulous. Funny, those songs are all about me. You know, sometimes I long for the old days when we were all in the closet. It was like war. We were spies, passing on forbidden messages: Camp. Bold. Varda the Homies. Sure, we were a persecuted minority but there was a camaraderie, a true spirit of belonging. Now it's all in the open, you can see us on television any night, discussing our problems. Homosexuality is old hat. Five year olds discuss all it's social implications. Good I suppose. But
I prefer the good old persecuted days. Have I ever told you how I first met Desmond?

ROSALIND: At least thirty times.

GERALD: He was so sweet, so innocent. I wish you could have seen him, that day, two years ago. There I was, lonely, unloved, getting over Antony who ran off with that Brazilian diplomat. I mourned his departure by waiting outside Euston station by the Paolozzi Sculpture, looking for lost boys. They come from the North, you know, the lonely ones; looking for work, for the buzz of the big city. Then I see him and I go over. Can I buy you a cup of coffee young man? He looks suspicious. He laughs. I belong to a special charity, I tell him. We provide refreshment for young people. He laughs. He is so attractive. So innocent. His name is Desmond. He comes from Darlington. He looks so cold I want to cuddle him. Where are you going Desmond? Not in life, but tonight. 'I have nowhere to stay. I'm on my uppers.' Oh my poor boy, how fortunate that you found me. Tonight you will stay at my place. Tomorrow is another day. Desmond's innocent eyes radiate joy as we go down the tube. 'Where do I sleep?', he asks when we enter my nefarious den. I'm so sorry. There's only the one bed. He blushes, chuckles and hurls off his clothes and jumps into bed. Oh! That beautiful provincial bum. I nearly die and I quickly shower and spray myself and slide in beside him. In the dark I creep closer to him, surreptitiously. 'Are you trying to bum me?', he shouts angrily. Me? Are you crazy? You think I am a common homosexual? My mission is social responsibility. It is to make lost beautiful boys happy; maybe for the first time in their lives. Time passes; I slowly make my move when suddenly he leaps upon me. 'Okay Mister, you've been trying to bum me for half an hour. You've asked for it.' With that he whips me around and he gives it to me.

I am in my seventh heaven. But as soon as he is finished I see such terrible anger in his eyes. He grabs me round the throat. He is overwhelmed by English guilt. He is going to choke me. Everything is going black, I shall be dead within seconds, but I have a sudden inspiration. 'Thank you. Thank you.' I manage to croak. 'You have saved my life.' 'EH?' He loosens his grip. 'What do you mean?' And then I explain. 'I am dying from a rare, incurable disease. The doctors told me only an injection of male sperm can possible save my life. Thank you.' He smiles. He lets go. I kiss him. He kisses me, and sleeps innocently in the crook of my arm. His mother writes to me regularly from Darlington. 'How kind you for helping my son in wicked and disgusting London. Thank you for taking him under your wing.

I shall be grateful always.' Last week she sent me a gift parcel, crammed with black pudding. But my sweet provincial Desmond, faun-eyed, has become clever and cultured and dangerous. Yet he is so beautiful. And I love him. And I hate him. Hate him. (*Overcome, he cannot continue and almost cries but covers it by pretending to yawn.*) What's the time?

ROSALIND: The time when most people die. Three o'clock.

GERALD: I must get my beauty sleep; give us a big hug my darling. You go to sleep as well. That is a command.

ROSALIND: Yes, big daddy.

GERALD: (*He lies down covers himself, sings quietly.*) 'Falling in love again – never wanted to. What am I to do? Can't help it. –' (*He muses.*) Do you know I'm allergic to sex, the very thought of it makes me swell?

ROSALIND: Do you know Gerry, if Ben were to die, twenty mad patients in St John's Wood would go bananas and rise up like assassins and pull jagged breadknives across their throats.

GERALD: And if we don't find the next pretty boy, I tell you we must die, I tell you we must die. I tell you I tell you – I tell – (*He continues very quietly, until his voice peters out.*)

ROSALIND: Gerald, what did I do to become the other woman? How did I become excluded from the human race? From being able to live an ordinary life? Sometimes I rage inside when I see a family on the Heath. I hate the child because she is not mine. I hate the woman because I am not her. I hate the man because he is not with me. I want to see that family explode, blown to pieces before my eyes. Yet I love life. But thank God I didn't have children. A merciful release for them.

I find it hard enough to cope with myself.

(*No reply.*)

Gerry? Okay Ben, row me over the purple sea into the dark inlet. I'll steer. That way we sure are to not get to where we were never going. Ben! Careful! When you loved me I loved myself. Oh grow up darling! Mummy, why did you leave me all alone in the dark? Where am I now that I need me? Sorry Ben, I can't forgive you. Make love to me. I want you inside me. Too late though to make a pretty daughter. No brushing her hair. No trips to Paris. No Nutcracker Suite. My eggs are all used up. Ben! Tell me I shouldn't do that Soap Opera. Tell me you have other plans and I am included. What's it like being dead? Shall I join you. (*Sings a bit of 'Gloomy Sunday'.*) 'Dearest, the shadows I live with are numberless; little white angels can never awaken you, not where that black coach of sorrow has taken you. –' 'Oh I do like to be beside the seaside –' (*She turns out the light. Again.*) Silly. Of course he's not dead. He's in Canada. Which amounts to the same thing? Goodnight.

(*A short passage of time.*

It is the next morning. Sunlight streams into the room. Vienna waltzes play from the radio. ROSALIND is on the phone.)

You are the same young man! You are. I know you are. And I am a woman who has reached the end of her tether. I tell you I cannot go on like this. It is not here.

I have searched everywhere. I have not found it and

you must send me another one. Today. Now. Are you all
enjoying yourselves at my expense? Do you understand
that I have an important audition, next week. My shoes
are falling apart. I am trying to keep up appearances.
How can you be so cruel? I demand that you find out why
you have not replaced my missing Giro. How dare you! I
have not cashed it. Talk to your superiors and phone me
back immediately. Do you understand? I am desperate.
Desperate. Thank you. (*She puts down the phone.*) Idiot! How
did he manage to escape from a condom in Cricklewood?
Surrounded by fools.
(*GERALD enters.*)

GERALD: Was that Ben?

ROSALIND: (*She snaps.*) You know perfectly well that Ben is
in Baffinland. Where have you been?

GERALD: The corner shop. I told you. I got everything.
Eggs. Milk. Bread. Passion fruit.

ROSALIND: Did you go upstairs?

GERALD: Not yet. Let sleeping dogs lie.

ROSALIND: What are you going to do about Dessy?

GERALD: What are you going to do about Ben?

ROSALIND: How dare you?

GERALD: Alright! I'll tell you what I'm going to do about
Desmond. In a few minutes you and I shall make us both a
boiled egg for breakfast. With toast and honey. Then
I shall go upstairs, pack his things, and tell him to get out.
Once and for all. Goodbye Desmond. You shall see. You
shall be my witness.

ROSALIND: Marvellous.

GERALD: This time I mean it. Do you believe me?

ROSALIND: Absolutely.

GERALD: And later today I shall start to think about the
future. I am determined. Oh! I forgot. This came for you.
(*He hands her a packet.*)

ROSALIND: Why didn't you give it to me immediately?

GERALD: A simply gorgeous young man delivered it.
I'm just getting over the shock. He was all in black; a
messenger of the gods of television. Open it and be deified.

ROSALIND: (*She opens the packet, takes out the script and a letter*.) Enclosed find story outline. (*She reads*.) Oh my God. This sounds – listen. A communal garden in Holland Park, a complex multi-faceted community.

I am meant to be Antonia, ex-ballet dancer –

GERALD: How old is she?

ROSALIND: Thirty five. Can I get away with being thirty five?

GERALD: Rosalind! Are you kidding? It's perfect for you.

ROSALIND: You sure? Listen. Antonia recently had a bad fall at the Garden; her brilliant career has come to an end. She teaches. She is in love with Dominick, a plain clothes detective from Bow Street Police station. Outwardly she appears serene, gentle; she smiles all the time but inwardly she is deeply bitter, a furnace of envy, hatred and frustration; she is manipulative; desperate.

GERALD: I can't wait. It is made for you.

ROSALIND: Listen to the dialogue! 'Daphne, your brother Dominick has such beautiful blue eyes; when he smiles I melt. Do you think he's noticed me? I know he's only a policeman, but does that really matter? Has he ever mentioned me?' Gerald! It's banal.

GERALD: Of course it is. That's the whole point.

ROSALIND: I don't understand.

GERALD: It's life. And life is banal. And I personally find it very moving. It's about real things. Trivial things. The things that obsess us. That's it's potency. Relationships. It's all about our own lives. It's vicariousness. It's as old as living in caves. It's living other people's lives. Will he love me? Why does she ignore me? Am I too old. Am I too young? I used to fancy him. But now I fancy her. I hate him. I love her. But she loves him. And he loves me, but I love her. Don't you see?

ROSALIND: I'm out of touch. Fact is I'm afraid of being recognised. Why did I choose to become an actress? We're children dressing up, playing at life. We are at the mercy of everyone; we solicit opinions from anyone. Postmen. Milkmen. Girls at check-outs. 'Saw you on the box last night miss.' 'Really? Was I alright? Mummy! Daddy! Was I alright? Did you like me?'

GERALD: Yes darling! I can see both of us are about to enter a new phase. Are you prepared to be stinking rich, desperately wanted and fabulously famous. I know I am.

ROSALIND: (*She dials. Changes her mind.*) No. Gerald, I've decided. I cannot go to the interview. I cannot consider playing this part.

GERALD: Rosalind, I am too frail to fight you.

ROSALIND: The truth is I've got nothing to wear.

(*The phone rings. She hesitates. GERALD answers, hands her the receiver. For a moment she thinks it's Ben.*)

Hello? Oh! Archie! Yes! It's arrived. Glanced. (*With surprise: almost shock.*) WHAT? Today? Are you kidding me?

GERALD: What's going on?

ROSALIND: I thought they wanted to see me on Monday. I can't. Not today. I've only just got the script. ARCHIE! You're a liar. Archie! You didn't tell me. What am I going to do? Archie! Be reasonable. Damn them! How can they be so inconsiderate? I'll try. Goodbye. The interview for this thing is in (*Looks at her watch.*) four hours time.

GERALD: Excellent. You will now not have time to drive us both insane.

ROSALIND: Gerald, I really cannot do it.

GERALD: Here we go.

ROSALIND: The fact is – I am totally, totally broke. I've lost my Giro. I desperately need tights. Shoes. My hair! How can I go to the BBC looking like this?

GERALD: No problem. (*He takes out his wallet and offers her a banknote.*)

ROSALIND: No. You've done more than enough. I shall phone them.

(*She takes up the phone, he puts it down again.*)

GERALD: You are the artiste. I the grateful patron.

ROSALIND: Fifty? Gerald, I can't.

GERALD: You will take it.

ROSALIND: I can't. I won't.

GERALD: It is my privilege. A gift from your passionate but platonic lover. Please. It is generous to take graciously. Please.

(*She still hesitates.*)

ROSALIND: Only a loan, mind.

GERALD: Absolutely. Soon you'll be as rich as Croesus and we'll dine at the Ivy and winter in Barbados.

ROSALIND: Thank you. I won't let you down.

GERALD: I am very proud of you. You are the only person in my life.

ROSALIND: But who shall I be? How shall I do it?

GERALD: Roscka. This is for the box. Be something light and frivolous and funny.

ROSALIND: (*Joking. She tap dances, sings.*) 'On the good ship lollypop, it's a nice trip to the candy shop –'

GERALD: You're far too young to attempt Shirley Temple.

ROSALIND: When they say to me 'Ms Fraser, what can you especially offer us?' I shall reply, Gentlemen! I can offer you incessant sex.

GERALD: Of course, I'm not a fool. I'm cutting my own throat. You'll shine out against all the others and get this job and within a year you will be fabulously rich and move away from here. And forget all about me and I shall be left all alone.

ROSALIND: In that case I shall do my best to fail. Just for you. (*She goes to him and kisses him.*) What can I say? Thank you. I shall have a shower.

GERALD: Marvellous. Please do your best, for me.

ROSALIND: I will. Goodbye. (*She goes out.*)

GERALD: Please let them love you. This is my true metier. I should have been a housewife.

(*He goes to the stereo deck, and now plays Jerome Kern. He hums and dances the songs as he continues working. Blackout.*
Time has passed. GERALD is draped in the armchair and is snoring. ROSALIND enters, her hair beautifully styled. She looks at him for a few moments, maternally.)
(*Jumping up with a start.*) Well?

ROSALIND: (*Quiet. Smiling.*) Very well.

GERALD: And?

ROSALIND: And they all lived happily ever after.

GERALD: You've been hours and hours. I was worried. You got the part.

ROSALIND: No. I did not get the part.

GERALD: What? You're kidding.

ROSALIND: I kid you not. I did not get the part.

GERALD: But you seem happy.

ROSALIND: I am. I've decided. I am a classical actress not a commodity.

GERALD: Didn't you read well?

ROSALIND: I read very well. They said I did. But they also said I was the wrong age. Irony upon irony. Why do people put you into that situation? Why do they expose you like that? The wrong age.

GERALD: They must be mad. You are ageless. What can I say? I'm so sorry.

ROSALIND: Gerald, believe me, personally I'm relieved. You know I had my doubts. Theatre? Yes. It's a world I can cope with. Now fame and fortune does not immediately beckon. We are platonic lovers for life.

GERALD: Good. All I want is your happiness. (*Then concern.*) You're not acting now?

ROSALIND: I thought you knew me. Now I can get on with my life.

GERALD: It's late. Why did it take so long? I was worried sick.

ROSALIND: I just felt like wandering.

GERALD: Unlike you.

ROSALIND: I walked and I walked. Suddenly I enjoyed the streets. The park. The children playing. I can still see the faces, still hear their happy laughter. Life is forever. And the bustle of Queensway. And Notting Hill gate. Then the West End. Regent Street. The river. South bank. I've been buried here too long. Have you been upstairs? What's happening with darling Desmond?

GERALD: I don't know. I've been avoiding him. Malevolent smiling spirit. I am not avoiding doing it. I am determined. I stayed down all the time, in case you phoned. It was lovely and peaceful. This room has such a marvellous atmosphere. I hope you don't mind.

ROSALIND: Never. Gerry, I'm so weary. I would like an early night.

GERALD: Certainly my love. I did everything. Swept.

Dusted. The washing up. Oh yes, hope you didn't mind,
I made a phone call. Remember that lovely Greg I met
last year in Marbella? That beautiful Armenian I told you
about, well, as soon as I get rid of Desmond, tomorrow
morning, I'm taking the plunge. What have
I got to lose? You'll love him. He smiles all the time.

ROSALIND: Careful. If he smiles all the time he's hiding
something.

GERALD: He'll hide nothing from me, dear. I assure you.
Roz. It's nice to see you in such a good mood. Get a good
night sleep.

ROSALIND: (*Solemn. Like a bride.*) I will.

GERALD: Yes. And we'll talk about everything tomorrow.

ROSALIND: Everything. Thank's Gerald. I feel so serene, so
happy tonight.

GERALD: (*He seems a little unsure and concerned.*) Goodnight.
See you later. (*He goes.*)

ROSALIND: (*She latches the door, pours herself a large whisky,
drains it down in one gulp, and then gets a tumbler of water.*)
'Now thy revels all have ended.'
(*She puts on Fats Waller singing 'Your Feet's Too Big' then
sits to write a note.*)
Thank you, Ben. Goodnight.
(*She puts the note into an envelope, and places it on the
mantlepiece. Then she writes another note.*)
Forgive me, Dear Gerald. Thank you for being there.
'Because I could not stop for Death, he kindly stopped for
me. The carriage held but ourselves. And immortality.'
(*She stands this next note next to the other one. Now she
takes the large mirror and places it face upward on the
table. Then she takes a box of pills out of her handbag,
empties the entire contents onto the mirror and arranges
them. She sets them out almost ritualistically before her,
playing with them, as if it were a board game, smiling
down at her reflection in the mirror.*)
No half measures this time. People fail because they don't
really want to do it. But there's no escape, once the Bogey
Man comes out of the cupboard and gets his hooks into

you.

(*Sound of children laughing.*)

'We passed the school where children played; their lessons scarcely done; we passed the fields of grazing wheat. We passed the setting sun –'

(*She is ready for the act, takes up a fistful of tablets, stuffs them into her mouth.*)

GERALD: (*His voice outside.*) Rosalind! Darling! (*He has put the key in the lock but the door won't open.*) You've locked the door. Rosalind! Please!

(*ROSALIND spits out the tablets, retches, almost being sick, but quickly manages to conceal these spat out tablets in some tissue paper.*)

Rosalind! (*He bangs on the door.*) Rosalind! Open the door. I must see you. Let me in. (*He sounds distraught.*)

ROSALIND: Wait! Wait!

GERALD: (*Still banging on the door.*) Please let me in!

ROSALIND: Go away. Please. Go away. Oh my god. Oh my god. Oh my god.

GERALD: Rosalind! You must open. You must.

(*The banging continues until ROSALIND unlocks the door. GERALD enters crying, clutching a note.*)

He's left me. Desmond's left me.

ROSALIND: Oh! My god! My god! Oh my god!

(*Then she quickly turns her attention to him. He thinks her despair is for him.*)

GERALD: Help me. Help me!

ROSALIND: My poor darling!

GERALD: How could he? How could he?

ROSALIND: There! There! (*She strokes his head.*)

GERALD: He wrote me a note. (*He thrusts the note at her.*)

ROSALIND: (*Gathering herself she jokes.*) I didn't know he could write. (*Reading the note.*) 'So, it's all for the best, mate. Cos I better get out before I do you a real injury. See ya. Thanks. Yours faithfully, Desmond.' What can I say?

GERALD: Please help me.

ROSALIND: (*Comforting him.*) Darling! You know as well as I. You're better off without him.

GERALD: Desist with the homilies. He's gone. He's gone.

How could he do this to me? I'm so sorry I'm doing this to you. So sorry. (*He cries again.*)

ROSALIND: If only I could help you. Don't cry. You'll be alright. (*She cuddles him, almost cradling, him like a child.*) I'll look after you. I'll never leave you. Come on Gerry, it's all for the best.

GERALD: How can you say that? I love him. I can't live without him.

ROSALIND: Yes you can. You can. Gerry listen, you cannot continue being the victim of a three year old child. You really must cut your losses; cut him out of your life. Once and for all. And somehow survive the withdrawal symptoms.

GERALD: Can I? Do you think so? Yes. I know what you're saying is right. Thank you. How could I survive without you? As you say, one door closes, another door closes.

ROSALIND: (*Also giving advice to herself.*) Please laugh. Crack your face. Smile for me. Come on. Remember? Laugh and the world laughs with you. Weep and you sleep alone. Pretend. Put on a face. Be someone else. Be your mad aunt. (*He smiles grotesquely.*)
That's better. That's much better. Have a glass of vino darling. That's what we need. I'll get some.
(*She goes to get the bottle and glasses. Meanwhile GERALD discovers the suicide pills wrapped in tissue. He is quietly horrified but conceals all this from ROSALIND.*)
Gerald! What am I going to do with you? I was just turning in…and the floodgates opened. Here my darling. A beautiful nightcap. (*She brings two glasses of wine.*)

GERALD: Here's to you. And here's to me. And here's to Mister Armenia and his beautiful moustache. May he come into my life and stay there, forever. Roz. You've saved my life, yet again. So now you owe me something.

ROSALIND: (*Laughing.*) I see. I save *your* life, so I owe *you* something? Fair enough.
(*They both drink.*)

GERALD: In life you are not allowed to play God. One does not have the power over life and death. Only God has that and thank god I do not believe in God. All you can do is cling to the parapet. Dearest Roz, you have no choice. You just have to get on with it.

ROSALIND: Thank you. So, you've probably found yourself a nice new man.

GERALD: Yes. And if this is to be the start of a new era, let us both face it together.

ROSALIND: Absolutely.

GERALD: Let us both face the truth together. I am ready for anything if you are there with me.

ROSALIND: Right. Corporal. (*She salutes.*)

GERALD: Roz, when is the right time for a good friend to speak out?

ROSALIND: Anytime. Now. What do you mean?

GERALD: Isn't it time Ben was exorcised from your life?

ROSALIND: Darling, I am not hearing this.

GERALD: Look! I have to say this because I love you. I've agonised and agonised. Ben doesn't exist.

ROSALIND: What? You poor thing. Desmond's flight is letting out all the pus of your despair. Good. Good. Let it all out. Come on. Come on.

GERALD: Oh. I know he exists somewhere. That he's probably real.

ROSALIND: Probably? How dare you! I shall be charitable. I shall believe you are distraught and forget what you've just said.

GERALD: Alright. He does exist.

ROSALIND: Oh really? Thank you.

GERALD: But not for you. You've built him up. Out of all proportion. It happens. Nothing to be ashamed of. I understand.

ROSALIND: Well understand this. Get out.

GERALD: Forgive me. I have to speak.

ROSALIND: You have to speak crap. I'm tired. Please go.

GERALD: I know you were once his patient –

ROSALIND: Oh you do believe that? Thank you. Tomorrow you'll be devastated and beg my forgiveness and I shall forgive you. Goodnight.

GERALD: But he is not, and has never been your lover.

ROSALIND: I have asked you to go –

GERALD: Please Roz, don't let this spoil things.

ROSALIND: This time you've gone too far. Go before you go even further.

GERALD: I know what you are going through.

ROSALIND: Not one word more.

GERALD: If we don't face the truth about ourselves we're doomed,

ROSALIND: (*Covering her ears.*) I will not hear this.

GERALD: You will. You must. Desmond has gone forever. Ben does not exist. And we do not exist if we believe in them. Listen! Listen! (*He tries to remove her hands from her ears.*)

ROSALIND: Bastard! You rotten bastard!
(*She slaps him hard, twice on the face. For a moment there is silence.*)

GERALD: Grow up.

ROSALIND: How dare you! You of all people! A pathetic quivering old queen; an old man in corsets with dyed moustache and pretensions of culture; a beaten up victim of endless sessions with rough trade. Get out of my life. Get out of my life.

GERALD: You? Call me pathetic?

ROSALIND: I am an actress. I have some standing.

GERALD: You're a child. Most women of your age are going to the ballet with their daughters.

ROSALIND: If you don't get out – I'll kill you.

GERALD: Stop acting. You always dramatise everything.

ROSALIND: You revolt me. You make me cringe.

GERALD: You're play-acting now.

ROSALIND: You talk a load of shit. So get out. GET OUT! OUT!
(*She lunges at him but he catches her arm.*)
I'll kill you. How could you do this to me?

GERALD: (*Pleading.*) Rosalind. Please. Face reality.

ROSALIND: What's reality ever done for me?

GERALD: (*Suddenly struck by remorse.*) Rosalind! Forgive me. I've gone too far. (*He cries.*) Why did you make me go too far? Help me. I hate you. What have I done? Why am I doing this? I'm not here. I'm dreaming this. Please forgive me. (*He is kneeling on the floor, almost rolled up into a ball. He sobs and sobs.*)

ROSALIND: Get up. Get up. (*But then she suddenly feels desperate for him.*) Gerald! Gerald darling! Please get up. Gerald. (*She touches him.*)

GERALD: Don't touch me! Don't you dare touch me.

ROSALIND: Gerald, I need you. I'm sorry. I didn't mean it. She just said silly things. She couldn't stop. She got carried away.

GERALD: Not far enough.

ROSALIND: We drink too much. Let's both forgive each other. And ourselves.

(*GERALD stops crying. She helps him to his feet and then they cuddle for a few moments, clinging and rocking together.*)

GERALD: My sister and I... We were so close. The past was such a wonderful place. I had family.

ROSALIND: The past is safe. It's not like life.

GERALD: But now is now. What's going to happen to us, Roz?

ROSALIND: We're going to be alright Gerald.

GERALD: If only I could believe that.

ROSALIND: We must act being alright. Act in order to get ourselves together, in order to act. Acting is being.

GERALD: Good. Perfect. But there's one thing that worries me.

ROSALIND: Yes?

GERALD: (*He goes to the mantlepiece, takes the suicide notes.*) These! (*He reads the envelopes.*) 'To Gerald!' and 'To Ben'.

ROSALIND: (*Snatching one of the notes.*) NO! Don't!

GERALD: This one is addressed to me. I shall read it. (*He opens the envelope. She remains impassive while he reads the contents.*) What does the other one say?

ROSALIND: It says Goodbye Ben. (*She tears the note into tiny pieces.*) It means... Goodbye Ben.

GERALD: Were you going to do it? Really?

ROSALIND: Yes.

GERALD: Thank you.

ROSALIND: What do you mean.

GERALD: And leave me here, all alone, to dispense with your corpse. Nice. Thank you very much. I exist you know. Outside you. I have a life to live. Cremate me, she says. How neat. How cosy. And use my ashes for an egg timer. Thank you very much. Rosalind! I've had enough. Do what you like. Kill yourself.

(*He is about to go. She pulls him back.*)

ROSALIND: What can I say? You above all should understand. The world getting smaller and smaller, until nothing else exists except a tight nut in your brain that says – switch me off. The concentrated pain is too much. Switch me off. I was somewhere that most people cannot know exists. But I tell you what. There seemed to be no other way out. The preferable option.

GERALD: So, you'll try it again?

ROSALIND: No. I don't know. Yes. Maybe. I can't predict the future. I'm far too busy trying to cope with the present. Gerald, forgive me.

GERALD: Listen Roz, if anyone came to you in the deepest trouble what would you do?

ROSALIND: Try to help of course.

GERALD: Exactly! You would share your heart; show them some compassion. Right?

ROSALIND: Right.

GERALD: How about showing a little compassion to yourself. And letting yourself off the hook?

ROSALIND: (*Something dawns.*) Thank you. Thank you.

GERALD: So what now?

ROSALIND: Ben's dead. I've finally buried him. Help me through the grieving.

GERALD: I have no choice. (*The phone rings.*)

ROSALIND: Ben!

GERALD: (*He answers it.*) Yes. Miss Fraser's residence. No. This is her friend and confidant. Yes. Oh! Really? I see. Yes. Tomorrow morning. Eleven o'clock. She will be there. Thank you. (*He puts the phone down.*) It was the BBC. They've called you back.

ROSALIND: Does it mean I've got the part, after all?

GERALD: No. It's terrible. They don't want you for the lead. But they are considering you for her closest friend.

ROSALIND: (*Small cynical laugh.*) Oh yes. Samantha. 'A reactionary soak and Kleptomaniac, of fading beauty.' Type casting.

GERALD: You mean you will consider doing it?

ROSALIND: Gerald, the state of my finances, I'd consider playing Grandma Moses.

GERALD: But you're far too young. Fading beauty? How dare they! Look at you! How beautiful, how glamorous you are.

ROSALIND: Darling! Gerald! Suddenly you've got cold feet. You were chiding me ten minutes ago, remember? That at my time of life I should be playing with my daughter. Well, it's a job Gerald. And if I get it I hope you will still boast that you know me. Gerald! Cheer up. You're a long time dead. It's work.

GERALD: I really am glad for you Roz. I'm delighted, I'm shooting over the stars. This time I'm sure you'll get it. Please be light at the reading.

ROSALIND: Oh course. I'll do *Berenice* by Racine.

GERALD: No.

ROSALIND: You're right. I must be light. Gerald! It's beginning to dawn. My Bank manager will smile at me and ask me to lunch. And do you realise, more people will see me in one night than saw Sarah Bernhardt in the whole of her endless career.

GERALD: (*Sarcastic, because he said it first.*) Yes darling.

ROSALIND: Soap Opera is so significant. It vibrates in the psyche of masses. It is the microcosm of the universal. The minutiae, the quintessence; the wavelength of common identity; the jubilation, the expression of the collective conscious. It is tribal; avatistic –

GERALD: (*Sarcastic.*) Atavistic. (*He tears up the suicide note and takes the box of tablets.*) You won't be needing these any more.

ROSALIND: No darling. Not for the moment. (*She sees his concern and laughs to reassure.*)

GERALD: Rosalind! We must celebrate. I know it's a little premature, but let's live dangerously.

ROSALIND: Haven't you got your beautiful moustachioed
Armenian coming later?

GERALD: I shall phone him in the morning. I know he's
eager. We shall have a party, tomorrow evening, all three
of us. (*He sings like Dietrich.*) 'Love's always been my game,
play it how I may, I was born that way, can't help it.'

ROSALIND/GERALD: 'Men flock around me like moths
around a flame, and if their wings burn I know I'm not to
blame. Falling in love again, never wanted to –'

ROSALIND: What am I to do? Can't help it. Good morning
Mr Hartmann.

GERALD: Good morning Miss Fraser. And what are you
going to do for us?

ROSALIND: Let me see. What shall I do? Who shall I be?

GERALD: Incidentally, how old are you, Miss Fraser?

ROSALIND: How old do you want me to be, Mr Hartmann?
I can be any age. I can be anyone. (*Phaedra.*) 'Listen. It
was I, Theseus who on your virtuous, filial son made bold
to cast a lewd, incestuous eye.' (*Irish. Playboy.*) 'Oh my
grief, I've lost him surely. I've lost the only Playboy of The
Western World.' (*Medea.*) 'To expiate this impious murder I
myself will go to Athens'. I myself.
(*She picks up her precious book of Chekhov plays that has
been by her bedside all along, she opens it and the bookmark
falls to the floor. She picks it up. It's the giro.*)
It's here. I found it. There you are! Wonderful! We live
again! (*She now holds the opens book against her.*) Who am I?
'I am – I am – I'm a seagull. I'm a seagull. I'm a seagull…
No, that's not it. I'm an actress. An actress.' Gerald, I
promise you they have no further hold on me. Ben! My
mad father. My sad mother. I'm rid of them. I've realised
that the cemetery is full of indispensable people. I am me. I
am alone, with tomorrow, if it happens. I am whoever you
want me to be. Look Gerry, I found it. (*She waves the giro
at him.*) Gerry! Can you loan me a little money until I cash
this tomorrow?

GERALD: It's my pleasure. (*He opens his wallet and gives her a
note.*) Here.
(*She kisses his forehead and puts on her overcoat.*)

Where are you going?

ROSALIND: Are the stores still open?

GERALD: This time of night?

ROSALIND: (*Not hearing him.*) I must get myself some new shoes. (*She hurries out of the room. GERALD sings.*)

GERALD: *Tu madre cuando te pario. Y te quito al mundo. Coracon ella no te dio. Para amar segundo. Adio. Adio querida. No quero la vida –'*

(*ROSALIND returns and takes off her coat.*)

ROSALIND: It's dark out there suddenly.

GERALD: It is rather late at night.

(*She sits beside him. He continues to hum the Latino song.*) *The End.*

www.ingramcontent.com/pod-product-compliance
Ingram Content Group UK Ltd.
Pitfield, Milton Keynes, MK11 3LW, UK
UKHW020721280225
455688UK00012B/451